MAN ON HIS OWN

MAN ON HIS OWN

Essays in the Philosophy of Religion

ERNST BLOCH

Translated by E. B. Ashton

HERDER AND HERDER

1970
HERDER AND HERDER NEW YORK
232 Madison Avenue, New York, 10016

Original edition: *Religion im Erbe. Eine Auswahl aus seinen religionsphilosophischen Schriften,* edited by Jürgen Moltmann and Reiner Strunk. © 1959, 1961, 1964, 1966 by Suhrkamp Verlag, Frankfurt am Main.

Sources: "Karl Marx, Death and the Apocalypse" from *Geist der Utopie* (first published 1918), Frankfurt, 1964, pages 297ff. "Incipit Vita Nova" from *Tübinger Einleitung in die Philosophie,* volume 2, Frankfurt, 1966, pages 151ff. "Biblical Resurrection and Apocalypse" from *Das Prinzip Hoffnung,* Frankfurt, 1959, pages 1323ff. "Christ, or the Uncovered Countenance" from *Geist der Utopie,* Frankfurt, 1964, pages 267ff. "Religious Truth" from *Tübinger Einleitung in die Philosophie,* volume 2, Frankfurt, 1966, pages 44ff. "Christian Social Utopias" from *Das Prinzip Hoffnung,* Frankfurt, 1959, pages 575ff. "The Nationalized God and the Right to Community" from *Naturrecht und menschliche Würde,* Frankfurt, 1961, pages 310ff. "Man's Increasing Entry into Religious Mystery" from *Das Prinzip Hoffnung,* Frankfurt, 1959, pages 1399ff.

CONTENTS

Harvey Cox

FOREWORD

After years of hearing about him indirectly, American readers will now be able to taste some of the fruits of Ernst Bloch's long and productive career for themselves. These essays, drawn from Bloch's more recent writing, will hopefully whet so many appetites that the translation of his major works will occur before too long. Ranging over an incredibly wide variety of subjects, from musicology to epistemology, from social and literary criticism to political theory, Bloch's books will eventually delight and stimulate many different people. Why, then it might reasonably be asked, should this first book-length collection of his ideas be introduced by a theologian, and a so-called "young theologian" at that? Whatever else Ernst Bloch may be he is not a "young theologian." He misses that condition on two counts. First, he is an octogenarian, an alert and hard working one but nevertheless a man born in 1885 (of Jewish extraction in Ludwigshafen am Rhein). Also, Bloch is not a theologian— even though some of his critics have occasionally hurled that epithet at him. Bloch is a philosopher, and an atheist at that, at least in his own terms.

Still there are reasons why a theologian should introduce Bloch to English speaking readers. Bloch's present delayed "discovery" has been largely the work of theologians. This became especially clear in 1965 when Bloch reached his 80th birthday

7

and a group of friends and admirers published a *Festschrift* in his honor, (*Ernst Bloch zu Ehren,* Suhrkamp Verlag). To the astonishment of many readers, who knew Bloch as an old Marxist, nearly half the contributors to the volume turned out to be theologians, among them some of the youngest religious thinkers of Europe. Why this interest in Bloch among younger theologians?

Bloch himself might enjoy trying to answer that question. One of the continuing interests of his life has been the riddle of why certain insights emerge at one point in history and not at another, why some men appear "before their time" and others seem to live in an age which has already disappeared. As a theologian it seems to me that while Bloch's work is certainly not of exclusive interest to theologians, there are compelling reasons why he is particularly relevant for us today.

The first reason Bloch fascinates us is that we feel very strongly, and quite correctly I think, that the world today stands *"zwischen zwei Zeiten,"* between two ages. We disagree on how those two ages should be defined. Some see us emerging from Christendom into a "post Christian era." Others see us moving from the religious to the secular epoch in theology. Still others insist that God is dead, that all forms of theism are passé, and that we are already in the period of post-theistic Christianity. Yet, despite the disagreements, most agree that we are now leaving one identifiable period behind but have not yet arrived at the next. We are experiencing what Bloch calls a period of *"Zeitwende."*

Such periods, claims Bloch, are particularly fruitful to study because during them, if often only very briefly, we catch a glimpse of man as he really is. In such periods we live in radical anticipation, hope, and expectation. This is valuable, says Bloch, because existence in hope should not be a periodic episode in man's life; it should be the basic posture of his existence at all times. Man *is,* Bloch contends, that creature who hopes, who phantasizes, who dreams about the future and strives to attain it. These features are not merely accidental to his nature but are utterly constitutive of it. To be human is to be on the way to something else. To be man is to be *unterwegs.* Man's nature

8

eludes definitive description because by the time it is described it has already begun the transmutation into something else. Thus Bloch helps us to seize the day, to enjoy and profit from the discomfort of transition, to see in the dislocations of our own period an epiphany of what is real in history at large. Consequently theologians, for whom the changes of today are especially momentous, see Bloch as especially significant.

But what does Bloch help us to see? How would his thought be capsuled if it had to be described in a few words? Bloch himself, Adolph Lowe reports, was once faced with this challenge. A few years back at a late afternoon tea in the home of a friend, someone challenged the old man to sum up his philosophy in one sentence. "All great philosophers have been able to reduce their thought to one sentence," the friend said. "What would your sentence be?" Bloch puffed on his pipe for a moment and then said, "That's a hard trap to get out of. If I answer, then I'm making myself out to be a great philosopher. But if I'm silent, then it will appear as though I have a great deal in mind but not much I can say. But I'll play the brash one instead of the silent one and give you this sentence: S is not yet P."

"S is not yet P?" Is this a mere evasion? No, in a sense Bloch had succeeded, despite himself, in passing the test of being a great philosopher. His life work has been built on the contention that the dynamic reality always eludes even the most supple agility of language, that it outraces words even while they are being spoken. Thus to say "S = S" is already to falsify the situation since in the time it takes to utter even a short phrase, the inexorable movement of reality towards a still undefined future has relativized the statement.

Does this mean that for Bloch the venerable law of identity in classical logic is passé? Yes it does. For Bloch's ontology, to claim that S must be S and nothing else is to fall into a static view of reality, a condition which can only result in hindering and slowing down the onward march of history, though it can never halt it. In short Bloch is suggesting a logic of change, a new logic appropriate to a time when we have discovered at last that change itself is the only permanent thing we have.

There is another clue in Bloch's one sentence summary. It is

9

the words "not yet." Just as other philosophers have written at length on the vast worlds that open to our imagination if we examine such time words as "love" or "is" or "time," Bloch peers into the creative sources of human existence by examining the words "not yet." Man is not for Bloch principally a product of his past either individually or as a race. Man is not to be described as "thinker" or "symbol maker" or "tool maker" or even as "worker." Man is the "hope-er," he-who-hopes. His essential existence tip-toes along the narrow ridge between the disappearing "now" and the ever newly appearing "not yet." And his basic stance, when he is true to himself, is that of creative expectation, a hope that engenders action in the present to shape the future.

What is the nature of the "not yet"? The future that makes man free? Bloch's answers are never fully satisfying. With a trace of teutonic titanism he proclaims himself the discoverer of this new continent. But like Columbus, he admits that the full exploration of the new world must be left to others. He is content to plant his flag in its sand, let his gaze follow its vast horizons, and speculate on what may lie behind its towering mountain ranges. Like that great investigator of the unconscious, Sigmund Freud, with whom Bloch likes to compare himself, he can demonstrate how the charting of the new land mass might proceed. But he does not pretend that the rough charts he has made are definitive.

The comparison between Bloch and Freud is an interesting one. Both are secularized Jews. Both thought of themselves as atheists but could not shake off their interests in religious problems. Both offended middle class sensibilities, Freud by meddling with sex and Bloch by becoming a Communist. But both retained in their private lives a conventional bourgeois style. Freud loved to play cards with old cronies in his antimacassar Vienna home. Bloch thrives on the *Gemütlichkeit* of Tübingen. Freud studied what Bloch has called the *Nicht-mehr-Bewusst,* that which has come to consciousness but has now passed into unconsciousness. Bloch has discovered the *"Noch-nicht bewusst,"* that which scampers teasingly on the threshold of consciousness, sensed only in anticipation, not yet fully realized. While Freud was interested in night dreams, Bloch is fascinated by day dreams. Fantasy, for Bloch, is not a mere frippery, not a waste of time, but a crucial key to how human beings think. Perhaps the most significant difference between the two is that while Freud did develop a method for examining the no-more-conscious, psychoanalysis, Bloch has not produced its equivalent for the not-yet-conscious. Or perhaps in Bloch's own spirit we should say he has *not yet* produced it.

In theology, the study of the "not-yet," although we do not usually employ Bloch's phrase, is called "eschatology." Although it has usually been the poor step-sister in the household of theology, eschatology, the study of the Christian hope, is today once again claiming a central place. Theologians such as Jürgen Moltmann and Johannes Metz are working today with the assumption that Albert Schweitzer was right when he saw Christianity as essentially eschatological. They see the need not just to recover eschatology but to rethink the whole theological tradition from the perspective of hope. As Moltmann says, eschatology is not just one doctrine among others; it is the *key* in which everything is set, the glow that suffuses everything else. Therefore eschatology cannot be merely part of Christian doctrine; it must be the determining characteristic of all Christian existence and of the whole church.

But how does Christianity recover its lost eschatological stance? Its daring hope for the future which has now been taken over and distorted by revolutionary movements? The trouble is that Christian hope has been either so postponed or so underplayed in the history of Christian thought that theologians today have an enormous job on their hands. How can we restate that hope, expressed in the New Testament in symbols of the resurrection of the dead and the triumphant return of Christ on the clouds, in images that modern man can understand? For centuries Christianity has persistently minimized any notion that the future would overturn the religious or political institutions of the day. Consequently the church has often become an objectively conservative force in the society. Yet the early Christians

hoped for something that *would* transform this world, and today secularized forms of this hope are altering the face of the
earth. How does Christianity regain a posture of radical hope, a
hope for *this* world? How can the church regain the *stance* that
was unswervingly oriented towards the future, but transmute the
content of their hope so that it becomes available to contemporary man? With this task set before us it is natural that we
should be impressed by a man whose life has been spent examining the *"futurum,"* the idea of the new, the *"Impuls der
Erwartung"* and the "principle of hope."

The interest in Bloch among theologians is not merely an un-
requited love. Like any really significant philosopher, Bloch
recognizes that he must deal with religion, so the interest moves
both ways. Still Bloch remains, for his Christian suitors, a little
hard-to-get and perhaps ultimately even unavailable. But this
resistance, in the intellectual as in the romantic, often seems to
excite interest rather than to dampen it. How does Bloch deal
with religion?

As a Marxist, he knows as Marx did that "all criticism begins
with the criticism of religion." Unlike most Marxists, however,
Bloch approaches religion neither with distaste nor with conde-
scension, but with genuine sympathy and untiring fascination.
He has displayed an interest in religion since his earliest years,
and that interest continues to the present day. For Bloch, all
religion finds its source in the "dichotomy of man between his
present appearance and his non-present essence," (*Prinzip Hoffnung,* page 1520), a statement that calls to mind Marx's own
assertion that religious misery is not only the expression of real
misery in a distorted and mystified way, but is also a protest
against real misery. Marx, however, emphasized the narcotizing
effect of religion (the "opiate of the people"), whereas Bloch
is more interested in why and how religion functions as an expressive form of protest.

What about Christianity? Unlike some twentieth-century theo-
logians who insist on a qualitative distinction between "faith in
Christ" and religious belief, or between "religion" and "the
Gospel," Bloch sees a continuity between religion and Christian-

12

ity. More in the style of a nineteenth-century theologian, or of recent theologians influenced by contemporary phenomenology of religion, Bloch speaks of Christianity as the purest and most consistent expression of this irreducible content of all religion. In its universal messianism and its inclusive eschatology Christianity becomes the religious expression *par excellence* of the hope-laden dissatisfaction which spurs man on towards the future. Bloch also believes, however, that there is a crucial difference between Christianity and many other religions in the way it copes with the present. While some religions stress the mythical and thus tend to become static and to serve as an apology for the status quo, Christianity's messianism gives it a critical perspective on the present and loads it with explosive potential.

Both friends and foes of Christianity may rightly suspect at this point that Bloch's estimate of its significance seems unduly generous. They should realize at once that Bloch is not talking about Christianity as currently preached and practiced. He has in mind what might be called the "essential meaning" of Christianity, a meaning which for Bloch burned brightly in the early church but emigrated into non-Christian movements when the church surrendered to the wiles of Constantine, sacrificed its eschatological hope, and allowed itself to become the sacral ideology of the empire. He believes that Christianity's great gift was to introduce the "principle of hope" into the world, that is, a way of seeing things from the perspective of the future, what they could become. He says that this essential Christian impulse, although it was throttled by the church, has popped out again here and there in such renegades as Thomas Münzer and Joachim of Fiore, but that its major vehicle in recent years has been movements of revolutionary social change. Christianity kindled a revolution which, instead of devouring its children, disavowed them.

In Bloch's view, not only man but the cosmos itself is an existence moving towards a still unfulfilled essence. Indeed he insists on this point so avidly that one cannot help being reminded of St. Paul's famous assertion in the eighth chapter of Romans that not only man but the creation itself groans and travails

13

waiting for its redemption. But here Bloch adamantly stops short of any agreement with St. Paul. It is not God who is the source of this discontent or the ground of this hope. Drawing on the same "left-wing Aristotelianism" that nourished Marx, Bloch contends that this restlessness of matter, its longing for form, is an inner characteristic of matter itself. Here he seems closer to the vision of Teilhard de Chardin than he does to those theologians who posit a God who beckons to the cosmos from a radically other future. Yet even here his position is not entirely unequivocal.

Bloch is a troubled atheist. He rejects the Christian propensity to hypostasize the future into an existent God. But he is also bothered by the nihilist alternative which sees man's hope merely as wishful projection into the void. Bloch wants to guard the unconditional openness of this future by arguing that it transcends all images and schemes that seek to give it content, but he refuses to assign it any viable facticity. He attempts to escape from this dilemma by talking about a "vacuum," an unfilled area which exerts a certain magnetic pull on man and on the cosmos. This moving point ahead of human history was once the cinema screen on which religious projections were flashed. Now we must no longer be deceived by the pictures. Still, for Bloch the moving point is no mere oasis, no cruel deception luring man on into destruction and frustration. But at the same time it has no substantial or existent reality. It is the constantly receding threshold over which existence passes in its endless quest for essence, a quest which, for Bloch, is never satisfied as long as man remains man.

Here the point of fruitful encounter between Marx and contemporary theology zooms into focus. Bloch balks at saying this open window to the future "exists." He is understandably afraid that to concede this would drag back into the picture all the static ontologies and superstitious notions of God that Christianity has for centuries erected, thus contributing to the constriction and stupefaction of man. But what Bloch does not realize clearly enough is that many Christian theologians today are equally reticent to claim God "exists" in the sense that makes

14

Bloch so uncomfortable. Tillich, for example, vigorously refuses to allow the verb "exists" to follow the noun "God." For Tillich the phrase "God does not exist" was central to his thought, since an existent being could not be the ground of all being and all existence. There is no real difference, therefore, between Tillich and Bloch on the question of the "existence" of God—they both deny it. The point of their essential disagreement is over the question of where the reality Tillich calls "God" and Bloch does not touches man. For Tillich it was "in the depths," as the source of our being. For Bloch, on the other hand, it is at the "forward edge," where man moves from the present into the future.

The truth is, however, that Tillich's influence in modern theology is now waning. The dialogue with Bloch is now in the hands of a younger group of theologians with somewhat differing emphases and interests. Although it is of course impossible to predict how the conversation between Bloch and these men will unfold, it is tempting to speculate on the contact points at which it will proceed. Naturally this can be done here, however, only with great brevity. Three groups in particular suggest this sort of comment: (1) the so-called "death-of-God" thinkers, (2) the "development" theologians, and (3) the "secular theologians."

For a death-of-God theologian such as Thomas Altizer, Bloch poses a serious challenge. He appears as a "threat from the left." For Bloch atheism is no issue; he has already accepted it. The death of God cannot become either the content of Christian proclamation nor the determinative condition under which theology must now proceed. It cannot be the proclamation since it is not new and not in itself very interesting. It cannot define theology's task since the mere disappearance of God does not answer what for Bloch remains the crucial question. What holds history open for man and man open for history?

What would Bloch think of Altizer's quasi-pantheistic mysticism? It is safe to guess that the restless old German Marxist would find the young American Christian's work disastrously defective at the very point at which Christianity makes its most

15

telling contribution: eschatology. Altizer's eschatology is in the past. God *has* died in Christ, and his reality now suffuses our whole world in a radically immanent way. Any notion of a God who "comes" in judgment or a Christ who threatens the kingdoms of the earth is missing from Altizer. Eternity has replaced history. Man, although he should love the world and his neighbor, has no need to open himself to the future since nothing really new is to be expected from there. But eschatology has a way of jarring inert worldliness, sowing seeds of discontent, and launching man into change and history. It would therefore seem reasonable to suppose that an appropriation of certain aspects of Bloch might restore an element of eschatology and therefore of social radicalism to Altizer's theology. Without it his position remains ahistorical with all the dangers of a conservative immanentism.

How would Bloch's thought engage those theologians who are seeking to develop the doctrine of God beyond its present state? Here the best example is the thought of Leslie Dewart. It seems unfortunate to me that in his provocative book *The Future of Belief,* Dewart never once mentions Ernst Bloch. Admittedly, Dewart tries to utilize scholastic thought even as he breaks out of it and shows its insufficiency. Bloch might have been a hindrance to this task. Still, Dewart's effort to push the present forms of Christian theism towards forms that will not elicit immediate atheistic counter-arguments might have benefited from Bloch's ideas on the ontology of the "not-yet."

Dewart, like Bloch, recognizes that the notion of God as a supernatural being, although it may have served a constructive purpose once, now acts as a drag on man's maturation and creativity. When combined with uncritical ideas about divine providence, the conventional doctrine of God saps man's initiative, undercuts his feeling of responsibility for history, and leads to a prolongation of childishness and dependency. Dewart tries to get the discussion on a new course by moving away from arguments about God's "existence" and focusing instead on the question of his "reality." He argues that the reality of God as that which enables man to be aware of and to transcend himself is experientially undeniable, although the word "God" may not be the best way to describe such a reality. He then tries to utilize the category of "presence" derived from Gabriel Marcel to describe the mode of our experience of God. For many readers, however, Dewart's argument, although fascinating, falls short of persuading completely, since the crucial question of the grounding of this "presence" in reality is left insufficiently developed.

Dewart correctly traces our present myopia about the reality of God to Parmenides and our mistaken insistence on equating being *real* with *existing*. He tries to suggest a possible doctrine of God that would grow out of man's experience of his own questionableness, his capacity for self-transcendence, and his irrefutable awareness of his own freedom. The trouble is that so many writers, Sartre for example, have used just such an approach without feeling any need for a God. Dewart admits that his ideas are provisional and tentative. What his book shows is that when we do leave scholastic categories behind, a new frame of reference will be needed, and that Marcel's somewhat illusive notion of "presence" may not suffice. Dewart's own interest in Marxism suggests that he could profit enormously from Bloch's thought, that the category of "hope" rather than that of "presence" might provide him with a more productive starting point in his exciting effort to facilitate a further stage in the development of theism.

What about that somewhat disparate group of thinkers who have been called "secular theologians," a group within which I would have to count myself, I think. Bloch's work provides an insight that will help enormously at just the point where the most vociferous complaints about our position have been lodged. How, we are constantly asked, does one prevent a theology of the *saeculum* from collapsing into a mere theological decoration of the world as it is? What is the source of prophetic criticism? If heaven has faded into oblivion, if the horizon of human history now defines the field of man's existence in faith, where is that Copernican point of perspective from which renewal and insight emerge?

From Bloch we might learn that a horizon is always formed by something, not by nothing. The hidden God, whose very hiddenness is disclosed in Jesus of Nazareth, provides history with its "frame," with what Marshall McLuhan might call its "anti-environment." Bloch helps us to see that this *saeculum,* this world-age, is bounded by the future towards which it hastens every day, a future it never attains but which continually prevents it from accepting itself as finished and final. With Bloch's help, we can be unremittingly concerned with the secular without sacrificing the transcendent. God is not above, or beneath us, or even just "within" us. He is ahead. Christian existence is defined by hope and the church is the community of God's tomorrow, eternally discontent with today.

This tiny volume of essays may begin a new chapter in the career of English-speaking theology. It will certainly bring to many people the voice of a man whom cold war politics and ephemeral intellectual fads have kept from us for far too long. I have often speculated on how different theology would be today if Ernst Bloch, rather than Martin Heidegger, had been our conversation partner for the past twenty years. Would we be as miserably lacking as we are in a theologically grounded social ethic? Would we be as disastrously out of touch with the revolution that is transforming the third world and burning the centers of our American cities? Would we have needed the catharsis of the death-of-God theology? Would we have allowed the ecclesiastical furniture shuffling of recent years to pose as a real renewal of the church? Might we have produced a theology that was truly radical in its impact on the world and not just in its rhetoric?

These questions cannot of course be answered today. Nor can we expect Bloch to do for us the work we must do for ourselves. Bloch is not just a Christian *manqué.* He does not help us much when we seek to spell out the *content* of hope for today's man. For Christians, that must come from a vision of what is possible for a world in which the God of Exodus and Easter is still alive.

18

Jürgen Moltmann

INTRODUCTION

What was an inner light becomes a consuming flame that spreads outward.

KARL MARX

"Where there is hope there is religion," Ernst Bloch wrote in *The Principle of Hope*. Nowhere does the underlying and inherited subject of all religion emerge so clearly as in Christianity, particularly in its explosive starting-point, the resurrection of the reviled and crucified Christ, and in its long history of hereticism. Rather than a static and therefore apologetic myth of a particular age and society, Bloch finds in it the "human-eschatological, hence explosive messianism" that always brings us back to the same question: *aut Christus aut Caesar*. And so he returns continually to the Bible, which "brought eschatological conscience into the world" and made the conception *incipit vita nova* an inspiration of human history.

But Bloch's reading of the Bible is not the one we are used to. It does not begin with the Creation, but with the watchword *Eritis sicut Deus;* and it ends not with God who has become human, but with man who has become divine. This is as atheistic as it is mystical, as pious as it is rebellious, and it is the reason why Bloch's philosophy makes religious and irreligious reading at the same time. Atheists are gratified to note the sarcastic

19

qualifications he holds ready for the transcendent consolations of the religious; yet his appraisals of the immanent and ersatz satisfactions of the non-religious are hardly less sarcastic. To the religious, Jews and Christians alike, Bloch seems irreligious; to the irreligious, to Marxists and positivists, he seems religious. He seems so because the old distinction between transcendence and immanence is no longer applicable to the historic dialectics of an eschatological future as elaborated by Bloch. What emerges here is a kind of *tertium genus* hardly known as yet. "Above Christian and Jew: messianism and the *Tertium Testamentum*," Bloch wrote in his first major work, *The Spirit of Utopia.* For him, the apocalyptic idea of freedom contains something absolute that will put an end to antitheses beyond those dreamed of by social utopians and revolutionaries; something that will change the understanding of all past contexts as well.

Bloch's own way of translating eschatological hope into philosophy, in order to make a *docta spes* of it, is as singular as it is unprecedented. His anthropology of "the not-yet-conscious" and his ontology of "not-yet-being" bring the first practicable categories into the unknown territory of hope and of the world process. As the same time, however, a negative knowledge preserves the ground of this hope, which defies ontologization. Even the *docta spes* retains aspects of folly. When priests become philosophers, fools become prophets. What triumphs at the conclusion of *The Principle of Hope* is neither Schelling's natural philosophy nor Marx's historical revolution. What triumphs is "the end" that banishes all the resolved historical enigmas to a realm of enigmatic provisionality—the end of which, according to Bloch, we know little more than the *index falsi,* the permanent negation of the negative, which spurs us on. The very greatness of this philosophy of hope may be that it turns all definitions of truth, virtue, and justice into "infinitions," extrications of the future and of freedom. Those who would pin Bloch down, to Marxism or to theology, are not going to meet the real Bloch. Time and again, reading and encountering his work will indicate new paths to unknown regions.

Life and Work

Man is a still undetermined being; hence a certain reserve is advisable in biographical notes. Ernst Bloch was born in Ludwigshafen in 1885. In retrospect he writes of this background: "Here the pure factory town of Ludwigshafen, ugly, without any history, founded on chemistry, but as full of hairy bruisers, boatmen and dives as a Jack London novel. And over there, across the Rhine, the elegant old theater, baroque observatory, and palace library of Mannheim, that philosophy-laden oasis." The situation typifies the conflict of a German nation behind time. Non-contemporaneity becomes contemporaneous. Here the incipient industrial landscape with its magnificent ugliness, social tensions, ruined nature, and uncertain future depends upon interest rates and markets; there, transfigured in the meantime, is the world of an apparently successful past. Here the Industrial Revolution, demanding that the freedoms of the French Revolution be extended in socialism; there the old world of the feudalistic German principalities, a world which in going down shines like a beautiful oasis for the man estranged from it. Here the assembly-line and managers and technicians without background, family, or past, with their eyes riveted on their own world of the future; over there music, baroque architecture, ancient art, tradition. As in a play by Bertolt Brecht, his non-contemporaneity of appearance and being, of tradition and modernity, invades Bloch's work. Utter incongruities blend into new horizons with surprising perspectives. Old stories, recondite fairy-tales, and philosophical profundities mingle with journalistic topicality, criticism of the times, and political purpose. It is a transitional form of thought, expressed with a vocabulary and style that are always provocative and startling. Here no theoretical system is built up like an old Gothic cathedral, stone by stone, as if to afford an encyclopedia of the whole. Bloch wants his thinking to be a "transcending"; and to bring the new and unknown of the future into the proximity of the lived moment. This thinking serves the ends of practice, experience, and

21

change. It moves like a ship that never stays in one place and yet holds an unvarying direction. It is full of the mysticism of the obscure, lived moment; and yet the thinker's eyes are open to fleeting encounters and superficial peculiarities. "To have plumbed thought at its deepest is to love life at its quickest," said Hölderlin.

The course of life reflects the singularity of thought. Bloch studied philosophy in Würzburg, Berlin, and Heidelberg, worked with Georg Simmel, and made friends in the Heidelberg circle of Radbruch, Jaspers, Lukács, Lederer, and others, before withdrawing as a pacifist from the overall national war fervor of 1914 and moving to Switzerland. There he wrote his first great work, *The Spirit of Utopia* (*Geist der Utopie,* 1918; revised edition, 1923). In it, Margarete Susman saw the flash of a new German metaphysics amid the gloom of the collapsing old world: "The utopian casts anchor on the bottom of the deepest, most fearful night." It is an expressive, baroque, and pious book; it offers a revolutionary gnosticism, a "God-conjuring philosophy" of "truth as prayer," as its last line says. The experience of alienation is enhanced to a tremendous God-forsakenness. "In ourselves alone the fire keeps blazing"; and Bloch turns it outward, fanning it into a consuming flame, to ripen the world for the "dread harvest festival of the Apocalypse." Here Margarete Susman saw the introduction to a great "system of theoretical messianism," and *The Principle of Hope* was to prove her right. At that time, others were not so perceptive. Bloch has kept faith with these Judaeo-Christian and philosophical-theological beginnings, though he would never repeat them with the same enthusiasm.

He lived through the glorious and yet miserable Twenties as a free lance writer in Munich and Berlin. In 1921 he published his case against reformatory Christianity, *Thomas Münzer as the Theologian of Revolution.* Münzer was the leader of the peasant uprising that was crushed with the battle of Frankenhausen in 1525. This militant chiliast of the kingdom, critic of the "gently living flesh of Wittenberg," and revolutionary romanticist struck Bloch as a pacemaker for the spirit of Utopia on earth. Christianity has attracted him ever since—not because of its ecclesiastical tradition, but through the subterranean history of its non-conformist heretics, from Marcion and Montanus down through the Cathari, Waldenses, Albigenses, Joachimites, Brethren of the Free Spirit, Hussites, Anabaptists, and Illuminati, all the way to Weitling, Tolstoy, and the religious socialists. In this "underground movement" the Bible is not read as it is in the Christian establishment. The demythologization that prevails there is completely different from the familiar one of our modern world. "Faith in God refers . . . not to a mythologically extant God, but to a future realm of freedom for God's children." "Insurgence" comes to be the professional ethics of the chiliastic Christian. Hence Bloch in 1921 struck a note which theologians are taking up only now in the attempts at a "theology of revolution."

Bertolt Brecht, Kurt Weill, and above all the unforgettable Walter Benjamin were among his friends. In those days Bloch wrote analyses of German "non-contemporaneity" for magazines, *Die Weltbühne* and *Sozialistische Monatshefte*. His collected aphorisms, essays, reportages, and reviews of a period in which German democratic-technological culture was thwarted and destroyed by right-wing romanticist reaction appeared in 1935, in the volume *This Time's Legacy* (*Erbschaft dieser Zeit*), when he was in exile. Also mounting up for a volume entitled *Traces* (*Spuren,* 1930), were visions, tales beneath the surface, burlesqued melodramas, snapshots from everyday life, in which sparks of unconditionality and of the future were struck from banality and simplemindedness. In Pirate Jenny's song from *The Threepenny Opera,* Bloch heard something like the melody of "the (possible) resurrection of the dead." "Hidden in the *citoyen* was the bourgeois; may God have mercy on us for what hides in the comrade," wrote this Communist sympathizer who never joined the party. Bloch is a master of the art of narrative which makes the familiar sound baffling, and brings out unexpected and quite different aspects of the conventional. He thinks in narration, and surprises in colloquy; he baffles, attracts, provokes, mystifies, and unveils at the same time. The reader of *Traces* will come closest to him.

In March 1933, under the unobtrusive title "The German

High School Composition," the magazine *Das Tage-Buch* ran a biting satire of his on the "Third Reich," which had just come to power. The public and police reaction forced him to flee at once. He emigrated via Prague, Vienna, Paris; in 1938 he arrived in the United States. There, in solitude (but also disappointed and forsaken in a Philadelphia without brotherly love) he wrote his magnum opus, *The Principle of Hope* (*Das Prinzip Hoffnung*, first published in East Berlin from 1955 on, then in Frankfurt in 1959). Here the rapturous "spirit of Utopia" has acquired measure and definition. The enthusiastic chiliasm of Thomas Münzer gains a solid footing. The "warm red" of unconditional passion for the coming realm of freedom combines with the "cold red" of critical-empirical social analysis; hope joins the categories of "real objective possibility" in the historic process. "Whatever is non-illusionary and really possible in images of hope will tend towards Marx, affecting (however varied and rationed out according to the current situation it may be) the socialist transformation of the world." What Bloch means is that the prophecies and hopes of mankind find their mundane aspects and must be conveyed in the open possibilities of the world process. From the real communication of hope and possibility he derives his basic categories: future, front, and "the new" (*novum*). But the grandeur and unconditionality of human hopes will also explode the schema hitherto known as "Marxism." Is Bloch a Marxist, or did he use Marxism as a building-block for his system of theoretical messianism? Although the question seems pertinent, it remains superficial. There is more to this work than Marx, and more is under discussion than can be fitted into the familiar pigeonholes of the ideological mind.

In 1949 Bloch returned from the United States to the part of Germany that seemed to him to offer a chance to "the new." But the Leipzig professor soon proved an uncongenial comrade to East German Communists. In 1957 he was ostracized by opportunistic students who held a mock-trial on the charge of a "revisionist version of Marxism." Cold-shouldered, isolated, soon forced into retirement, he became homeless in this "homeland of the proletariat." News of the construction of the Berlin wall on August 13, 1961, reached him while he was visiting the Federal Republic; instead of returning to Leipzig, he accepted a guest professorship in Tübingen. His impressive opening lecture there dealt with the central problem of his thought and life: "Can hope be disappointed?" His reply was that it could be disappointed, or else it would not be hope. But it remains hope, against all the temptations of nihilism, for the world process is inconclusive. It has not been victorious anywhere, but neither has it been frustrated anywhere. Exiting from its disappointments and embarrassments, hope regains itself in inconclusiveness. "Even the end of Christ was his beginning."

In 1961, finally, there appeared the latest surprise from Bloch's pen: a book on *Natural Law and Human Dignity* (*Naturrecht und menschliche Würde*). The great themes of critical enlightenment, freedom, and justice, and the French Revolution's "liberty, equality, fraternity," were now subjected to messianic interpretation. "No socialism without democracy, no democracy without socialism" (Rosa Luxemburg). There will be no human dignity if want is not ended, nor will there be human happiness unless the law is just and men can live with their heads held high. Here Bloch works out the forgotten and repressed problem of man in the affluent Western societies, and by means of all things, a concept of natural law that is generally thought to be conservative. But when man's true nature has not yet been found, the natural laws do not recall a past primordial state; instead, they "anticipate conditions in which injury and insult cease" and man achieves the "*eunomia* of walking upright."

Today one finds the octogenarian Bloch at his desk near Tübingen Abbey, where, at the outset of the French Revolution, the "Christian Jacobins" Hölderlin, Hegel, and Schelling conspired on behalf of freedom, reason, and the kingdom of God, lest their hands remain idle. He is also to be found making incendiary speeches at public rallies against the new German "emergency laws," and at the head of students in quest of their freedom. His life reflects his writing; and conversely, time and again, his thinking finds the necessary point of "con-temporaneous non-contemporaneity" between hope and the prevalence of seemingly hopeless conditions.

Atheism for God's Sake

A *Festschrift* for Ernst Bloch appeared in 1965 to celebrate his eightieth birthday. Of the eighteen contributions, five were purely theological in content and two others at least quasi-theo-logical. Surprised critics remarked on "too much theology" in honoring one who was, after all, an "atheistic thinker." No doubt, it is an odd phenomenon that of all disciplines, it should be Christian theology—always harshly criticized by Bloch—that feels provoked by him to renew itself. Do the messianic pathos and the homiletic posture of his language impress theologians and Christians? Are they stressing the eschatological vein and tacitly ignoring the atheistic emphases? Do they offer grandiose misinterpretations in their zeal to appropriate even this thinker and exalt him as a twentieth-century Father of the church?

The first thing to be said is that theology itself is today under-going a great transformation. Demythologizing biblical criticism, social criticism of the institutions of the church, and ideo-logical criticism of Christian preaching and ecclesiastical pro-nouncements are the marks of a new critical theology. We can hardly be concerned to appropriate alien elements at the very time when we are discarding everything we have for so long jealously and uncritically guarded as our property and privilege. Since Vatican II and the 1966 Geneva Ecumenical Conference on Church and Society, the two major Christian churches have set out to revise their common condemnation of the French Revolution and the social revolution of the nineteenth century. The "holy alliances" are dissolving. In these circumstances Bloch's philosophy is a useful solvent for lazy compromises. It puts religion and revolution on a path leading to common origins and to possibly parallel future goals. Throughout ecclesi-astical history the elimination of heresies has left the church more unified, but also poorer. The modern divisions between faith in the Creation and natural science, between eschatology and revolution, have opened a new schism in Christendom within contemporary society; the only way to overcome this will be a critical processing of the revolutionary chiliasm of the modern age. The reactions so far evoked by Bloch's philosophy indicate that instead of turning into Blochians, theologians feel encouraged to go their own way. However stimulating Bloch's utopian materialism may be for a new dialectical theology of nature and society, theologians are not going to engage in a possible remystification of nature. And however helpful Bloch's theoretical messianism may be in restoring the forgotten Christian eschatology to a meaningful theological dimension, theologians will not be so carried away as to overlook the cross in hope, and the faith that is the ground of their assurance. The literal concurrence seems most remarkable in Christology, where Bloch, like Athanasius, champions the *homoousios*— Christ's being of one nature with God. But what theologians understand to mean the complete incarnation of God in Christ means to Bloch, on the contrary, the complete deification of Christ and man.

Christian theology in the past has mostly followed the Platonic principle that "like alone knows like." God alone knows God. We know God in the Holy Spirit. In consequence, a likeness unto God was a requirement of his cognition. This is why Christian theologians have never been able to make themselves understood to any but the religious, those who are already asking about God. But there is also a line by Heraclitus, to the effect that things are known only by their opposites. Opposites attract each other, and so it is only by the non-divine that God is known as "God." The godless know God as the Other, as that which is unlike themselves. God knows the godless by justifying them, as St. Paul says, by always being their God "who justifieth the ungodly." Reformation theology knew this, and so does modern dialectical theology. Should the atheist who finds in himself no kinship and no likeness to God be closer to that divine maker of new life from nothingness than the religious man

27

who thinks he is a reflection of God? There is a form of atheism (like Feuerbach's) that takes the Old Testament ban on images seriously. There is an atheism for God's sake, like Bloch's. And there is an atheism that is negative theology. Are Christian theologians who talk of God for the sake of the Crucified not obliged to return continually from the realm of dogmatic answers to the realm of critical questions, and to have that realm of dogmatic answers open the way to freedom rather than block it with transcendent positions?

Yet atheism itself is not so unequivocal. "Only an atheist can be a good Christian," Bloch had written. In my contribution to the *Festschrift* I reversed this: "Only a Christian can be a good atheist." Bloch accepted the offer. But what is atheism? Is it the abandonment of a God different from man (as Feuerbach thought), so that God and man will come to be of one essence? In that case atheism would be the acme of mysticism. Or is it the perfect insight into the different being of God and man, in the expectation of future correspondence and communion? An atheist for atheism's sake knows no God as the wholly Other—or as that which makes man quite another—because he views himself as God. An atheist for God's sake, on the other hand, destroys all images, traditions, and religious feelings of his own that unite him with God in an illusive fashion; and he does so for the sake of the inexpressibly living, wholly different God. His atheism is negative theology.

Finally, God's defenders are not necessarily closer to God than God's accusers. It is not Job's theological friends who are justified, but Job himself. In the Psalms, protest and jubilation ring out in the same voice. Wherever in history the combination ceased to work, the theologians would learn as much about God from atheists as the atheists could perhaps learn from the theologians; and correspondingly, Christians may learn as much about Jesus from Jewish critics as the Jews can perhaps learn from Christians.

There are communities in the order of answers. They are always denominational and partisan and particular. But there is also a community in the order of questions, distinguished by

28

greater universality, open-mindedness, and solidarity. This is the expectancy of every creature. It is also the expectancy of Christians sighing at the non-redemption of the body and at the "unfreedom" of the world. In such community, Christian theology may join hands with the "atheistic" principle of hope: first, in fighting all those who would break man of the habit of questioning and casting doubt on his unhappy circumstances, so as to make him a well-adjusted functionary or consumer; and secondly, in finding the "traces" of man's coming homeland and helping him fight for freedom and justice in a society that would entwine him with itself.

KARL MARX, DEATH
AND THE APOCALYPSE*

1. The Socialist Idea

When considering the nature of the State we cannot be too ruth-
less in excluding any feelings of awe and solemnity. If it fails to
provide for economic efficiency and thus becomes obsolete, it is
nothing. All the other aspects of the State—oppressive or sopo-
rific—can be dispensed with; everything apart from the regula-
tion of bleak and functional matters just has to be dropped.
Once the fears and lies depart, the State may find it hard to
exist at all, let alone to excite esteem.

And how does it win respect? Perhaps on account of what it
inhibits by coercion? This, says Anatole France, is equality before the law: that rich and poor alike are forbidden to steal
firewood or to sleep under bridges. The inhibition of real in-
equality is so slight that in fact it amounts to protection. Or
does the State prove its Solomonic fatherhood by purveying
public justice? The weak are unshielded, but the slick are in-
vulnerable; people distrust the courts. There is no real concern
for individuals and for cases; paper and pedantry rule, and the
entire field of legal protection is methodically as well as
topically circumscribed by the horizon of property. Since legal

* Pages 31–41 translated by John Cumming; pages 41–72 translated by
E. B. Ashton.

training is of a purely formal nature, the talents peculiar to the exploiting class (a head for figures, censoriousness, and canny calculation) find ready soil in this formalism; and of course the contents of any odd economic order can be fitted without contradiction into the abstract amorality of jurisprudence. The plaint is not merely that most lawyers (like taxis) take on anyone who happens to come their way; not just that a judge in a civil trial is like a bad clock that won't function unless shoved hard by one of the parties, and lacks any personal impulsion to get at the truth; no, the law as a whole, and the greater part of the criminal law as well, is simply an instrument by which the ruling classes maintain the legal safeguards that *protect their interests*. This applies not only where trickery carries on its usual trade and wins in court; it applies even where the State takes a hand in the investigation and prosecution of crimes. The forms of punishment used, far from antithetically establishing the Right by their very crudeness, turn penal retribution into an immoral barbarism and the protection of society by penalties into the most inept prevention and most futile pedagogics that hindsight could possibly conceive. If there were no property, there would be no law and no need for its sharp-edged though hollow categories. The rest is the administration of palliatives or, as "justice," cure of souls.

But this wretched coercion would offer rewards too—handout presents. There are citizens it seems to value—*its* citizens— and above all, servants to be exalted. Hence the effrontery of wage laws, the conferring of dignities, the State clergy, the claim to be God on earth. Yet what more could bureaucracy mean, than that the right man should fill the right position in a purely technical administration. As for the divinity of the State, war and other forms of self-righteous terrorism have clearly shown us what kind of god inhabits the power States. Or are we to take the murderous compulsion of universal military service on behalf of the stock market and this or that dynasty as a proof of the moral substance of the *polis,* when we have just passed through one of history's most infamous hours, with the State once again blithely used as a springboard for the Furies, for the logic of natural catastrophes? It has gone so far that eventually the State is impelled to cut loose from the very business interests whose managing board it has become in bourgeois countries. In accordance with its feudal a-logical essence, the coercively structured State culminates in the war State; this proved an autonomous abstraction of power in itself that business interests, the causal infrastructure of the past, came to look like a kind of ideology in comparison—so utterly had the State, regardless of all bourgeois definitions and all socialist misconceptions, unveiled itself as a heathenish, satanic, coercive being in itself.

Though for a time it may continue to function in a bolshevist form, as a necessary transitional evil, in any socialist perspective a true conception of the State demands its withering away— its transformation into an international regulator of production and consumption, an immense apparatus set up to control *inessentials* and no longer containing, or capable of attracting, anything of import. Under socialism the State becomes an organization whose purely administrative and technical Esperanto will underlie the various national cultures; these may well constitute the next valid category of social cohesion. Conceived thus, the State signifies only a relatively stable fragment of economic history, sometimes of military history, and in principle of administrative history. At none of these stages does it contain anything independent, any product of the mind that is not ideology. At each of these stages (the last in particular) solely the clarifying frictionless operation of its regulative method in the midst of illogical life allows the State its justification and its sole, wholly instrumental and negative logic—a logic of need.

Therefore the right initial action ought to be as sober as possible, a boring into these things from below, so as to set them in motion. Marx taught that one must never seek or try more than is possible at the moment; that what counts is always only the very next step. The corresponding factor in revolution is the knowledge that, with justifiable selfishness, the oppressed wage slave found his proper function in revolutionary action, and saw it as a means of elevation. Marx names private interest as

33

in most cases the strongest motive force. The proletarian has nothing to lose but his chains, so his own interest—indeed his mere existence, and how much more his existence adequately conceived—is tantamount to a dissolution of capitalist society. In question here is no longer the natural growth of poverty (and not the "stratum" of bondsmen only mechanically depressed, so to speak, by the weight of society but still within society, as in the feudal age), but the emergence of a wholly new class, of social nothingness, of emancipation in itself. To this very class, and to its class struggle—which is an economic revolution *a priori*— Marx offers his magnificently paradoxical combination: the heritage of all freedom; the beginning of world history (after pre-history); the first genuine, total revolution; the end of all class struggles; and deliverance from the materialism of class interests as such. The alliance between the poor and the thinkers —between an egotism powerfully kindled by the *vis-à-vis de rien* (the life with nothing to look forward to), and the moral purity of communism—is said to be already in effect; or, as Marx put it: philosophy cannot be realized without the abrogation of the proletariat, and the proletariat cannot abrogate itself without the realization of philosophy. In particular, this alliance seemed possible to Marx because the proletarian as such already stands for an abrogation of society, because in capitalism society has reached the last of its dialectically possible, dissoluble forms; socialism accordingly posits no more visible class tension, and no contradictory, recoiling factor. In general, however, Marx never doubted this alliance between self-interest and *an idea* of this kind. It did not even strike him as a problem. That it seems possible at all is obviously because man's pursuit of his happiness is not altogether depraved, and because, if the pursuit is a revolutionary class interest, its ethical determination—or determinability, at least—will be defined by the simple fact of a *communal will*. Finally, the alliance seems possible because interest, to be effective, can no more dispense with the idea and statement of its suffering and of its will, than the idea can dispense with the course of the world as its own eventually refuted, duped equipment. Of course, such random usage, this kind of

Hegelian doctrine of the cunning of reason, is not the way to deal with the sublime; and in Christian ethics, in Kant, in Schopenhauer, we find an unvarying contradiction between the interests of the creature and the paradox of virtue, the idea of the good. Yet in a world as wretched as ours, the first step evidently requires a compromise with regard to the individual: one in line with Marx's despair of any political evidence of the good. Besides, the proportions that Marx assigned to the two factors (to the voluntaristic one of self-interest and to the panlogistical and, as it were, providential one of the idea) are by no means clearly defined. He wanted to act volitionally and to change the world; that was why he refused to wait for conditions to arise, but taught how they might be brought about; why he posited the class struggle and analyzed the economy for variables suited to active intervention. On the other hand, there was the occasionalism revived by the Romantics and above all, in a grandiose reversal of the irony of the subject into that of the *object,* by Hegel. This doctrine of world reason which makes use of everything, and now makes use precisely of the subject(s), could not fail to affect Marx.

And so the man who expelled any element of fetishism from the process of production; who would analyze and exorcise all irrationalities of history as merely unclarified, uncomprehended (and thus, in effect, fateful) obscurities of the class situation and productive process; who banished all dreams, effective utopias, and religiously garbed teleologies from history: the same man now treated the "productive forces" in the same over-constitutive, pantheistic, and mythicizing way; and accorded to the design of a "productive process" ultimately the same power of using and guiding which Hegel had granted the "idea," and even Schopenhauer his a-logical "will." Precisely this manifestation of the problem of proportionality between "subjective" will and "objective" idea proves the necessity of thinking it through in principle, and metaphysically—as Marx did not. History is a hard and a mixed voyage; there is only a chance that long-continued *activity* will turn into time, into its own *objectivity*—that it will change and transform time into a point of least resistance, or indeed into an allied private dynamics of objectivity. This clearly puts the problem on the same level as that on which the Council of Trent discussed the relations and proportions of freedom and "grace," and their possible synergism.

In the past, everything would mostly be reduced largely to hard cash; or there was the other way—the soul shining in, but always from above. The businessman has the laugh in *earthly* affairs, where the levers are in his hand; a misunderstood Jesus offers encouragement in the *ideal* field, trying in vain to arouse shame by not resisting evil. Marx at last created separate sensitivities: to externality, which so easily hardens the heart, and to the goodness of a man who would bring freedom by himself alone. Only afterwards does he unite the two; he is guided simultaneously, so to speak, by Jesus with a whip and the Jesus of brotherly love. Sometimes the conquest of evil may be managed in more quiet fashion, as by the proverbial horseman who simply didn't see that he was crossing a frozen lake, and—more profoundly—in exceptional situations, by the saint who succeeds with the kiss of love, ignoring evil creatively. Yet the rule is still that the soul must accept guilt in order to destroy existing evil, lest it incur the greater guilt of idyllic withdrawal, of seeming to be good by putting up with wrong. Dominance, or power in itself, is evil; but it takes power to counter it. The categorical imperative must carry a gun wherever and for so long as power can be crushed by no other means; and wherever and for so long as anything diabolical maintains its violent resistance to the (undiscovered) amulet of purity. Only afterwards can dominance, the "power" of even the good, and the lie of the "right" of retribution, be dispatched as neatly as possible.

Marx thus approaches this *third* way with a mental apparatus, a variant of the identical revolutionary concept, that is complex enough to let him counter mentally the sins of capital in capital's own purely economic terms (as the detective is homogeneous to the criminal), where nothing but economics need be considered; complex enough, too, to conceive of a higher life only afterwards, when the idea has been given room and freedom to move, and when the monstrous lies (including the unconscious embellishments, excuses, façades, and variables of purely economic functions) can be ousted by the currently and ultimately true idea of society.

This is a dual procedure. Instead of trying to determine economic conditions by psychological means, by means of a "league of the just," Marx extracts the economic from the psychological, and derives the psychological from the economic. Or—as he defines the essential maxim of the scientific socialism—that is his achievement, it is not men's consciousness that determines their existence; it is their social existence that determines their consciousness (the seedbed of their ideas).

By itself, of course, the sobriety of such a view is ultimately barren. Man does not live by bread alone. Outward things, no matter how extensive their importance and our need to attend to them, are merely suggestive, not creative. People, not things and not the mighty course of events outside ourselves (which Marx falsely places above us), write history. His determinism applies to the economic future, to the necessary economic-institutional change; but the new man, the leap, the power of love and light, and morality itself, are not yet accorded the requisite independence in the definitive social order. To put it another way: if the primitive mode of supplying human needs, the sequence of feudal and capitalistic economies, did determine spheres (at least) of a distinct moral and cultural life, then the discontinuance of all private economic components in the eventually successful economic method of socialism, must also have its distinct moral and cultural consequences. It must result in an equally "correct" *a priori* way of thinking and of culture that cannot be defined simply as "freethinking," as the banal atheism whose ideals socialists have taken over from bourgeois philistines. Of course, no adequately founded socialism could have emerged if Marx had been submissively pious, and if he had held on to the Arcadian state of a world requiring only rational distribution to give everyone all that he needs. No proficiently grounded socialism could have emerged if Marx had reorganized only the economy of consumers, and not (above all else) that of the producers; and if he had not done so with a practical eye to the inevitability of industrialization, and with an unromantic, cool, confining and vigorously disenchanting materialism. But it is precisely when this confinement lasts too long that man will be entirely economically harnessed, and that the pressures on him will be merely reduced, not relieved. After all, in the end production will again be out of the hands of those subject to the pressures, and a ghostly process of universals, of a self-eventuating economy, will take its idolistic and occasionalistic course, unbroken even in the future. This tallies with the fact that even where Marx did not soften his main drive to a "revolutionary development," it was still aimed at capitalism alone (a relatively young and derivative cancer) and not equally at the age-old, lasting core of all enslavement, cruelty, and exploitation: at militarism, feudalism and the supremacist world at large. Here the very identity of the adversary served in many ways to stunt, confuse, and dispirit the age-old socialist movement. In a religious perspective (closely linked with the above) there can be no doubt that indiscriminate ideological suspicion of any idea, without the urge to exalt an idea of one's own, will discourage rather than promote lucidity; nor can there be any doubt that Engels' assumption of a dialectical-synthetic restoration of a state of liberty, equality, fraternity as found in the old communist *gentes* falls short of a clear and strong, ideal constructive counterpart to the socially constructive effort. Heart, conscience, mind and spirit, the communion of all the living, brotherhood, Philadelphia, the end of secretiveness—on earth; these were more closely reflected in the French Revolution, that truly more than "bourgeois" outbreak of the history of heresy. And in these days, finally, with all things reddened by the desperate twilight of God, and neither Atlas nor Christ still able to uphold his heaven, there seems to be no particular philosophical merit in the Marxist fixation on an atheistic *status quo* that offers the human soul nothing but a more or less eudaimonistically furnished "heaven on earth" without the music we ought to hear from this effortlessly functioning economic and social mechanism.

38

What we can say, as a result of the strong emphasis on all (economically) deterministic factors, and of the latency of all the extant but still enigmatic transcending factors, is that *Marxism is near to being a Critique of Pure Reason for which no Critique of Practical Reason has yet been written.* Dialectics has voided the economy, but the soul and the faith it was to make room for are missing. The actively astute view has destroyed everything—much of it deservedly, of course, as with the private idylls and shallow reveries of the settlement-builders and secessionists of socialism, the men whose wish to distill the best of the world into a beautiful earth-on-the-side for themselves only made the rest of the globe spit. Certainly, too, there were grounds for repudiating the far too Arcadian, abstract utopian socialism that has repeatedly emerged since the Renaissance as a secularized mode of the millennium; often as a mere shroud without substance, an ideology for very sober class purposes and economic upheavals. Yet this helps us neither to comprehend the inherent utopian tendency, nor to grasp and judge the substance of its miraculous images—even less to dismiss primal religious desire. Throughout all the movements and goals of worldly transformation, this has been a desire to make room for life, for the attainment of a divine essence, for men to integrate themselves at last, in a millennium, with human kindness, freedom, and the light of the *telos*.

Not until then will the deceivers really quake, and the Right make its appearance. The conjurers will call up no more spirits, and dust will no longer be thrown into people's eyes. But more is needed than half-enlightenment of the kind that dispels the old heretical dreams of a better life instead of sifting and inheriting them. In this way alone, not by the pitiful means of popular atheism, can the mercantile would-be heroes, the wholesale-dealers and the power brokers, be ideologically strangled and their drapery stores padlocked. Only a man who combats it not only from earth but from the falsely abandoned heaven will be able really—that is to say, unseductively—to expose the humbug of the bourgeois-feudal ideology of the state; and then "enthusiasm for egalitarian indulgence" will no longer be the

39

only stirring element of the communist social theories, as it seemed to a Prussian State theologian named Stahl. Certainly men will work without the compulsion of need, and they will work much better and far more productively. Boredom and human unhappiness suffice to assure that. As an adequate motive in lieu of profit one will be able to use a man's joy in his skill, or at least in his factual office, as is now the case with teachers, civil servants, politicians, artists, and scientists. Not to mention the chances of evaluating this motive socially, the tremendous possibilities of raising contempt on the one hand and prestige, honor, and fame on the other, which more than make up for any monetary inducement.

Superficially only, Marx's far from laissez-faire "State of the future" exhibits some dangerous affinities: in Hegelian references to Prussia, to a universal State, to organization pure and simple—which makes it so much easier, so much more urgent, to feel obliged to raise him to a higher level, to the new, most intrinsic adventures of the life he liberated, to the question of what his society is for. In other words, the social construction that has been stopped short, cut back too severely, is to be returned to the utopian superiority of Weitling's, Baader's, Tolstoy's world of love, back to the new puissance of Dostoevsky's human encounters, back to the adventism of heretical history. Thus the distant totality of Utopia presents the picture of a building without a single economically profitable part: with everyone producing what he can; everyone consuming what he needs; everyone, according to the degree of his contribution, of his moral and intellectual ministry, openly taking, and taken on, mankind's way home through the dark of the world.

This is the only way to understand the new life that has become both radical and orthodox, and the only way in which the most exact order and sobriety of theoretical economics can be combined with, and legitimized by, political mysticism. All the wretched snags are removed and handed over to a cooperative society as the private sphere is abolished; but real privacy and all the socially irremovable problematics of the soul loom larger than ever. In the heights of the building (which requires socialism to become honest and clean) they will be combined with the Church—with a necessarily and *a priori* socialist-oriented Church facing new contents of revelation. Nothing else can create the space for community, for a freely self-chosen community *above* society (which merely lifts the burdens), and above a social economy thoroughly organized along communist lines, in a classless, and therefore non-violent, order.

But a changed Church is the carrier of widely visible goals; placed in a life beyond labor, it is the conceivable realm of the flow of traditions and a nexus with the end; and no order, however successful, can do without this last link in the relational series between the collective "we" and the problem of a final purpose. Then, at last, men will be free to deal with those uniquely practical concerns and questions which otherwise come only at the hour of death, after a lifetime of unrest has done little more than lock away the essentials. It is as Baal-Shem says: the Messiah cannot come until all his guests are seated at the table—and this is first the table of labor, then the one beyond labor, but immediately after, the table of the Lord. The kingdom of brotherly love provides the organization of the world with its ultimate metaphysical guidance.

2. The True Ideology of the Kingdom

But I want to be. And what is left for us at the end?

Will not all inwardness now seem still farther above us? For we must *die* without much delay, and corpses may not require such expansive wrappings, in order to go the way of all flesh. The inner wealth of brotherhood will be the same ephemeral spectre, rotting into tree bark like the spurious treasure of Rübezahl, the German mountain spirit, unless it shows it has the strength to withstand even death, and conquer death; and thus not only to undergo it but to be strongly above it as an essential part of eternal life. For the last time, therefore, we repeat an "intention" of further fulfillment—which here, of course, stands against more than phrases from the battle of Cannae and the

41

ensuing withdrawal of *creator spiritus:* So that's where we could end up, where we had to end up. Pay the piper, call the tune, says the German proverb. But this dance around calf and calf-skin at once, with nothing behind it, remained surprising none-theless. It means we have no genuine socialist idea. We have been more impoverished than the poor beasts; if our god is not the belly, it is the State; everything else has deteriorated into fun and games. We will stand waiting and longing; we have a short span of knowledge, but no action and—which helps ex-plain the lack of action—no scope, no vista, no ends, no inner threshold to sense and to cross, no core, and no conscience that would gather what is.

But here, in this book, a beginning has been posited exactly, with a new grasp on the unlost heritage; as rekindled here, the innermost, the beyond, is not a cowardly As-if denying the At-all along with the Not-yet, nor is it an unsubstantial façade. Instead, rising above all masks and bygone cultures was the One, the goal of every quest, the one dream, the one conscience, the one salvation. It swept forth from our unrent hearts, from the most profound, most real ground of our daydream, from the last thing that remained to us, the only one worth remaining. But what this book (which makes no peace with the world) car-ried through to, was our unapplied essence, our secret head and figure, the germ of our concretion and the core of our creative principle. This we heard interpreted here in the instance of a simple jug, interpreted as the *a priori* latent theme of all "repre-sentational" art, and finally interpreted as the center of all musical magic—in the last possible self-encounter as the con-ceived darkness of the living moment opens up and hears itself in the essence of the unconstruable, absolute question, in the "we-problem" of collectivity as such. It had to be said that these depths are reached by the *internal* way alone, also known as self-encounter—by the preparation of the inner word with-out which all outside vision is nothing, not a magnet, not a force that will attract the inner word on the outside as well, and will help it break through mundane error. Ultimately, of course— *after* this vertical, purely *internal* concrescence—the broad river ought to spread out, the wide *world* of the soul, the expanding, vibrating diapason of the problem of collectivity, the *external, cosmic* function of any utopia as against privation and death and the accumulated shells of physical nature.

In ourselves alone this fire still blazes, the last dream in Augustine's sense: *Deum et animam scire cupio. Nihilne plus? nihil omnino.* In ourselves alone the absolute light keeps shining, a *sigillum falsi et sui, mortis et vitae aeternae,* and the fantastic move to it begins: to the *external* interpretation of the day-dream, the *cosmic* manipulation of a concept that is utopian in principle. Finding this concept, finding the right for whose sake it behoves us to live, to be organized, to have time—this is where we are headed, why we are clearing the metaphysically constitutive trails afresh, calling for what is not, building into the blue that lines all edges of the world; this is why we build ourselves into the blue and search for truth and reality where mere factuality vanishes—*incipit vita nova.*

But we still live ever so briefly. We dwindle as we mature. Very soon we shall turn yellow and lie rotting far beneath.

We do paint images of what lies ahead, and insinuate ourselves into what may come after us. But no upward glance can fail to brush against *death* which makes all things pale. In our being and experience, nothing seems to take us beyond the caesura and let us vibrate beyond it.

We always stand outside. From our viewpoint there is no elucidating the strange case. Some who have returned at the last moment describe as colorful, if not indeed as happy dreams, what had seemed to bystanders like spasms or dreadful convulsions. But an old Jewish saying describes the gentlest form of death as like having a hair picked from our lips, and its more frequent, more terrible form as like having a knot ripped out of our throats.

Thus there is little, at first, to guide and assist us. When it is time to die, good wishes are not even fathers to the thought, much less to things in being. Nor can this be helped by means

of the comforting pictures we find roundabout and do not need
to approach otherwise than proverbially. In itself it makes no
great difference whether we say that all heights are lonely—
surely without being put under further obligations by the corresponding parallel between a mountain peak and Goethe—or
whether such parables as larva and butterfly, winter and spring,
or the lure of the new dawn seem to give us an external demonstration of life hereafter. And yet, although the leap from dying
to death will continue to defy experience, it still seems as though
in ourselves it should be possible to find more evident grounds
for the prospects of what endures, and what remains identical
on both sides of the caesura.

For we feel distinctly how we walk about in ourselves. It is
something we are aware of; we can hear the steps even though
the one who walks remains a shadow. We cannot reject the
impression that in us a hand controls the glove and may perhaps
take it off.

That death is the end pure and simple is thus a meager bit of
visual evidence; it doesn't say very much. One may be indifferent to what follows—as if life, which changes constantly, were
worth telling about, but death were a stable state whose determination sufficed once for all. But this very *skepsis* is far from
establishing a fact. When it really poses as a statement of complete personal extinction, or even as a mere statement of the
likelihood, it is by no means a cautious delimitation, a chapter
ending for lack of material. It is a theory in itself, a theory about
something unknown, which can be countered from the outset
with theories of personal indestructibility whose hypothetical
weight is entirely equal.

In short, it may be doubtful whether we could find the thought
of dying in ourselves if we had not previously seen death around
us, and had not accordingly taken our empirical place in it. It
is quite certain, however, that every single relational act is not
only accompanied but ultimately sustained by the relation of
"I feel, I will, I think," with the result that the I (the synthetic

point of view) will almost always shine into the perishable, oblivious workings as a self-assured being that is the way it is. Here lies a germ that is indestructible, a germ that is precisely the veiled I, *the dark, the question, the substance, the ground, the core of all our self-encounters*—no less shadowy as an act of consciousness than as an object of consciousness bent on objectifying itself, and yet the most real support of our personality. For to us this enduring thing is thoroughly given; at each moment we can find it phenomenologically, in order to make it evident to our minds. That we must die, on the other hand, is discoverable only empirically; and that in each case there must be some psycho-physical parallelism, that the death of the body must destroy the being of the soul, that there can be no life of the soul without corresponding physiological acts—this is a mere working hypothesis of physiological psychology (since Bergson, full of holes even in its special science, and purely regionally inferior to the phenomenological evidentiality of being-in-oneself, of the psychical substance).

Though external experience does not take us across far enough and unequivocally enough, we do—*pour être heureux ou malheureux il suffit de se croire tel*—have at least the phenomenological faculty to make out adequately that the being of the soul is different, physically superior, incomparable, and ultimately unaffected. In other words, that the core remains identical on both sides of the caesura. As Schelling ventured to prophesy on the strength of a Hyperionic illumination: "For the souls of those entirely replete with temporal things will indeed shrink very much and approach a state of annihilation; but the ones who in this life have already been full of enduring, eternal, and divine things will be eternal in the major part of their being." The human person does not simply step forth from the cogs of the body like the apostles on an artificial tower clock, destined to pass away with the body's empirically comprehensible mechanism. The soul in its eidetically real character is posited as indestructible; and its resonant, personal, personifiable qualities make the body and its death seem empty playacting like most of the other bungled works of extant empiricism.

45

Such is the detachment with which we often watch our own transformation. And yet, the least thing we are carrying with us is a significant yardstick. We could not suffer so much under shortcomings if something in us were not spurring us on, if there were no deeper chords seeking to drive us far beyond anything that has to do with the body. We would not be granted to do what we do all the time (and what is our very demonstration of the power of our not-yet-conscious knowledge, forebodings, and awe): to expect, intentionally, what lies ahead of us, what we are destined for—unless we felt as children do: that some day it will open, the box that is always locked and hides the secret of our origins.

What we see at work here is a vast, unfinished mass of voli-tive and apperceptive tendencies, a true spirit of the utopian soul. It is partly the fault of this spirit that pain and joy can only be felt—pain so strongly, joy so much more weakly—and are so much harder to grasp and to bring into form. It is also partly because of this spirit, however, that the happy and valuable ele-ments of our life, those that have become our gains, can be so much more accurately and essentially held fast in memory, at least, in this strongly post-mortal, highly metapsychical gift of ours. Of course, the great yardstick is no less truthful in showing us vile caricatures and deficiencies of ourselves, and finally, above all, our own anaemia—definitively understood as the sub-ject's inability to stand, to bear, to guarantee purposive chains that extend too far and imply too long a view. No matter how sure a man who looks at his beloved may feel that this soul cannot pass away—or, in analyzing the inner point of it, that man's inmost being cannot die—beyond this limit, beyond definitiveness and the immortal soul's manner of bearing the approach to it, the most evident phenomenology cannot make out a thing. What does appear now, clearly visible at that very limit, is the promised point from which the question of death is *extensively* illuminated by the encounter with self, exalting the problems of our historic and mystical existence against death, disturbances, and the eventual doom of the world.

Here, above all, we are changed, and now the self-certain "I"

46

makes a total exit. But while it used to seem as though such scope were to be gained only by a decline, by a degrading organic or social adjustment of the daydream that shows us the goal, there is now a leap: a desultory exitus-exodus in the collective "we" itself, posited on its own level. In the organic or social sphere the "I" was affecting, reinforcing, guiding something else, something it was merely on good terms with. It becomes objective in that sphere by joining itself like a violin string to the thousands of things and social facts it encounters, on the basis of their vacillation and vacuity—an objectivation that will, of course, make the "I" in itself ring more fully, widely, and deeply.

But now Zion's daughter stands facing no one but herself in her very own jeopardy, in the very gravest *de te res agitur,* which is precisely how death challenges the soul to metapsychical-metaphysical *probation* in the world, and in supra-mundane horrors. Here we reach the most inward and "most outward" point at once, the most direct passage from one to the other, the soul's most direct entrance into the "world"; we reach it on the free, great, scenic stage of decision, the ultimately most real part of metapsychics; we reach it in the form of death and its inherent metapsychical *challenge* simultaneously compelling *the full scope of the metapsychical sphere.* Here the inner light becomes wholly extensive, not a glow cast upon the field as in sociology, but a ray beamed out of the dome. In other words: if in view of death, against and above death, the inner man comes wholly into the open—if the hostile prick of death, the blow of doom, involves the most central application and rebirth of inwardness—death serves as the master-test of our journeyman years. It tests the height we have reached, the value of our inner metapsychics; it examines its strength, its utility, durability, and suitability in mobilization and in the most terrible reality; it introduces a factor alien to the subject and thus summons us directly from the subjectively ideal sphere, from the freely suspended realm of ideal self-definitions, to the "cosmic" realm of danger and diffusion, and of the gathering from the bustle of this world of death in which the self finally proves itself, after all. In short, death compels the *birth of metempsychosis by metapsychical force.*

As a result, our duty here, and our problem, is to allow what we have grasped as permanent in ourselves to triumph over our empirical views and shortcomings—that is to say: since we cannot experience history in its entirety, to conquer it by the strength of metempsychotic diffusion, and finally by means of the Apocalypse as the absolute work of the Son of man.

THE STRENGTH OF METEMPSYCHOTIC DIFFUSION

And yet it means a good deal to be able to die. There is a certain freedom of movement: a freedom to depart, at least, whether for good or only in the way of mists and clouds that rise and yet keep circulating. We can thus assume either that we are completely separated and can never return, or that a young life, a life from the beginning, is newly granted, unlocked, and poured out to us, over and over again. The former, harsher assumption, which takes all things to be definitive already, makes up the simple doctrine of the immortal soul.

In Judaism and Christianity the contrary view, that the soul migrates, is mentioned only covertly, if at all. On the Jewish side discussions of what happens in the beyond are few and far between; Sheol, the realm of shadows, covers all secrets. Only now and then could things concealed between the lines (or, better, in the lines) be read as pointing to the other view, to metempsychotic trains of thought. In Job 1, 21, for example: "Naked came I out of my mother's womb, and naked shall I return *thither.*" And in Genesis 3, 19: "Till thou *return* unto the ground, for out of it wast thou taken"; in Deuteronomy 33, 6 (according to the Aramaic translation of Onkelos): "Let Reuben live, and not die a *second* death"; in Ecclesiastes 1, 4 and 9: "One generation passeth away, and another generation cometh . . . The thing that hath been, it is that which shall be; and that which is done is that which shall be done; and there is no new thing under the sun." It also seems that Exodus 20, 5—

"For I the Lord thy God am a jealous God, visiting the iniquity of the fathers upon the children unto the third and fourth generation"—ought to be interpreted as referring to the same "I," especially if one recalls the Yahweh who would not destroy Sodom for the sake of ten righteous men, and who, when those ten were not found, had angels lead Lot, his wife, and his daughters out of the doomed city. These are just a few verses, of course, and stressing a "thither" or a "return," or taking "generation" to mean the same soul, will not enhance their probative value, quite apart from the fact that these changes in emphasis were made only later, in a Cabbalistic interpretation. Jesus also left these questions wholly unelucidated, and spoke only of a final resurrection on the Last Day; and so—despite occasional hints as in Matthew 11, 14, where John is said to be the reborn Elias, and although the Church had to make arrangements for a long wait, whereas Jesus had thought of the Last Judgment as directly imminent—the doctrine of immortality, the *abbreviated* form of metempsychosis, has remained essential Christian dogma, according to the New Testament as well. Post-Christian Jewish rabbis, on the other hand, had an increasingly vigorous recollection of metempsychosis as an intracosmic force of the spark across death. A line by Rabbi Meir Ben Gabbai succinctly discloses the whole intensively moral fundament of this doctrine, this mundanely embedded and effective postulate of our white magic against the black magic of death: "You must know that this work [the multiple transition of souls] is an act of God's mercy upon Israel, so that souls may become worthy of the light of the Supreme Light, and that, as our rabbis of blessed memory have said, all Israel may come to share in eternal life."

Wherever the speaker is not the "Messiah" himself, who indeed empties all happening, but where initiates speak of an *en route*—in all secret doctrines of the world, not just in the Buddhist one, but equally in the heart of the Sudan, in druidic Ireland, in Sufism, in the Cabbala, among the Cathari, throughout the old form of Christian Rosicrucianism—we find that the last assignment of neophytes as well as the regular, comparatively determinable *arcanum* in the mysteries is the second, subdivided, more just, more loving, more complex form of immortality: the transmigration of souls. In the aspect of a repeated life (as Lessing also emphasized, significantly, in his *Education of the Human Race*) there will not be, then, too much death and termination for one man alone.

Besides, whereas dying may be sufficiently grasped in the continued life of our souls, what place—not to mention anything else as yet—should we assign to birth, to the *descent* of the soul that has been created from the beginning, as even the dogma of immortality puts it? Why, once this incarnation is admitted for a single time, should it be confined to singularity? And what compels us, for the sake of such singularity, to cling to the consequence of a dully, continually unrolling number of souls? If there is nothing but the Last Day to limit that number, we may conclude, of course, that the world ends when God wills it —or rather, that its end has been a divine forethought from the beginning; so that it will probably come at the right moment, and the world's total soul-substance will have been used up and embodied as soon as there is no further need for it.

But it is also possible (and perhaps more justifiable in view of the random character of all creation) to argue the other way round: if the Last Day is to define the number of souls, the number of souls also defines the Last Day. In other words, if that day is so conceived, it will come when the meaningless, bad, finite number of souls has finally been exhausted by their singular births—with the unbearable result that the purely mathematical concept of a fulfilled quantity will take the place of the concept of catastrophe in the philosophy of nature, or of the metaphysical concept of a leap in the divine mystery. According to the inner-world's transcending idea, the value idea of metempsychosis, on the other hand, the mere *number* of souls has long been complete; what is still missing and therefore, of course, poses problems more profound than those of quantity, is the *maturity* of the souls; this alone will then determine the end.

That we are allowed to depart from earth—that we differ from things, which remain, and from the animals, whose death

50

is amateurish, without an "I," a memory, or achievements—
means that we have a more profound right to return to earth.
We take ourselves along, then, as we have become and have
come to be our own, inwardly, each in his way and still unfinished, without knowing ourselves. But often the vibrations
from down here will reach so far that even though a true "fore-
death" can scarcely be suffered, a man may think about his
inner luggage for the dread journey over the pitch-black seas on
which he sets uncertain sail. "Life's frenzied chase is drawing to
a close . . . Come! See if on the hearth a fire glows," says C. F.
Meyer's Ulrich von Hutten, weary unto death; it is this inwardness we carry into a beyond filled with its reverberations, with
its afterglow. "The dream was better," a saint exclaimed, down
here on earth. The least that remains, the least that applies, is
what Jean Paul reports of the last hour of this life: "When
everything in the broken spirit withers and dies—rhyming,
thinking, striving, joy—then the night flower of faith is still
green at the last and strengthens you with fragrance in the final
darkness." And shining still more deeply is a smile that does
not fade and allows no faltering, a smile from eyes that can
give us light in death; there is the richly transcending sound that
"shivers over" us, the living, and makes the dying sit up and
hearken upwards:

Roundabout they heard and knew not what they were hearing.
But the seraph reached for the soulful web of his lyre
And unsteadily, still in the throes of joy's sweet torment,
Down the luminous strings his wavering fingers ran . . .

Thus Klopstock, in the twelfth canto of his *Messiah,* on the
death of Mary, the sister of Lazarus, who died because she could
not bear the enchantment which the heavenly voice poured into
her breaking heart. Yes indeed: death uncovers here a deeper
sense of hearing—a sense by which death can be grasped, by
which our life can be victoriously entwined with death, like a
single Now, morally passed by the disembodied in the indicated
shadow-state of the beyond. If men knew who they were, the

51

re-embodied would have no trouble recalling their previous existence. But we do not know our true *Existence,* do not know who sleeps in the dark chamber of the lived moment, and so we lack a yardstick by which to tell our souls in other, earlier forms. We cannot make sure of their identity the way Novalis' Heinrich von Ofterdingen in the hermit's cave sees the metamorphoses of his figure depicted through the course of time.

But the *last* pictures have always been dark and incomprehensible, even when certain forms of its dream would surprise and enchant the soul; and likewise men lack the clue of *decisive* recognition, whenever such self-remembrance is claimed in later days. "My name is Nobody," Ulysses told Polyphemus, and the gloomy truth is that for purposes of final identification this remains the human name. Yet even though apparently denied a deeper insight into these things, let alone a recognition of ourselves as the same migrants, we still have the overpowering impression of which so many accounts of insight and memory tell us; and that votive offering in Delphi at the sight of which Pythagoras swooned with the cry "My shield!"—and which was the shield of Achilles—still hangs in every major event. Our memory itself is a most peculiar gift in which the internality of the lived moment is preserved for another time; and the concept of metempsychosis, the union of Epimetheus and Prometheus, is capable of adding to this gift an even greater metapsychical enigma—hope—without contradiction.

This, then, is why all the pictures of our past come rushing by in moments of mortal danger; this is what made the dying Pericles boast of having caused no wrong to be done any citizen; this is why, according to a profound Cabbalistic tradition, the same angel who burned as a small flame on the head of the foetus, who during the mother's pregnancy showed the soul around the higher regions, will now, when the end comes, return as the Angel of Death. He comes to the deathbed—and man recognizes his twofold guardian. By this fearful gauge and indicator of beginning and end, he can see how far he was thrown back, how much closer he came, and how large a debt to his original image his life has left open or paid, as the case may be.

"My deeds are my possessions," says Buddha. "My deeds are my inheritance, the mother's womb that bears me; my deeds are my only kin; my deeds are my refuge." All ancient initiations were meant as transitions, as perambulations with oneself: "I passed through the gates of death"—the seeming coffin, the coffin of Lazarus—"and set foot on Proserpine's threshold"— here the soul that has been captured by the nether world, by Pluto, by the past, by matter, recognizes itself as the same— "and having moved through all the elements, I saw at midnight the sun shining as though at noon"—poverty, grief, threatening extinction of the light, a total December night of the world, the birth of Horus, Mithras, Christ, the Messiah. What Apuleius has to tell about the death mysticism of the Eleusinian mysteries sets forth the content of all comparative esoterics, the Christian ones included.

But the departed souls should become young and embodied again; they are looking for us, down below, and the breasts, the flowering body, are their means of attracting us and clothing themselves. The lovers' embrace is the bridge that bears the dead back to life. They are the guests and the hosts as well; the will of the unborn is felt, though not exhaustively, in male strength and female allure. No soul, however lucid it may have become, leaves the inner-worldly circuit; the lucid ones will leave it least of all. The saint returns too, and returns in the flesh, intervening in the fates of the living. "The saint sacrifices as he eats," says Buddha again; he practises the great renunciation of still being here; being a teacher still, and lingering still on the plane of not knowing. Even men of genius enter the historic lists unaccidentally and unsubjectively, as it were, as the heirs to their own altogether discontinuous maturity, which could never be acquired in a single lifetime. Mythically akin to this is the motif of instruction in the returning sons of deities; the birth of Christ would have been the embodiment, the sepulchral journey, the all-pervading earthly journey of the man-oriented deity—the Son of man in God himself—if men as well as God had not failed in this supreme reincarnation, this contact between all of heaven and all of earth.

Thus the souls live to the last in a circuit of shared responsibility between here and there—a "there" that is not truly "over
there" unless the "here" will finally, fully appear in it. And to
the last they function as the organs of that great march of souls,
that *cosmic process of self-cognition,* which the errant, disjoint,
unknown god of souls or Holy Spirit pursues according to the
true gnosis of metempsychotic doctrine. It is in the world as a
passage, and in man as the world's head, the site of eventual
preparation, resurrection, and hot problematic circulation of a
universal idea that has not been found as yet.

HOPES AND CONSEQUENCES OF BEING PRESENT

But now it was a matter of being too strictly confined within
ourselves. The dark accident of birth moved us into particular
circumstances, into a short life with distant, invisible goals. The
problem that arose above all was who experiences this life in its
entirety, and whether, above this existence as it is, it may be
possible to set up something that concerns us constantly and
jointly, something that *all* can see ultimately. There the doctrine
of metempsychosis, this penetrating application of an assured
collectivity to the world's sundering course, should prove the
strongest antidote to the contradiction between our brief time
and the time of history, which is beyond experience.

First, of course, it will be asked whether the consolidation of
such a curved path is desirable at all. Is the external side of life
neat enough to be entrusted with the execution, the unbroken
execution, of reward and punishment? Above all: are the higher
powers so moral, are we so wisely governed, do we even want
to be so wisely and patriarchally governed that our karma will
be dictated to us like an assignment, with the negative items
pedantically balanced as in school, under penalty of backsliding
and suffering in the next life? Is it not more pious to stay with
an unordered life than to bow to such merciless discipline as is
represented by the inexorable causality of suffering, purification,
and bliss? And finally, if we do have a used soul, if the individ-

ual does pick up the threads of his work precisely where he dropped them in a previous existence, must the consequence for basement dwellers—who had the same start, after all—not necessarily be cowering despair? And for the better endowed, whose luck, talent, and place among the chosen will then truly strike them as their "heritage," must it not be the iciest pharisaism of "status"? Are the mediocre, the ones whose lives flow in a lukewarm twilight, equally compounded of night and day, not the only ones to whom the karma doctrine will sound a note of better days, a song of comfort? There is a good deal of truth in all these objections. But here the resolution must come from the thought that, after all, the journey is by no means forced upon us heteronomously, by circumstances and a God who is added in.

It is not only that all of us, as we grow old, can take note of dying. The air of death is what really makes us mature, and from our first hour we transform this air historically as we breathe it. This divides our life, gives stages and color to it, works out an attitude and a face, saves us from the immobility of the child or adolescent. And this cognizance goes farther: on subsequent paths our beating core has left the death-beat behind independently, along with the rest. What remains is dirty enough, but nothing can be less attached to us than the emptied corpse; so it may be painlessly flushed away after death—that tremendous excretion. We have not only escaped here, so that the slamming of the door will catch only our cloak (which does not belong to us anyway, except as a shell or a specimen of the real one), for it was too late for its destruction, and the leap of the soul, even the leap to the individual, historic soul, had already occurred. We also have been able to make death, which is as indeducible organically as gestation, serve our own light in ways that more than half express strength rather than misery. It is not only *within* this life that we found the Goethean "die, and be transformed" at work—that we forced many a dark energy of death to play the devil who must build St. Martin's chapel, who could serve as the engine of self-renewal, could mortify selfishness, could turn into nights of love and relaxations of our

55

limbs, into the very death of our worldliness. We also have used death and its essentially most evil and most horrifying power, this bolt of lightning hurled with satanic intent and at least tragic effect against everything that is significantly human—we have used death even *beyond* our one life, extracting from it the idea of multiple beginnings, the ichor from the witches' cauldron, a broad, parting and recurring and thus vigorously intermittent *diffusion of our ego over all history, an intermittence to various historic beings of the soul,* with the dream of a final, as yet un-coined, fully-ripened presence of our selves at the world's end.

This is why everything here is determinable only from the I, and not from without. And why the travels of the soul, the karma, and our own ability to be the cause of our future life (*nota bene:* of its purely characterological make-up)—why these constitute an instrumental outwitting of the external and su-perior, of the unchanged, unrelated automaton of the world. They are not at all, as it might seem at the outset, an out-rageously meaningless pan-logistical system of the real machinery of chance, luck, and success, conclusive all the way down to Desdemona's handkerchief. A karma of the soul is certainly not a causal determinant of the course of the world. It is cer-tainly not the moral and pan-logistical explanation of fate, *tyche,* and automaton, of the pure mechanism of events—much less their vindication. What the soul derives from wandering is solely the power to compel its external fate, to make use of it, to bring it into ironical accord with itself, to employ it like death as a tool kit for most unworldly purposes, to pervade it intel-ligibly in the midst of, and through, empiricism. Hence, to get back to the point: this is how we roughhew, not our innate, but our expressive bodies. Thus our seemingly unassailable charac-ter may well be open to historic alteration by us in eternity, just as it is in time. Thus all social and other fates, all wrong or missing encounters that have affected or hampered us here, may be anything but unique determinants of the soul's fate. Subjec-tively, at least, the radius of action that is born with us would go beyond the social differentiation of the moment, and it would therefore equip us not to regard it as the ultimate in a merely singular presence.

56

The rule would then be: nothing in life is singular; no accident is irrevocable; the five foolish virgins could find oil even after midnight; the *status viae* extends far beyond death, which is far from placing the rocklike stamp of a *status termini* upon us. And though, in keeping with the ephemerality of all realizations on earth, an organic and social pessimism remains ultimately inextinguishable, it is precisely as an individually affecting enclave of meaning, an enclave which can ultimately be excised from "fate," that the ability to work on our real "son of man" is not foreclosed to us in the perspective of *our own recurring, unsame sameness.*

Thus the last things, which we feared we would not see, are also coming very close to us as we live over and over. We must set the switches; we bear the agony of setting the course; but at the same time we go along. As ourselves, not merely remembered, we go the good, living way, the way of the goal; we follow it to the end because we *are* the way. Wieland's Hercules chooses, and chooses to act; he feels not at all like "a fool who died so that, being no more, he would catch unfelt existence on the lips of other fools."

The stone falls to the ground, but consciousness, once achieved, flares steeply higher and higher, bearing gold with it. At the very last it was still doubtful what might endure in the total experience of this life; but now, wherever we are true to ourselves, wherever we hold on to the core, we do live a continuing life as ourselves. Not at all times, but intermittently—and above all at its end—we live the entire life, the broad, historical life that is assigned to "mankind" as a whole. Or, put another way: if we make several appearances, our existence can spread over the whole of history. It would have become possible for us in different centuries to be on stage as the same human beings. It would be possible to live our own history—though unaccompanied by any recollection of our identity, since our deepest subjectivity can never be experienced. As indicated also by the resurrection of all the dead in the dogma of simple immortality, we would never be removed from living choirs and could be existing subjects at history's final event. *Everything could pass away, but the house of mankind must keep its full*

57

numerical strength and must stand lighted, so that some day, when the holocaust rages outside, we can be helped by the human achievements that inhabit it; and it is precisely from metempsychosis that such thinking leads to the point of genuine social, historical, and cultural ideology. It would be unthinkable to understand past ages, let alone to deduce a rhythmical historical recurrence of living (that is, individualistic) and "abstract" (that is, theological) times, if there were not an alternation between two different historical spirits—a change of poles, so to speak, which today, for instance, lets us look upon Greece and the Renaissance as the work of strangers, and understand the primitive man, Egypt, the Gothic Middle Ages, and above all the ineptly interrupted Baroque as the work of our brothers, if not of our own selves. Thus metempsychosis correctly divides history into two realms, a lower, earthly one and an upper, invisible one, between which this rotation of the two groups and times occurs, with history, or the typology of the next period, always receiving its *essential* causal stamp in the upper realm as that of the departed, the intermediate realm between here and the beyond.

And above all, above the history which we can keep repeating and around whose meanings we can play, metempsychosis simultaneously arranges for the presence, the tested presence, of all subjects at the *end* of history. It guarantees the concept of "mankind" in its absolute entity, in its then quite concretely complete numerical strength. What men do makes up the world's age of virility; and their time, the time of the circulation of their souls (historical time with its vast and subjectively, at least, well-founded and deep-rooted chains of purposes) makes up the true, constitutive mystery stage. The waters pour off; earth's fiery flow is extinguished; even the great mutations of the organic world have long lost their strength—but men have stayed at work, and now it is they who will finish the broad, historical, subjective metaphysics: the life of time (which overtakes all as it thunders against the heavens), and of its restless exemplification in the name of God.

FORMS OF UNIVERSAL SELF-ENCOUNTER,
OR ESCHATOLOGY

Too much round about us is still halting, and ultimately we are still in a state of not-yet-being.

It is only inwardly that we could no longer be permanently affected, that we have taken another road and built a house of our own.

But most of us work without knowing what we do, on grounds of mere low, jejune goals. Thus our vehement joint effort is spearheaded by no thought save that of economic profit, a meager, barbarian content whose sterility will soon suffice to bring it to a dead stop. The appearance of other, more idealistic endeavors avails little against it, for as long as they are denied decisive functions, and the power of decisive change, the co-operative and intellectual factors will remain as random as the business factor will remain a senseless breaking of records. One is a pure matter of the belly, the other a lie woven around the business side—or else, after hunger has been stilled and luxury given free rein, it is a kind of sport, of clowning, fun and games, a science in itself, research into the psychology of gnats or (as Dostoevsky declared mockingly) a treatise on the Hanseatic importance of Hanau, and on the special and obscure reasons why Hanau in those days had no such importance at all. The mind is reduced to a bottomless and fundamentally shameless figure of speech. It would take only a single turn, of course, to make the night of our fragmented doings lucidly surveyable; even under a spell men face in one direction, and the orders under which they work on the establishment of liberty are sealed.

For there came restless reaching, the work we had others do for us, and the iron service rendered by mechanical force. Yet relief by means of technology is to come, as a result—life's henceforth irresistible blessing, which makes it possible to abolish poverty and allows the revolutionary proletariat to relieve men forcibly of economic problems. To come, too, is the progressive reception of alien *mores* and phenomenologies into a

59

common point of view, not determined by colonialist policies
but following the old program of the idea of mission. To come,
not to be thwarted any more, is the federal approach of peoples
to each other, the reduction of their differences to a parallax of
the distant star, the "multiverse" of a world republic, so that the
waste of segregated cultures may cease and the fellow-man (that
which we mean by the name of morality) may at last be born.
To come, finally, is the rebirth of a *polis*-less, paracletically
permeated church that will call anew on a fraternal element in
human life, and preserve anew the fiery, unifying signals of the
travel companionship and spiritual confederation of men.

The course of liberation, as we have seen, is thus not aimed
at facilitating somnolence or generalizing the pleasurable, com-
fortable leisure of the contemporary upper classes. We do not
propose to end up with the world of Dickens, or to warm ourselves at the fireplaces of Victorian England, at best. The goal,
the eminently practical goal, and the basic motive of socialist
ideology is this: to give to every man not just a job but his own
distress, boredom, wretchedness, misery, and darkness, his own
buried, summoning light; to give to everyone's life a Dostoev-
skyan touch, so that he will be clear about himself and his moral
party-affiliation once the walls of the body tumble—of the world
body that shielded us from the demons—in other words, once
the ramparts of the realm of earthly institutions are razed.

And all this is now preceded by a breath from afar off. The
soul lights up; truly creative thought awakens. What appears
called to active intervention here will surely come in time, from
the viewpoint of a philosophy of history; it will be justified even
if received and witnessed, not by the people who happen to live
at the time, but only by whatever is ahead of its time. What
stirs in this book: the urge to know what is to be done and to
unlock the world of the "I"; to set out in earnest, at last, to end
the immoral game of a "world enigma" and its apparent book
solutions; to place ethics, and a philosophy of being open to
enormity, at the most constitutive point of the seventh day of
Creation—these very first sketches for a system are already
written regardless of a living public. Dictated by conscience and

a philosophy of history, they are written for another kind of service and guidance: for the human spirit in ourselves, for the divine spirit in the state of this epoch, as indices of its level. Every book has an intent, an *a priori,* and the ultimate strength of this utopian book is meant to be that of two hands holding a cup and carrying it to the end, filled with the libation of the self-encounters and of music as the earthly blasting powders and tropical essences of the *telos,* lifted up to God on high. In no other way can the inherently useless, anarchic, and far too objective literary side of intellectual structures be brought into a framework and into relief, by way of a historical-theological background that will let us assign a flow, a direction, a serving value and a metaphysical place to whatever works men create above themselves—the metaphysical area of another test, a restless mobilization; the area of genuine socialist ideology; the area of the grand strategy of civilization and culture against human viciousness, against the world's all-confusing stupidity and lack of values; the area of a strategy dictated by the conscience of the kingdom.

Nothing can permanently thwart us here, apart from ordinary dying. But of course, this is exactly why the ever-active adversary looks for ways to hit, deceive, and perplex even a soul that has escaped by transmigration. The fact that inwardly, in the shade of the towers we have built, nothing will strike us any longer is the very reason why, for our four hundred years of total migration and emancipation, the bad conscience of the end has been seeking at least to slow down the process. Thus, to begin with, evil does not approach us as pride any more, but on the contrary as slumber, lassitude, concealment of the "I," and distortion of the beyond. It approaches us in far more dreadful fashion, for the situation with regard to God is now reversed: men have ceased to believe in the devil and no longer have an eye for the cashiered side of transcendence—and this is what makes for the adversary's real triumph and facilitates his revengeful design. There are two points, above all, both aimed precisely at the two criteria of discovering philosophical truth, which serve to unfold the malice of this Satan in God, this element which we have overtaken and which hates us now and seeks revenge. For one thing, it may harden our hearts and seal them against our neighbor. And then, in a more thorough intervention, it may so closely restrict our will to be, may make us so quickly contented, that any definitive fire will die down. The venomous, breathtaking frigid mist seems able not only to harden hearts and fill them with envy, obduracy, and resentment, with bloody scorn for the divine image and light, with all the causes of the only true original sin, which is *not wanting* to be like God. No, the bad conscience of the end can also sap our minds, make them callous enough for the next part of this original sin: phantasms, contentment with the world, the state as an end in itself, mundane omnipotency through devil-worship; and thus toleration of the distance, unwillingness to be like God, as the intrinsic, conscious formula of Anti-Christendom. But all this is not the *most* intrinsic trump card of the Anti-God. The soul is not yet sufficiently withered for it, still being mixed with too many counterforces; the last-minute outburst of bitterness against all power, against any apparatus of rankness, against all pointed or indenting works of evil, has been too explosive; and finally the pangs of absolute conscience at the coldness of the heart, and also at all glittering seclusion will be too vigorous. Pillage overtakes the bogus temples of imagery, of works, and of any cultural dead hand. But the very fact that our radical overlight starts burning here more strongly, burning through the world and the mirages, shows us the last, the most dreadful, the absolute counterblow: what *other* forces, long ignored, remain for us to unharness; what a disturbing, frustrating force may be exerted by the plain stupidity of God-forsaken, value-free causality; how well the vengefully inflamed demiurgic element knows how to fall back upon its very own potent and impotent artifact that is still our living space; and how terribly ultimate and absolute a form of dying and means of death remains available in *physical nature,* which is the unfeeling stage of our kingdom.

True, we alone of all the downward castaways have moved out of it. But as we did so, the lower realm drifted on without a soul; the wheels kept turning, and a kind of blind, vacuous, accidental shoving became the rule in this life. This may hit us at will, dealing frustration, death, and calamity. So the lower realm affects us extraneously enough, but often also as if taking its revenge in the lost letter, in the bad doctor who happened to live nearby, in the extra glass of wine the railway engineer consumed before the crash—even though it was steam that propelled that engine. An *olla podrida* of mishap and serviceability comes upon us—so foolish, so maliciously arbitrary are the causal connections of this world. We are right in their midst, amid a thousand random disturbances and concatenations, the prey of accidental affinities—but we say too much if we call them "chance," and ascribe blindness to nature, that monstrous rock that slipped out of our hands and is now taking its value-free course down the precipice.

Flaubert captured this agony of our lives, and its silly, unnerving stupidity. The world is a tower in which a captive is held, and there is no humanizing the tower. The world is Ixion's wheel, to which mankind is strapped; it is not what it seemed to astral myth-makers under the pagan spell: a Zodiac close to Christ, which macrocosmic man might be transferred to without losing any of his depth. In dawn, dusk, spring, and sun, external nature does give some dull, broad advance enactments of inner mysteries, turning the morgue into a mental scenario as if the external sun were indeed hiding a Christ—but the correspondence is oblique, at best.

There are no feast days in the natural summer; the sun of the spirit does not cast its brightest light until Christmas; in every creaturely and natural view, Christianity is a paradox; in the Apocalypse the heaven departs as a scroll when rolled up; and not without reason does the Cabbala teach how the very ruins of nature gave birth to the evil demons bent upon destroying the realm of men. Mere physical nature is an embarrassment in itself. It is the fallen house in which man did not occur, a rubble of life that has been defrauded, has died, has been corrupted, has strayed, and perished. It is the kingdom of Edom as it was and as it exists outside Israel—the nation of men and kingdom of the spirits; and it is at all times a dangerous point of attack

63

for the Ahrimanic counterblow of premature perdition, of an anticipated Apocalypse.

Here we feel a gentle motion of the ground that seemed no longer to extend to us. But we have not entirely escaped the mysterious events which by all appearances work in the realm that lies beneath us and bears us. The process from helium all the way down to lead—this weight loss, this explosive decline to the simpler configurations of electric charges—is a perfect unrolling, a disintegration of past density, and on the whole the first chemically comprehensible indication of that physically long-effective entropy that sets out to raze and level the old, strongly vaulted physical structure.

Here a warning signal of the end is already perceptible, a soft, distant tremor. A small, strange, previously unseen cloud heralds the approaching storm: somewhere behind our backs, in the subterranean processes of radioactivity—no longer merely of entropy, the Second Law of Thermodynamics—physical nature is crumbling. As we see it, of course, all this goes on calmly and disconnectedly enough; but should the leap have no place in a process that has so much to do with the end? True, entropic cooling could not be the only factor in the physical end. Here the weights of the clock drop only very gradually; the decline of the potential is extremely slow, still quite commensurate with endless physical time, and besides, as a mere slackening of the universe, the process in itself is anything but desultory and explosive. However—quite apart from the fact that the radioactive discharge has occurred only now and thus in a historic context, if not indeed in a functional connection with the place occupied in history by our present human work—if the incipient swaying of the ground *is* so utterly unrelated to our differently structured age, would this not be the very *discontinuity* that makes us lose our footing and which most perilously parts the moments of vanishing matter and religious maturity? Is it not by such a discontinuity that nature, this barely enduring coffin lid, this laborious, deathly-clear rubble heap of worlds which God, according to the Cabbala, shattered because man did not occur in them—that this monstrous, headless stage prop, this hard, tarnished, godless shell, is put at the mercy of every malign metaphysical incursion, without a chance of celestial resistance?

We know, we can know by definition, that as a process the world has an end in time as it has a beginning. The not-knowing that sustains it is not a permanent state in its yawning relativity; metacosmically, it must be limited either by absolute futility or by absolute universality. Hence the attenuation and constriction of whatever does not help us beyond the burning vapors. We are not spared the terrors of the year One Thousand, and the many preachers of doom who have since risen only to be disappointed cannot compromise Jesus' words of the Last Day, that will flame as if from a jet. The main blow is yet to come, and the counter-movement to the goal, a movement which eventually can no longer be rationed, shows what a dreadful Achilles heel has been left by the sickness and possible death of matter, by a weird nature that has not bloomed and is devoid of man and not yet called to itself—what a standing invitation to any poison and blast, to the properly netherworldly explosive act diverging in principle from the day of maturity: to the *natural act* of the Apocalypse.

For when we die—even though we always die as men who would still need a lot more life to "finish"—the earth remains, and the weapons can be passed on. But when we are strangled and suffocate; when the mountains and islands are moved out of their places and the sun becomes black as sackcloth made from hair, and the moon becomes as blood; when for us, unready and unsheltered as we are, all time in the world and the world's very face are extinguished in the raging, satanically directed thunderstorms of the world's midnight, in the inconceivable collapse of all fundaments and firmaments—then we stand to face the end naked, by halves, lukewarm, unclear, and yet "finished" in the sense of the tragic situation, although shattered by desires, connections, and lengths of time quite different from those of our work, and of the time it has laboriously wrested from Satan. Now *Satan's* apocalyptic moment holds sway, and at this premature, satanically arbitrary but irrevocable closing hour of our

65

work, nothing will carry weight except what we have achieved in purity and preparedness, in possessions of the soul and thoughts of the mind, in *having become at all*—nothing but the vocal cognition of *our name, of the finally found name of God* —lest all be in vain, lest the journey be cheated of its goal and all its recuperations such as life, souls, works, or worlds of love perish without a germ remaining in the dust of cosmic waste. Only a good, thoughtful human who holds the key can attract the dawn in this night of annihilation, if those who have remained impure do not weaken him, and if his cry for the Messiah is illumined enough to stir the saving hands, to make quite sure of the grace of arrival, to rouse the inspiring, grace-bringing forces of the Sabbath kingdom—in other words, at once to consume and to conquer the crude, satanically stifling fire of the Apocalypse.

This is by no means a matter of our admission or non-admission. Who should or should not admit us; who should judge us —*nil inultum remanebit*—lest he be judged? That we and a God are foiled is the only judgment passed, on us and on him, and it is frightful enough. To be just, therefore, however needfully the eye turns toward revelation, the tribunal in the Revelation of St. John calls for mutuality. Like Ivan Karamazov, we would rather stay with our unavenged suffering and hot, unquenchable anger than see the rest (quite innocent children as well) condemned to suffer for the purchase of eternal harmony. Why, asks Ivan Karamazov, are the children (who can have nothing in common with the whole adult complex of sin, retribution and reconciliation) also turned into material to manure the soil of future harmony for others? "I admit I cannot understand why all this is so arranged. . . . Oh, Alyosha, I do not want to blaspheme! I do understand what an upheaval of the universe it will be when all things in heaven and on earth and under the earth blend in one song of praise, when all that lives and has lived cries out: 'Thou art just, O Lord, for Thy ways are revealed!' When the mother hugs the fiend who threw her child to the dogs, and all three of them sing with tears in their eyes, 'Thou art just, O Lord'—then, of course, the crown of all knowledge and all cognition is reached and everything will find its explanation."

But Dostoevsky refuses to make this outcry. The children's tears are unpaid for—they can never be paid for, neither by revenge nor by forgiveness; there is no one in this world of ours who has the right to forgive that, and if the sufferings of children must be added to make up the sum of suffering required to pay for truth, then truth is not worth the price, and Ivan Karamazov as a man of honor declines the ticket to ultimate harmony. That is to say: we may have to see everything and to be present when it happens, that precious world finale at the moment of eternal harmony which will suffice to still the outrage of all hearts, to make up for all the atrocities men have committed, to atone for all the blood they have shed, to make it possible not just to forgive but to justify everything that has happened between them. And yet, in Ivan Karamazov and in us, there lies a power that will not acquiesce, a power which Dostoevsky, in a line of unheard-of profundity, calls having faith in God but scorn for his world, and as much scorn for the end result, the pan-logistical day of judgment and reconciliation.

Let us therefore put our own faith not in "him that is," the subverted one, but in him who is valid. One cannot simultaneously want or worship the world, the Lord of the world, and that which cures the world or cures us of the world. For the oblique rule which somehow governs the course of extant, natural things, it would be truly unfitting to tolerate all earthquakes, shipwrecks, and wars and to start worrying only at the sinful confusion of human hearts.

At first there was no trend at all except a vaguely anthropomorphic one; but with Adam, with Jesus, there emerged a twofold direction: the mundane God, more and more distinctly turning into Satan, the adversary and the stumbling block; and —moving on with Jesus, with Lucifer—the God of future ascension, the essentiality of inner radiance, of the Shechina or proper glory of God. What holds us here in its bungling and then vengeful hands, the inhibiting, persecuting, blinding spider, the devouring and being devoured, the venomous scorpion, the avenging angel, the demon of chance, disaster, and death, the homelessness of all sense, the dense, banal, hardly penetrable mountain range that separates from all Providence, the sorcerer of pan-logistic "piety"—all this *cannot* be the same principle that will some day sit in judgment and will pretend, then, to have long been watching over us in unfathomable, supra-rational ways and to have had us at heart, regardless of the world's "fall" which would be due to our pride. There is this double "I" in God, as our own depth, mingled at first, unclear, undivided, but then quite clearly awakened and set forth exactly —insofar as men would take the path of wanting to know better, insofar as the serpent returned in Christ and made the true revelation more closely audible, defying the wrath of the demiurge. In other words: insofar as our Luciferian being rebelled against the principle of the erring, manless, physical beginning of the world—rebelled really, in building the tower of Babel, and rebelled ideally, in the Fall of man and of angels—and insofar as prophets and Christ himself proclaimed the will to create, to know, to be like God, that so-called "original sin" of the past, as the supreme postulate.

This, however, comes entirely from our heroic component, from Lucifer, the insurgent who comes home at last, from the subject's will to know better, from the rebel with a cause. It comes from the core of intensity, from the chieftain of concealed subjectivism, now recognized as no longer a *mediator* but a *conqueror,* the germ of the Paraclete. It comes from the banner of Michael and the halo of Christ as simultaneous proof of the feeble, far distant, ultimate God: the utopian idea, the idea of the good, which will no longer fight Lucifer and—like the blackened sun, that truly and solely fallen night figure of the demiurge—present him rather than itself as Satan. The goal of that fight, to be sure, is to have men meet the day of the physical world's removal with purified souls, with the finally found *universal* of their souls, with the untorn paracletic genius of man's innermost, with word from the essence, with the cue of that Holy Spirit which in itself would have nature, this rubble pile of error, vanish so completely that no tombstone, much less a hell, would be needed for the wicked or for Satan. True, the life of the soul vibrates beyond the body; there is something like a germ plasma of the soul, and the loss of the body does not affect transphysiological immortality. To vibrate beyond the destruction of the world, however, the soul's life must be "finished" in the deepest sense; a lucky cast must have latched its ropes to the poles of the landing beyond if its germ plasma is not to be swept down the chasm of eternal death, missing the goals that matter most in the organization of life on earth: our pinnacle, eternal life; the unlocked, established inwardness; the immortality that is trans-cosmological as well; the sole reality of the kingdom of souls; the *pleroma* of the Holy Spirit; the foundation *in integrum* out of the labyrinth of the world.

3. The Countenance of the Will

We live and do not know why. We die and do not know whither.

To say what one wants now and afterwards is easy. But no one can say what he wants at all in this so very purposive existence. "I wonder why I am of good cheer," says an adage carved into medieval doors.

And yet we here, suffering and benighted, can hope far afield. If it remains strong enough, if it is pure and undistractedly aware of itself, hope will not fail us. For the human soul encompasses all things, even the beyond that is not yet. The soul alone is what we want, and thinking serves it. It is the sole space of thought, the content of its language, and its object—an object scattered all over the world, concealed in the darkness of the lived moment, promised in the form of the absolute question. And because that which is cannot be conceived any more, only reconceived and reduced to a matter of the soul; because good wishes, as they can be fathers to the thought, can also become fathers to things, which alone are truthful; because of this eventually unfactual, anti-mundane, world-dividing homogeneity of thought and of *not being, not-yet-being,* the *creative* concept deals now only with empirical factuality and with its logic, no

69

longer with utopian factuality, with the constitutive fantasies that are inaccessible or transcendent, if not indeed the "metaphysics" forbidden by Kant.

This should not be understood to mean that we can merely show the beyond to be "possible." A river can freeze over under certain conditions. That plants can feel is possible under hypothetical conditions, assuming certain premises that have not yet been confirmed. That there can be desert spirits is possible under problematical conditions, assuming premises so far unknown and perhaps wholly outside our present faculties of experience. But *that we shall be saved, that there can be a kingdom of heaven, that an evident insight into dream contents establishes them for the human soul, that correlatively confronting them is a sphere of reality, no matter how we define it*—this is not only conceivable, that is, formally possible; it is *downright necessary,* far removed from all formal or real indications, proofs, allowances, and premises of its existence. In the nature of the case it is postulated *a priori,* and hence of a reality that is *utopian, essential,* and exactly given for the intensively inclined. It lies in the concept of the lucid, holy soul, the beautiful, timeless soul whose exegesis and teaching has here been undertaken by methods of thought, but on the objects of faith alone: "He that overcometh, the same shall be clothed in white raiment; and I will not blot out his name out of the book of life, but I will confess his name before my Father, and before his angels." Thus good will has no limit, and the true thought sounds the one and only magic word we seek, the one that need but ring out to make every creature unveil itself, the word that need but stir to make the God-bearing soul unlock its dream, its foreboding that will ultimately be the truth of the whole world.

Hence to the end: as we think of suffering and longing, we ourselves step through our inward mirror. We disappear through the small, painted door of the fabled palace and are not seen again, neither in this world nor in another. The all-moving, all-concealing moment has come and burst open, and time stands still in the interior space of absolute, present revelation. This also was suggested messianically in Christ's return, and what is blown up explosively is the without, the sum of obstacles, the satanic demon of death, of the world's encrusted *ritardando*— whatever is not of us, the many individuals hoping for themselves, and of our heavenly glory, or what may hamper us even —while inside, in the Gothic chamber of the self-encounter, this entire vast and seemingly so real world will some day hang on the walls like a mere picture of innocuous remembrance.

If the soul is the sole object of our will, however, it also unveils the will itself. The driving force in its depth is at the same time the content, the only arrival, the covering of the drive as its philosophy vibrates through the world once more, opening everywhere the doors to Christ—that is, to the self-adequation of human longings—and correspondingly revealing the secret man, this always-intended, always utopian presence, this identical substance of what is meant by all moral-mystical symbols. Thus we are both wanderers and compass: coinciding at last with themselves, the intensities that were the enigma *before* the category are and remain now, *after* the category, the sole intended solution, appearing even above the transcendence of the idea, which had been supreme. The thing in itself used to appear as that-which-is-not-yet, that which is drifting and dreaming in the darkness of life, in the factual blue of the objects and at the same time behind all thought, as content of the deepest hope and awe. Now—according to the last unity of intensity and light as *their* self-revelation—the thing in itself can be defined more accurately as the *will to our countenance,* and finally as *the countenance of our will.*

It is to this that our vibration penetrates anew, eliciting the inmost. None of our structures may keep making itself independent. Man must no longer let himself be absorbed by the means and false objectifications of his own self. Just as machine and state should be held down on a merely unburdening level, works of the mind must henceforth be no more than means of the soul, storage bins or means of logical invention capable of being translated or retranslated into soul. Whatever has been humanly alienated is worthless. All cultural objectivities are irrelevant except as educational fees or inflated paper money, since in the name of God—to whom we owe purity as he owes us salvation—nothing but ethics and ethical metaphysics counts as gold coin on the Latter Day. "Know ye," an old manuscript of the Zohar says in that sense, "know ye that there is a twofold view of all the worlds. One shows their outside, namely, the general laws of the worlds in accordance with their outward forms. The other shows the inner being of the worlds, namely, the essence of human souls.

Consequently there are two degrees of action, the works and the orders of prayer; the works serve the outward perfection of the worlds, but the prayers serve to make one world contained in the other and to lift them upward." In such a functional relationship between unburdening and spirit—between Marxism and religion, joined in a will to the kingdom—flows the ultimate main system for all subsidiary currents. The soul, the Messiah, the Apocalypse which represents the act of awakening in totality —these impart the final impulses to action and cognition, and make up the *a priori* of all politics and of all culture. This is the direction in which everything about us can be colored, accelerated and decided. Nothing is complete; nothing is conclusive; nothing has a solid core. The point is to collect the sundered lower parts, to let our heads grow further out of history, to make the State accompany the fraternal community, and finally to bring the seed grain of the self-encounter to the dread harvest festival of the Apocalypse. "But mirrored in us all is now the light of the Lord, *with countenance uncovered,* and we are transfigured into the selfsame image, from one light unto the next, by the spirit of the Lord." For we are powerful; only the wicked exist by virtue of their God. But as for the just— there God exists by their virtue, and in their hands lies the sanctification of the name, the very nomination of God who stirs and moves within us as a door we sense, as the darkest question and inmost rapture, and who is no fact but a problem laid into the hands of our God-conjuring philosophy, and of truth as prayer.

INCIPIT VITA NOVA*

1. The Alluring Threshold

Not all beginnings are new beginnings. Though each morning seems fresh, though all the birds of May seem the very breath and voice of youth, often (how often!) each new thing is nothing new.

The alarm shrills us out to a day that is usually just like any other day. The bud is promise of spring and summer; but if we turn them to no special end, they are hardly more verdant than last year's spring and last year's summer. "The sky rejoices in the morning's birth," says the poet; but for the clerk, spring is only the alarm going off in daylight. We cross the threshold of the new year into one that differs little from the last. Still, the onset of something always has a particular fascination. A beginning is promise itself: the comforting sign that the stale and tired will be renewed. The colours of commencing can be tender or ardent: bud-, child-, or bride-tender; ardent like dawn, the universal incandescence of spring—or revolution. But strangest of all, as soon as this beginning is hoped for in history, it becomes a notion of a future far-off time. Of its own volition, life-as-history (not the individual life) seems capable of youth only when aged. The implications? Much anguish, and a world of ice to be melted.

* Translated by John Cumming.

73

2. *A New Life Begins*

PHOENIX, RENEWAL AND REFORM

The possibility of new life has never been obvious. Least of all in static epochs and closed societies where everything seemed destined to be (and to remain) as it always had been. But even in such times and places, as soon as a man reached mid-course in life, time would run down and away. Hence, in fairy-tales, the theme of the fountain or well of youth which brought at least organic renewal. It is found in travellers' tales of far-off lands, and in many legends (in Florida as well as India). In terms of the static society it is significant that rebirth was always expected to come only through a miracle or prodigies. And the unique water of salvation that would transform the whole man did not flow from natural springs or wells, but was thought to be administered by the mystical virtue of baptism or a sacred infusion. Only this would truly wash away the vileness of sin and the works of death. Similarly, fire, the most radical agent of "purification," achieved a significance that hardly originated with Zoroastrianism. The phoenix of the East, which burns itself only to rise again from its ashes, was used as an allegorical figure of rebirth. One of Ovid's didactic poems (*Met.* 15) shows to what degree the story of the phoenix was still alive, and effective as a legend of regeneration (later also known as "renaissance") in the reign of Augustus. Ovid presents Nature herself as the *"rerum novatrix"* (she who renews or repairs) by whose virtue Rome was remade. Subsequently (mainly because of Albertus Magnus, who deprived it entirely of its function as a figure of natural life and transferred it to mystical theology) the phoenix became a symbol of every form of renewal: renewal despite and indeed through self-immolation.

But a dramatic (and not only allegorical) process of dying and transformation (*"Stirb und werde!"*) occurred in the Mysteries. The faithful believed in them as means of growing into renewal, and towards the *novum*. To sprinkling with water, leaping through fire, and the application of magic seals, was added the equally ancient ritual of metamorphosis in which the *mystes* "mimed" the resurrected god of the particular Mystery. The Orphic Mysteries, for example, initiated the adept into the death and resurrection of Dionysus-Zagreus. As the ancient world drew to a close, there arose the Mysteries of Isis and (in Syria) those of Attis-Adonis; they allowed the same participation in rebirth. The "miming" of the deity was often so exact that the initiate, as in primitive cults, put on the mask of the Mystery-god.

The dramatic and symbolic ceremony of rebirth can be traced still in the imagery of St. Paul, who enjoins his faithful to put off the old and to put on the new nature (of Christ) (Eph. 4, 22; Col. 3, 10). *Bonus intra, melior exi* ("Enter as a good man, but depart as a better"), reads the inscription on the mosaic pavement of a temple of Aesculapius in Africa; for the dominant theme of the Mysteries was complete regeneration in the resurrected god—*ego sum Osiris* (I *am* Osiris). And Christianity bore the pathos of *renovatio, reformatio* (renewal as reform) through the centuries; even though its profound content was certainly not a precise conjunction of rebirth with an acceptance of the notions of antiquity. Indeed, with the prophets, the Bible became the source of a quite unique current of rejuvenation. With St. Paul it had some aspects in common with the Mystery religions, but almost wholly for appearance—if not for propaganda's sake. The only fresh content of the new myth, the *muthos* of Christianity, was that there was no imitation of the resurrection deities of ancient times, but the Resurrection and the Life were claimed to have only just occurred as a complete "renewal" or *novum* of history. Only the dead though now living Jesus initiated those who had faith in him into the daily renewal of their inner nature (2 Cor. 4, 16), and substantiated the promise of a new heaven and a new earth made in the "Thy dead shall live, their bodies shall rise" of Isaiah (26, 19). Only the star which no eyes had gazed on before, which showed the Magi the way to an event that had never yet been witnessed, illumined the New Jerusalem seen by

75

the author of the book of Revelation, and poured its light into the completely revolutionary message of the ruler of the holy city: "Behold, I make all things new" (Rev. 21, 5).

Ultimately therefore, a public as well as central conception (though in no way a concept) of the beginning of a new life (the *incipit vita nova* formula) came into the world only through the Bible. In this case, the fountain of youth of the fairy-tale did not break forth from wherever it had been gathering since an unknown date (in some far-off space, or in a recollection of some ur-legend of Attis or Osiris). Instead it emerged in its own right, as a *novum* in time; as if before Jesus there had been nothing in any way really new, but only longing for, and suggestions and expectations of, this one new thing. As a later mystic, Angelus Silesius, put it: "God who ne'er became, in time's midst comes to be / What yet he ne'er has been, through eternity." And so, for the Christian consciousness, *incipit vita nova* had its unique starting-point in history, which was chronologically indentifiable as "under Pontius Pilate." So that when the divine helper (the Paraclete) appeared at the end of history (John 16, 7), the same new beginning would start the process of complete renewal in which not one stone would be left upon another. There was a similar change in the concept of Creation (at least in the sense of a second Creation) to one *in re,* not *ante rem;* since it was now the genesis of the Right, the Evangelists shifted it to the mid-point, and the author of Revelation to the end of history.

SAVIOUR-KING AND TRULY NEW AEON

In novitate vitae ambulamus [We shall walk in newness of life] (Rom. 6, 4).

The day (having no alternative) begins as a morning. But also, considered historically, as a morrow. It banishes the night and begins as a fresh entrant; as that which is to come, after today, in the future. This is why I stressed at the outset the strange fact that as soon as the beginning is hoped for in history, it becomes a concept of a time far-off in the future.

For it must make something whole; it must compensate for anguish; and anguish piles up only in the course of history.

Through night to the break of day; *per aspera ad astra;* after clouds comes fair weather; thunderstorm and rainbow; in a mythical form these contrasting archetypes express a consciousness of a dialectical relation. But the distance of the far-off time itself is an expression also of weakness: the weakness of those who long for salvation; the weakness of conceiving the static society as one alterable in time—but by a miracle, through prodigies, or the ultimate appearance of a miracle-worker or miracle-king. In this case "miracle" implies not only an interruption of the usual course of events in life, but that—quite apart from this formal effect—whatever it will be, will be a miracle in itself. Even when considered in terms of its own content, the miracle can also be conceived of in a negative sense, as a chastisement which makes things as they are change very much for the worse. But in most legends a miracle implies that things will prosper, and is therefore quite positive; in such cases the content of the miracle is the miraculous or the *novum* as the absolute space of salvation—its very substance. If this is to be bestowed uniquely by a saviour-king from above (who effects no shaking of things from the foundations below), in the end (even outside the Bible) the morning will be a morrow, and the dawning a future.

Judaism adopted this messianic *framework* only from the time of the Babylonian captivity. Both the Egyptians and Babylonians looked forward to a miraculous ruler at the end of time. The Persians not only had legends of the return of Zoroaster as saviour; the theme was an essential part of their religion of redemption, in which Zoroaster finally divided the light from darkness and inaugurated the triumph of Ormazd, the good deity, over the powerful Ahriman. Expectation of final salvation and even of an imminent conclusion to things also permeated ancient Roman thought from the time of Augustus on, but was always designed to point to Augustus himself as the emperor of peace. In this case, Persian and Egyptian eschatologies were drawn on to supply the longing for salvation

77

with images of sovereignty. There is a very clear instance of
this in Virgil's famous fourth Eclogue (which the Church later
interpreted as a reference to the birth of Christ):

> *The last great age, foretold by sacred rhymes,*
> *Renews its finished course: Saturnian times*
> *Roll round again; and mighty years, begun*
> *From their first orb, in radiant circles run.*
> *The base degenerate iron offspring ends:*
> *A golden progeny from heaven descends.*

Virgil's *Saturnia regna* are of course the Golden Age.

Therefore the *incipit vita nova* itself, which almost at the same
time (according to the Gospel account) an angel announced to
shepherds in a field, was familiar to the non-biblical world as the
"fulfillment of time," and as time's *ultimum*. The panic of peni-
tence (and felicity) spread by John the Baptist, together with
this message that the kingdom of heaven was at hand, was indebted to Mandaean and Persian (at least as much as to Jewish) conceptions of the Messiah. Expectation of the end was
widespread; so widespread that the idea of the eschatological
creation can hardly be thought of as peculiar to the Bible. This
is true too of the *framework* of messianism. But what is peculiar
(and decisively so) to Scripture and its after-effects, is the setting of the *content of life itself* in the ultimate life begun (the
esential *vita* of the *incipit vita ultima*).

Something discernible in the Christian assimilations to the
images and liturgies of the Mysteries is applicable here too: a
unique current (a current of rejuvenation) which met the
streams of non-biblical Messianism, but soon parted from them.
For here we are confronted with an oppressed nation longing,
because of oppression, for a new life. The bored, the blasé and
the sated, lords, sensualists and masters, do not search the
Bible for the sake of novelty. Virgil's Roman audience may subsequently (in the course of time, as they say) have drained the
cup of life to the lees and mused over its insipidity. But those
who laboured and were heavily laden had little opportunity even
to put it to their lips. They were never in a position to be smitten
with weariness of the amenities of the cultured life. They were

waiting for the new life that would mean an end to bondage—on this very earth. To this extent, the new life would be an actual breakthrough: a bursting of the fetters and not a series of ecstatic *frissons* (sensual or spiritual). The restoration of the magnificence known in David's time was certainly a national revolutionary suasion at the time of Christ, but not for the upper stratum of Jewish society. The theme of the returning and magnificent saviour-king had no fundamental effect on the *incipit vita nova* of that time. The never-forgotten utopian archetype was the basic one of the exodus from Egypt to Canaan, in search of the promise that had never been fulfilled. A much older archetype, it later came in contact with the Persian messianism of lords and masters—from which it differs in essential content.

The main implication is that a class society would not recur in the final aeon which the messiah was to inaugurate. Despite all invocations of the Golden Age, the opposite is true in the case of Virgil's ecstatic hymning of Augustus; and particularly in the socially privileged heaven of the Egyptian, Babylonian and Persian images of redemption. The initiator of the ultimate age, on the other hand, was a son of man who had nowhere to lay his head, and whose message the ruling class answered with the cross. Not Caesar but his opposite established the new kingdom: and not as an empire but as a mystical democracy. Only as such has the "Behold, I make all things new" of the book of Revelation continued to operate in all heretics who revolt against "Babylon the great." The full scope and resonance of that voice rings out from Patmos and down the ages, long, long undimmed: even in the tribune Cola di Rienzo in the non-aristocratic stirrings of the classical Renaissance; but even more in Joachim di Fiore and his prophecies, and in Thomas Münzer—who took them quite seriously as prophecies of the Commune into which Christ would be resolved.

The fierce anger of John's revelation itself is shown as provoking a cataclysm through which tyranny collapses under the debris of the entire universe, and gives way to the descent of the new Jerusalem. Precisely this kind of essential identification of

79

the End with *disruption* would have been impossible in the non-biblical, patrician eschatologies, in spite of their use of a common thunderstorm-and-rainbow archetypology. The full genesis, the genesis of human adequacy, is found only in the prophets of the Old and New Testaments; they alone distinguish the new aeon from the old by the cessation of bondage. This was the sole watchword of messianism throughout the centuries that followed: liberation from the burden of oppression and the stench of decay; a breakthrough into fresh air and open spaces; the promotion of a humane future together with a humanism of nature that make this messianism the *a priori* of every actually revolutionary rebirth or new birth, including the Renaissance itself. *Incipit vita nova* is the Dantesque formula that inaugurated the new age. Its roots are in modern economics; but no one can deny that the current which fed the ideological growth of its roots, and which made and makes even the name "new age" possible, rose from the unsatisfied pathos of a new aeon still animated by Christianity.

KEEPING FAITH WITH HOPE

A clear distinction must be made between renewal and the new life. For renewal implies recourse to what has been (however inimical it may be to what has since come to be); whereas the new life implies advance towards what has as yet never appeared (however much it may still rely on the dialectics of history). Nevertheless renewal has often enclosed the new life; and then the so-called "rebirth" has had a regressive effect on birth. This was so even when there was absolutely no question of a mere invocation of a long-gone past, even when it was much more a question of an aboriginal return to the source: Renaissance, rather than Restoration and Romanticism.

Originally the call for (say) a "return to nature" was not accompanied by the sound of a hunting-horn; *retourner à la nature* was no invitation to a combination of stone-age savagery and a masked ball. The response to Rousseau's summons came from a young class—the rising middle class struggling against what had grown un-natural; therefore it demanded the recommencement of history. But as history was turned back from its unnatural path to the starting-point of "nature unsullied," once again the sentiment of a lost paradise largely obscured the essential contents of a new beginning. For the subversive Rousseau in Geneva, "nature" became a call to battle for a humanity without disfigurement; for a future that would sustain not the bourgeois but the *citoyen*. Precisely "degeneration," alienation from nature, predetermined the origin of property, the resulting division of labor, and the establishment of social classes. But, as in his *La Nouvelle Héloise,* the future was still reduced to an idyllic pastoral and colored with fake rusticity, the basis of which was a "return to nature"—the retrogressive sentiment enclosed in the doctrine of *perfectibilité*. Rousseau himself, with the notion of a dawn of creation free from sin, looked back to the ecclesiastical doctrine of a prelapsarian state; in other words, to the doctrine of *recollection* as the predominant content of hope. Recollection here is the fortunate memory (i.e. tradition) of a fulfilment that has never existed, but compared with which all that follows is a perversion brought about by the Fall. In the Rousseauian summons there is also an echo of revolutionary sectarian theology and its obscure reminiscences of primitive communism (rather like those in the legend of Paradise).

In particular, where there was no striving towards revolution, but only a call for an unflawed reformation that would remove "abuses" and "accretions," the *vita nova* (indeed the *vita ultima*) went quite into reverse and moved towards a restoration of the state of paradise. Bernard of Clairvaux, wishing to restore "pure Christianity," asked for simplicity, and equally conceived of the potent *novum* as restoration: the soul warped by the Fall and by the sins of the generations (the *anima curva*) was to return to its primordial *similitudo Dei* or likeness of God, and be made by the action of grace the same *anima recta* that it was in the dawn of Creation. This model is a partial anticipation of the "rebirth" of classical antiquity, and the return to a primordial nature (although in this case, of course, the duty and substance of the *anima renata,* the reborn soul, were quite different). Ultimately, from the viewpoint of philosophy, all these notions are lineal descendants of Platonic anamnesis: of that most static of all teachings which holds that all learning to know and creativity are "calling to mind," or recollection. Consequently there can be no creation of anything new, but only an uncovering of what is buried, a removal of encrustations from primordial realities. Therefore the New is new only for the man who comes to know it, but never substantially new in itself. The history of mankind shows, however, that the exclusive pathos of this theory of reminiscence was untenable; it was dispersed as hope rose to predominance. Nevertheless, its forward-looking correlative not only became part of the history of the instruction of mankind by the Supreme Being (for comprehension of him), but entered into the very conception of that Being. The *novitas vitae,* the "newness of life" spoken of by St. Paul, would indeed occur in an intrinsically divine event: in a descent of God himself and in the unheard of becoming man of the *Ousia*—the divine Essence.

Finally, from an entirely different direction, the modern philosophy of generation and process (which corresponds to the increasing release of productive forces) came to oppose the mere *restitutio in integrum,* a return to an earlier integral condition. Although the "reprise" or restitution of the initial thesis in the synthesis following the antithesis (the apparent return formula of the Hegelian dialectic) could indeed slip into the virtual snare of anamnesis, it was just as capable of emerging from it, being of course antithetical to it.

The whole character of dialectics is process and production. Not even the "restitution of the liberty, equality and fraternity of the primitive communist *gentes,*" which Engels was to speak of later, could bring any primitive tribes to the "commonwealth of freedom," to the never yet achieved *novum* at the summit of fully developed forces of production. The commonwealth of freedom looks back to the undeveloped primitive commune in an affectionate though distant way; it does not unite with it in a circular movement of return to some location in pre-history.

If there were a beginning struck by the lightning of the end so that the ultimately new was the primally old disclosed, such a beginning could be only the most obscure of all problems, and hardly a solution before its time. In no way is the beginning set far back in time; it stirs and prompts where it lies enclosed, in every moment of being. Viewed from a less metaphysical perspective, and therefore more within the visible range of the materially formative process, whatever is conceived under the title of the "Golden Age" is clearly and properly (in spite of the primitive commune) not something prehistorical but a still utopian destination. Nevertheless, it cannot be denied that the category of the new still remains interlaced and bound up with that of renewal, even though the latter is disproportionate to it.

What is the reason for this, and is it anything other than a false relationship? In fact it is to some extent a true one, if the reference back is not made to what is already past, in the sense of that which appears already finished and complete enough not to make any progress requisite (as something developing after it, and from it). No, the *genuine* reference-and-return is towards what is still in the future, and therefore *what has not come to be in the past;* ultimately it is a return to the *still underived derivation* of all that happens. To the impelling "so that"—or the intensive origin of life, and reason for there being life. Only this provides justification for the interlacing of *renovatio* and *novum;* as justification, however, it is obviously minute, barely adequate, and lies *only* in the *final* synthesis of the very last content (the *what*) and the most primal intensity (the *so that*) of universal being. The substance of the "what" is actually the same as the intensity of the "so that": the intensity which will be disclosed at the "end of history," and which is the impelling factor of realization in the world. But this driving force of the content, of the content of *so that,* together with the *realization of the realizer himself* as the ultimately valid new thing; this utopian and radical *novum* has nothing in common with a receptive renewal of anything that already has *been,* and *happened,* and is merely *lost.* From the potential fruition of the root, the conjunction of the new and renewal obtains only a possibility: that of being able to conceive of any conjunction at all of last with first. But the root of the manifestation itself is no past existence (or even landscape) of a golden age or earthly paradise that has already been and gone; for the root has never flowered yet as the manifestation of that which it is. And in the end, *incipit vita nova* (and even *incipit vita ultima*) does not arrive at a beginning that has already shone forth; on the contrary, it means the end of a beginning, and an end to its questioning, its enigma, and its obscurity. There is only one direction in which the seeds of times past tend, the historic modes or forms on the way flourish, and the consolatory fantasies of a lost paradise that must be found again seduce. They tend, flourish and seduce only towards a supremely astonishing fruition. In that which is new there is only one true form of return: to what was always intended but has never come to be. From this source, as they draw from the inexhaustible spring of *Eunöe,* or remembrance, even the apparent repetitions of the heritage of culture obtain their productive power.

This is the basic form of recollection, which is precisely the same as loyalty—but loyalty to hope. It is the unfailing conviction that utopia must be created in time (*Ceterum censeo . . .*— but this time *Ceterum censeo utopiam esse historice creandam!*). As watchwords, both "It is accomplished" and the much less smug and banal "It *was* accomplished" signify a betrayal of this faith. The world is developing in history, and continuously coming forth; yet as it does so, it leaves its history behind. The sun of Homer (or of Hegel, or of Marx) will shine (no physical sun) only if at each dawn in history it rises anew from the spreading ocean.

3. Taking the Measure of the Ultimate

Yet something that gets attention only because it's lofty and dies a long way off, isn't really important. The question "What's it got to do with me?" is pertinent here (and very human) precisely because it's subjective. Perhaps it was provoked by the thought that the far, far better new state was too, too far off *in time*. A very obvious thought if we human beings, living our lives now, are to be roused because of (and to sweat for) a future consisting of nothing but the good things that we must sacrifice in the here and now: *Après nous . . .* the *après-nous!*

Such is the case with the rhetorically sublime though essentially insipid ends of vulgar marxism. Thus in Artsybàshev's novel *Sanin* (published after the abortive 1905 revolution in Russia) Sanin himself asks (an unashamed materialist): "Why should I get myself hanged so that workers in 3200 A.D. can have as much food and sex as they want?" This is Sanin's reply when his former comrades rebuke him for refusing commitment and opting for the good life instead. Doubtless his decision is a wrong one, but not so easy to prove wrong—even when, in addition to sufficient food and sex, the posthumous end projected into the future is a particularly lofty one. Perhaps it is seen as a commonwealth of freedom without alienation; or as the hope that men might be able to live in peace and concord with themselves and their world. But whose life (think how short it is) would fit a vision of such immensity of range and substance? A reasonable question; all the more because not Sanin (and not epicurean anarchism, or the total solipsism of Stirner's *The Ego and his Own*) but his abandoned revolutionary élan (even though—and precisely because it has understanding and true love of mankind) will sacrifice the present in order, as Ivan Karamazov says, to feed the soil of future harmony.

Criminal obsession can also sacrifice the present; with an end that justifies the means, and with a means that makes the end unjustifiable. And even when the soil is more moderately manured, there is direct evidence that love of humanity and the human individual before all else have been ignored. Revolutionary reasoning, on the other hand, well understands the reasonable question already posed about the way in which our present life accords with lofty, far-distant ends, for with it the question can move between existential concern and the objective itself.

Only *abstract* utopianism (and not that form concerned with the concrete, and immanently joined with its own epoch) has proclaimed mere *distant and lofty ends,* while ignoring inter-mediate connexions and present ends. The form of *incipit vita nova* which is attached to the present respects immediate ends in theory as well as in practice; but while these present ends are enclosed within the possible range of a human life, they must *at the same time* set their sights on the distant goal of a society without alienation. The perspective must offer help, though not violent oppression; it must inspirit, though not mediatize. It must not leap over the route to the ideal, but follow its stages without abandoning the ideal.

So far, so good. This kind of viewpoint certainly observes the dictates of common-sense—that variety of reason which rejects too much *après-nous,* and an ultimate *sans-nous.* But a defect has developed in the actual depositions of a socialist *incipit vita nova;* a defect that has persuaded many to see even the concrete end far ahead as a utopian abstraction: so that in such con-cretions utopia is apparently predicted not for the year 3200, but as something that will come on the feast-day of St. Never-ever. Indeed, if there had never been cause to lose faith in the new paradise of the East; if criticism and revision had been extended to outdated and (above all) inhibiting premises in Marxism, and the real basic principles of the commonwealth of freedom were just round the corner: even then Sanin's question would resound with threefold vehemence. For it has to do with that most certain of all empirical, and most emphatic of all metaphysical phenomena—the *death of the individual.* Death, that most personal cut of all, won't allow the individual to ex-perience even the distant objective that's only round the corner; doesn't permit him fully to experience even the moment of its attainment. "Let us eat and drink, for tomorrow we die" (Is. 22, 13; I Cor. 15, 32); this saying which the Bible so despises might have been tailor-made for the readjusted though doubly mortal ego: doubtly mortal because in an absurd world not only the individual life but the sum of all future individual lives, and of life's achievements, would be wiped out in the non-sense of an existence apart from human existence. In such a conjoining of ephemerality and universal Sisyphusdom, tedious agnostic

86

and secular versions of what was once called "immortality" are of little help: for example, living on in one's children, the return of the individual leaf's sap to the undying tree of the human race, or fading through death into all embracing Nature. The icy indifference which Nature itself seems to show to the sum total of our individual and (ultimately) our historical ranges of objectives (from abandoning us to glacial loneliness in the universe, all the way to total extinction through the big freeze of cosmic entropy) will (as far as the existential solipsist is concerned) in the end deprive all great objectives of value and stature alike. It is an inescapable and serious barrier to excess in any attempt to transcend; a special *mene tekel* against abstract utopianism, and against every objectified and static notion of being within the *incipit vita nova,* which would then in no way be grounded upon or looking towards not-yet-being.

But will even a notion of being that is conceived in full perspective offer in itself an adequately formulated reply to Sanin's question—an answer that satisfies all its implications?

Of course Sanin's query is too subjective to allow a proficient reference to the category of danger—still the most enduring determinant in the possible (though scarcely guaranteed) process of salving (or saving) our world. And too individual, especially when (in the case of a very distant and lofty objective) what is in question is the combination of possibility and futility that Beckett portrays as "waiting for Godot": a combination to whose metaphysical guile more things than an excessively individualistic attitude are subject.

So far, so bad—if there is nothing to hold fast to. But there is the return question: Can any single man be as excluded as he imagines? He is himself always present at the point of intersection of human relations; if these have atrophied or decayed, then more than fifty per cent of the retreating (or even rejected) ego will be reflecting not itself, but these very relations, in the state they are in. And could this solitary "I" feel an emptiness and a rejection, or sense the presence of an incommensurate wall (even a wall of the absurd), if there were nothing stirring within this "I" and hurling itself against the wall? By this action, of course, it implicitly transcends the barrier—more than by virtue of the vapid contentment prescribed in the West (without experiments), and in the East (with unsuccessful experiments). At any rate, the actions of transcension itself cannot be reduced to nothingness—not even where the *harshest anti-utopia,* death, so immeasurably outbids (and underbids) all forms of earthly darkness. Without doubt there is no successful specific against death, unless so central a design of the *incipit vita nova* is to be posited in the images of intentions and ideals produced by religions. Even in Lessing's *Education of the Human Race,* the ancient myth of a transmigration of souls persists; and the Church teaches the myth of Christ's resurrection as a unique event, which occurred then, for the first time, and which ever since has contradicted the effect of death. This has become (and more than ever has remained) a matter of faith; but what has also remained, here precisely, is an undermining of the supports of a fatality, that of all fates is least open to the understanding and least essential to the known course of the process. Hence the evident wariness when making the assertions it is still possible to make, as in this instance: "The kernel of true Existence has not yet entered the process; therefore it is not affected by transient features of the process. When faced with death it is within a protective circle of that which is not-yet-living . . . 1. The kernel of true Existence (for it has *not yet come to be,* is as yet undeveloped) is wholly outside the territory of becoming and ceasing to be, neither of which has even yet taken hold of our kernel in any way. 2. If the kernel of true Existence had come-to-be, had developed, and at the same time, in becoming, had been brought forth as the good (product), then this *success* would make it that which is absolutely outside the territory of death; for death itself, together with the waste matter of the process (of which insufficiency death is part), would be irrelevant and extinct" (*The Principle of Hope*). If this wariness, this fore-sight, agrees with what has been the unique concern of religions until now, then it is true to say that, at this point, demythologization would be necessary—right up to the religion in hope. Undeniably, however, nothing in traditional re-

ligion (no part of the treasures that rust, moths and—above all
—the acid of close analysis devour) can survive when it comes
to the Nietzschean crunch of "God is dead."

The reflexes and hypostases projected into its heaven by a
defunct society of masters and slaves are open to analysis; in
this respect there is no decisive distinction to be made between the "pagan gods" (say Baal or Zeus) and the baldachino,
or even the throne of justice or mercy in the still heteronomous
regions of the Bible. Accordingly, *precisely in this sense,* the
contention that only an atheist can be a good Christian must apply. The Romans were perfectly consistent (if unaware of the
implications) when they called the first Christians *atheoi.* But
of course there is the *topos,* the image and idea into which even
the purely ideological images of gods were converted and hypostatized; into which passed the unconfounded scriptural religion of the future, of the exodus and the kingdom. There hope
appears as the very quality that incites and stirs; appears as the
pioneering counter-force to the manipulations of fear and the
degradation of an ideologically profitable insurance company.
As a counter-force it has room to exert itself constructively only
when the guarantee under which the opium of assurance is issued is cancelled, together with the promise of a generous pen-
sion in the far above (absolute untruth, yet the least crack in its
fabric is the release of nihilism). Only open human history,
"pioneer history," is filled with *creator spiritus:* with presemblances, arduous and difficult breakthroughs and extensions
beyond what has already developed, and across the incessantly
hideous gulfs of bestiality. It goes forward as the experiment of
that which is not yet really successful, or what is absolutely
worth stating and affirming, of what can be lived under; and does
so with the only real "eschatology of the present," which is
known as creative expectation. Pertinent here is the judgment
of Franz Baader, a speculative theist (too speculative, except
that he speaks from the viewpoint of Christianity): "A basic
human prejudice is to believe that what men call a future world
is something already made—and fully made—for them; something that exists apart from them like a ready-built house which

they have only to walk into; whereas that world is actually a building which men alone construct, and which rises only as they arise." In fact, everything that arises in this way demands an exploration of the being of the world itself as potential being-on-the-ascent, as matter that objectively might allow itself to be, and could be, raised from its own alienations.

A support without its own virtue has no real uprightness, yet without the mediations of nature it has no ground; and both virtue and ground are in the process of development. Similarly, a sound *incipit vita nova* requires both its right time in human history and its right place in the world (and the world would be incommensurate if it were not itself a perspective). Hence the universal formula that applies at the *beginning* of philosophy: *S* is not yet *P;* no subject already has its adequate predicate. The history of being itself is the experimental attempt to identify its impulse and origin; the impulse and origin of that history which it is man's task to illumine. *Incipit vita nova,* then, implies especially (in the same impulse and course) the predication of the obscure *existere* in everything; a predication made to the "what" of its as yet undiscovered essence: made indeed to its not yet present *unum, verum, bonum*—the One, the True and the Good of its meaning. In this impulse and course, hope is moving; with close-range objectives in mind when the long-range end is considered, and (with regard to the thing that really matters) with the long-range end in mind when the close-range objectives are in view.

It is precisely hope (to the extent that it is joined to a world that does not surrender) that neither falls into despair nor sinks into quietist confidence. *Incipit vita nova* is still too much a *beginning* to allow that; and of course shows it in the irrevocable significance of its being a beginning—which is to be demanding and to demand to be. This it demands with an aversion to misery and social bondage that despite everything can never again be rescinded; and yet with that regrettable absence of support, significance and profundity from life's end-purpose which (in the long run) it is impossible any longer to mask. Both forms of concern (concern with a moral background, and concern for a meaning that touches and stirs the creative imagina-

tion) can march forward separately, but can only strike together. The onset of the *first, moral* cause, as the demand for
and willing of a better life and man's upright carriage, offers the
insight that under neo-capitalism the old servitudes are only
upholstered and painted over, whereas under state communism
they are only congealed and renamed; but that in neither case are
they disposed of. (A gradual improvement in prison beds does
not mean that the commonwealth of freedom has arrived. It
has a different face.) And the onset of the *second, metaphysical*
cause, as the demand for and willing of unity, support and
profundity, offers the insight that concrete utopia is the *signum*
—the sign for this time; and that the notion of *docta spes*
("learned hope"), and of its dimensions and its postulate, once
grasped, will never again depart from this world.

The aura of the continually threatened and precarious attempt to find what is redeeming and whole is inherent in the
tendency and latency of the world process, as long as the process
of the world endures and can endure. That which is still open
keeps it running dialectically, criticizes all its alien forms (and
forms of alienation), feeds the most important sources of vital
energy (beyond death as well), and leaves the horizon of its
"where to" and "what for" still sufficiently unregulated to be
productive—and even to allow a rising above that horizon.

As yet this aura offers no more (but also no less) than a
fore-glow of daylight; but what it promises the world in this
offering, those who inhabit the world must hold to: this loyalty
is the concern of the *subjective* factor of possibility, although
its adjunct *objective* factor implies a real possibility of something
for us in present, given existence. And so the foremost saint
in the philosophical calendar is Prometheus; not only as a rebel
and a thief, but as the patron of adventurousness. For it is this
quality which makes premature both a wholly solipsistic nihilism
and a pan-patriotic optimism. The most inalienable of all categories for the development of our life, literature, philosophy and
practice are certainly man holding himself upright, and the as
yet undetermined and undeveloped actual content of his po-
tentiality.

My intention here was to show to some extent how these

categories might be kept open in experimental man, in this experimental world; while remembering the ancient warning, *Principiis obsta*—which I gloss thus: Keep faith with the beginning, whose genesis is still to come.

BIBLICAL RESURRECTION
AND APOCALYPSE

It is surprising for how long a time the ultimate fear was neither thought nor dreamed about on the Jewish side. The Jews were as immanently oriented a people as the Greeks, but one whose life had an incomparably more vigorous direction toward the future, toward goals. And yet the desires and the images of life hereafter were but slowly forthcoming, although by then they had become cheerful about it, or vengeful. Previously the end was put off and aside—to Sheol, the distant nether world—by long life and well-being on earth. There was ancestor worship in old Israel, and there was a cult of the dead, presupposing a belief in life hereafter; but this was part of the magic taken over from the Canaanites, not an element of pious faith. When Saul has the witch of Endor bring up Samuel's spirit he is committing a sin; besides, the rising spirit is not described as a man but as one of "gods," *elohim* (Sam. 28, 13) —as a superhuman being, *not a soul*. The same applies to the strange and demonstrably very early verse about Enoch: "And he walked with God, and was seen no more, for God took him" (Gen. 5, 24). These, like the taking away of Elijah by a whirlwind, are great exceptions and distinguished as such; above all, however, it is to "gods," not men, that the immortal names refer. Could it be that Enoch, with his life-span of 365 years, designated a former sun god? And did Elijah not ride a "chariot of fire," as these gods did? Man's fate, in any case, would long continue to be Sheol, the nether world of the grave; it was still that in the Book of Job (about 400 B.C.), although evocative of Promethean resentment: "If I wait, the grave is mine house; I have made my bed in the darkness. I have said to corruption, Thou art my father; to the worm, Thou art my mother, and my sister" (Job 17, 13f.).

The breakthrough of immortality did not occur in Judaism until the *Prophet Daniel* (about 160 B.C.), and the impulse behind it did not come from the old wish to live long and well on earth, now with a transcendent extension. It came from Job and from the prophets, rather, from the *thirst for justice;* this was what turned the wish into a postulate, and the post-mortal scene into a tribunal. The belief in a hereafter came to be one of the means to allay doubts about the justice of God on earth; above all, the very hope for a resurrection became a moral-juridical hope. The Egyptians already had far more elaborate procedures of judging the dead, but something essentially new, apt to disturb the peace of mind of the masters and the rich in particular, was added in late Israel. For now the basic motive behind the call for a resurrection grew menacing: it was to *make up for the judgment missed on earth.* "And many of them that sleep in the dust of the earth shall awake, some to everlasting life, and some to shame and everlasting contempt. And they that be wise shall shine as the brightness of the firmament; and they that turn many to righteousness as the stars for ever and ever" (Dan. 12, 1f.). This was the moral invasion of pious faith by the hope of resurrection, independent of ancestor cults, magic rites, or God-men; and it was the first such invasion. The seemingly earlier portents in a few Psalms—above all in Psalm 49, 15: "God will redeem my soul from the power of the grave; for he shall receive me"; also in Isaiah 26, 19: "But thy dead shall live, my dead bodies shall rise again"*—actually date from times as late as that of Daniel; they are interpolations like the complex of Isaiah chapters 24–27. Of course, according to Daniel not all the dead will awaken, only many of them: only the pious Jewish martyrs, and of the wicked none but the worst fiends—and even those not yet to any hell, but to shame and contempt and to witness the triumph of the righteous. The *universal resurrection itself,* that of all men, was first proclaimed in the metaphorical language of the Ethiopic book of Enoch toward the close of the first century B.C. It took its coloring from the Egyptian judgment of the dead, from the Persian doctrine of a world conflagration. The Book of Enoch not only generalized Daniel's promise; it also introduced it for the first time to the lavishly depicted scene of hell, heaven, and last judgment. And the Ezra apocalypse of the first century A.D. turned the judgment into the final revelation: "For after death shall the judgment come, when we shall live again: and then shall the names of the righteous be made manifest, and the works of the ungodly shall be declared" (2 Es. 14, 35). The age-old Egyptian idea of the Book of Life, in which the weight of human deeds is entered, also played a part. The scribe god Thoth, who kept the record at the Egyptian judgment of the dead, returns as Yahweh's angel, even as Yahweh himself. And the entries were begun annually on the Jewish New Year's Day and finished on the Day of Atonement, the highest and most solemn Jewish holiday—a post-mortally directed day of penance which significantly is quite unattested in pre-exilic Judaism and unmentioned in the so-called Book of the Covenant, in the order of feasts (Ex. 23, 14ff.). Even so, the judgment book myth itself was interpolated into the old texts, as in Exodus 32, 32f., and cited also by the first Isaiah: "He that is left in Zion, and he that remaineth in Jerusalem, shall be called holy, even every one that is written among the living in Jerusalem" (Is. 4, 3). This was preserved

---

* This translation follows the German version used by Bloch. Its meaning agrees with the English Douay Bible—"My slain shall rise again"—rather than with the King James Version's Christian anticipation: "Together with my dead body shall they arise." —Translator.

in Luke 10, 20: "Rejoice, because your names are written in heaven," and it continues to ring out in the ecclesiastic Requiem: "*Liber scriptus proferetur in quo totum continetur.*"

Now, of course, along with the strengthened wish pictures and dream glimpses of justice being meted out at least by a last judgment and what lay behind, the time had come to reinterpret supposedly earlier testimonies. Especially impelling was the report in Genesis on Enoch, the antediluvian patriarch, and his being taken from earth; in late Jewish literature he was considered the first of those who had escaped from Sheol, or indeed from death. A Book of Enoch came into being, a "Book of the Secrets of Enoch," a fanciful account of the other-worldly mysteries the patriarch had come to see; the New Testament's Epistle of Jude celebrates Enoch, "the seventh from Adam," as a prophet of the Last Judgment (Jude 14, 5). The utopian resurrection eventually became orthodox despite obvious resistance, probably put up by the circles of the "epicurean" Sadducees ("which deny that there is any resurrection," Luke 20, 27). About the time of Christ a Sanhedrin decree was issued: "No part in the future world goes to him who denies that the revival of the dead can be proved by the Torah"—in other words, by the five Books of Moses, reliably devoid of any article of such a creed, unless one should count the above-mentioned ancestor worship that went little farther beyond customary magic than some local cult of tombs. Soon, ridiculous images of the end came up and got even into the Talmud—a future leviathan, for instance: "This is the monstrous fish whose meat the chosen eat after the twilight of the world, and of whose skin a tent is made for the righteous of all nations to live under in bliss." The sea monster became a kind of manna of the beyond, one which does not diminish when eaten, and which goes to show that even leviathan, the terror of the deep (Job 41, 2–26), will one day benefit the blessed. Later, teaching with renewed powers, Maimonides laid down the immortality of the soul and the resurrection of the body in the thirteen articles of his creed. Salomon Reinach's comment in his *Orpheus*—that these articles were as far removed from biblical Judaism as the

Catholicism of the Council of Trent was from the Gospels—is not quite justified, for the emotional ground for Maimonides' concern with the resurrection had been prepared throughout post-exilic Judaism, and the moral-juridical ground since Daniel.

Behind the fear of physical death there arose the horror of the second death, of the damnation awaiting the unrighteous. Jesus, in particular, lived in this faith that had become thoroughly accepted by the people; it was out of this faith that he spoke, when he threatened as well as when he promised to save. He cited the resurrection as a matter of course, an act that would be dangerous for most men (Matth. 11, 24; Luke 10, 12); in his sect, the belief in resurrection and judgment was part of the doctrine from the very start of Christian life (Hebr. 6, 1f.). It added to the radiance of heaven, to the effect exerted, above the political promise of the Anointed, by the promise of eternal life—of victory over the second death, behind the first, merely physical destruction that leaves the soul to either heaven or hell. After Daniel—finally also under Iranian influences—immortality thus became part of a tremendous drama involving not only the individual future but the cosmic one, a drama of world conflagration and sheer night, with sheer light behind it. And the point of the Latter Day came to be that all men will be present; it will not take place before soulless nature and the generation that happens to be the last. The world of the Apocalypse, in which late Judaism had arrived, would have struck believers in it as subjectless and irrelevant if it had not affected and endowed a resurrected assembly of all men since Adam.

More ardent, now, was the will to be on the right side, on the winning side. Jesus first appeared as a healer; it was as such that he appealed to the people, not politically, let alone by delivering from sin. He fought the first death and the diseases that led to it; he began by healing the lame, the blind, the bleeding; he awakened a corpse. This, not penance, is what the early, the wholly shamanistic miracle tales are about. Penance was not added until later, homiletically, inherited from John the Baptist, and again in an awakening conjunction with the

97

second death. Hence the word that is anything but inwardly, the magically materialistic word, "Whether it is easier, to say, Thy sins be forgiven thee; or to say, Rise up and walk?" (Luke 5, 23). Luke's interpretation is already pneumatic: the Jesus of this verse healed to let it be known that the son of man has power to forgive sins. But he was acting as the bread of life, not just as a forgiver of sins; and his victory, after the baptism of his death, was won completely as the resurrection and the life, as the believed in first-fruit of all those destined to rise, as the bringer of the second or heavenly life against the second death of hell. Deliverance from death-dealing sin was the root or the trunk of the tree, but the cherished fruit of the Jewish Christianity of the time—and even more of the Gentile one— was deliverance from death. Thus the word that is so reminiscent of a holy *taurobolium:* "Whoso eateth my flesh, and drinketh my blood, hath eternal life; and I will raise him up at the last day" (John 6, 54). And, even more, the definition which in the least factual, most pneumatic Gospel summarizes all signs and miracles: "I am the resurrection, and the life; he that believeth in me, though he were dead, yet shall he live" (John 11, 25). How different this sounds from the gods of Antiquity! They were strangers to death, but also to revival. There are instances of their appearance in the final hour, as Euripides has Artemis come to the death bed of Hippolytus. But what she promises him, instead of immortality, is a temple and post-humous fame, and then she, who has never tasted death, leaves him to die. "Into thy hands I commend my spirit"—no Greek could say this to one of his gods. Until then, of course, immortality had not greatly concerned Yahweh either, and so we find Jesus outbidding him as follows: "Your fathers did eat manna in the wilderness, and are dead. I am the living bread which came down from heaven; if any man eat of this bread, he shall live for ever" (John 6, 49 and 51). And yet the substance of eternal life itself, the *substance previously posited as unknown,* is now claimed and posited in the Father, too, as made known by Jesus: "But is now made manifest by the appearing of our Saviour, who hath abolished death, and hath brought life and immortality to light" (II Tim. 1, 19).

98

Jesus leads a second exodus away from Egypt, away from the Osiris-type of existence: "For he is not a God of the dead, but of the living; for all live unto him" (Luke 20, 38). And even without the Pauline sacrifice character, the Easter miracle is believed in the incipient participation in that substance: "For as the Father hath life in himself; so hath he given to the Son to have life in himself" (John 5, 26). It is thus precisely the ones baptized in the death of Christ who are to be baptized in his resurrection also, in the real Enoch, or real "first-fruit of those who have risen from death." From this point the impulse, or the Paschal utopia, was imparted to Christian art—above all, as we have seen, to organic, metaorganic, Gothic art. It was not meant to become stonelike; on the contrary: "The Tree of Life as perfection divined and represented in the form of Christ" (*The Principle of Hope, supra*)—this came to be the last landscape of Gothic wish fulfillment. Life was to have made its escape from death—though always only the life of those whom Christ had justified; there was no escape from the second death of the damned, no escape from hell. Hell was made as inevitable as heaven; *heaven and hell together form the locale of the exit,* a locale that is now wholly generalized. Of God's entire creation nothing remains but the duality of punishment and reward, screams and choirs, hell and heaven.

As for the time of entering into one or the other, there are two views, juxtaposed even though mutually exclusive: a patient one and an impatient one. For the instant of death no sooner was there, competing with the end of the world, than heaven or hell could be man's fate *at once,* not only on the Latter Day. Hell in particular was now conceived as an imminent future; at the sinner's death bed it was already waiting with claws spread, eyes hungry, maw agape. Besides, sheer hell was adopted and anticipated by the cruel judiciary of later Christian times; procedures such as breaking on the wheel, impaling, drawing and quartering and witch-burning would not wait for the devil. And life throughout lay open to incursions of the Christian beyond of the damned: garrets and crossroads, gorges and forests—most of them still virgin—were all haunted by souls unable to rest, by directly post-mortal horrors. In the dogma, purgatory was placed right upon the heels of life; but to Dante, heaven and hell also had already happened, and no Last Judgment could alter this iron state of affairs. On the crypt of the *Inferno* only the lids had not yet fallen shut; the rectangular sarcophagi in that silent, somberly burning hall filled with human agony were waiting only to be closed for eternity on the Day of Judgment. The end of the world adds hardly anything else to Dante's pools of sulphur or circles of light; the Book of Life seems to have been opened already. Jesus himself did pile all horror and all salvation essentially upon *a day yet to come,* though near at hand—but for paradise, at least, there were exceptions: for the believing thief, for example, and for Lazarus whom the angels carry straight into Abraham's bosom, without burial and resurrection (Luke 16, 22). All this agrees on one point only: that man's fate in the future world depends upon his conduct and his permeation with Christ in this world. Death ends the sowing; there follows only the harvest, and a flatly dualistic one at that. Inconceivable pain and inconceivable joy crown our short life with a contrast which no previous expectation of a beyond had known, not even that of Egypt. It is the Manichean conflict between night and light, the clash of two great, independent powers, which the Church spurned everywhere else but "absolutized" in its beyond.

The contrast was not always so enduring: Paul affirmed the eternity of hell in Romans 6, 23, but denied it in I Corinthians 15, 21–29; Origen, founder of the doctrine of purgatory, allowed that all spirits, even the demons, would some day return, purified, to God. But the Church, in one of its harshest dogmas, made the punishments of hell eternal; it was precisely the new God of love whose cruelty in this point far outdid even Ahriman's. Dogmatically, of course, the punitive state of sin, the *aversio a Deo,* was never regarded as anything but a *reversed image of transfiguration.* As heaven is nature turned into light, hell is its transformation into a world holocaust that makes the negatively transfigured nature feel continually on the brink of extinction. In fact, the Catholic utopia of vengeance reduces hell to the other vista of the same God: the damned

100

have the same apperception of divine love, but in the form of loss and rage only, having spurned that love. And paradise, the *vita aeterna* above the contrasting dungeons of the *mors aeterna,* seems so much more exalted: "Eye hath not seen, nor ear heard, neither have entered into the heart of man, the things which God hath prepared for them that love him" (I Cor. 2, 9). At this very pinnacle of wish fulfillment against death, man virtually becomes divine—and not just in heretical mysticism, but in the most correct of all places, so to speak, in the *Catechismus Romanus* (I, cap. 13, qu. 6): "While retaining their own substance, those who delight in God do assume a certain and virtually divine form, so that they will seem to be gods rather than men [*tamen quandam et prope divinam formam induunt, ut dii potius quam homines videantur*]."

So, in such vast pictures of hope, it was the *future* Apocalypse which triumphed after all, triumphed over that first, individually post-mortal permission to enter paradise "this day," without the world's coming to an end.

Aside from purgatory, the dead are now no nearer than the living to the mysteries of the transposed, mythologized utopia of either vengeance or triumph. It is *toward* those mysteries, rather, that the dead body sleeps. Only Christ's return will end the Advent period for both the quick and the dead, though the dead have already made their record to that end and the open book at the end of days will merely reveal it. The doubt of divine justice, previously soothed in so many ways, now found the last, the only way which empirically, at least, could not be refuted any longer: retribution on the Latter Day. The Church, of course, used the Apocalypse solely as an instrument of its rule, as the picture of a future *ecclesia triumphans* rather than as the victory of the slain over the great Babylon, whom it had indeed turned into. Even so, the thought that all the living would be paid back after death, and all the dead after the great roll call—this thought kept its significance as a revolutionary wish fulfillment for those who labored and were heavy laden, who did not know how to help themselves in reality or had lost the battle. Though postponed *ad calendas apocalypticas,* the day of judgment was to be expected any moment, and it was most imminently expected in revolutionary times, during the Albigensian Wars and during the German Peasant War. There Daniel's preaching of Christ had another ring to it than it had in the churches, and so had *"Dies irae, dies illa, solvet saeclum in favilla,"* and *"Iudex ergo cum sedebit, quidquid latet, apparebit, nil inultum remanebit."* Nothing will stay unavenged—this is the effect of Daniel's postulate of immortality, a moral-juridical effect, not a comfortably persevering one, and this came to be its grandeur. At the end of days, aside from having risen, the hanged Jesus himself returns as a judge.

This is the same archetype that has accompanied so many crushed revolutions—the same that lies in the cry, "We shall be back," and means to say that the one-time martyrs will be back as total victors and avengers. It is an arch-utopian archetype even though the Apocalypse that contains it, has in its fixed duality of hell and heaven reproduced and eternalized the duality of the old class society as well. In the Apocalypse, the returning Jesus is not depicted as a meek sufferer any more, and neither are his followers: "And I saw heaven opened, and behold a white horse; and he that sat upon him was called Faithful and True, and in righteousness he doth judge and make war. His eyes were as a flame of fire, and on his head were many crowns; and he had a name written, that no man knew, but he himself" (Rev. 19, 11f.). Not even as a memory does the New Jerusalem contain death, the old enemy: "And God shall wipe away all tears from their eyes; and there shall be no more death, neither sorrow, nor crying, neither shall there be any more pain; for the former things are passed away" (Rev. 21, 4). In Egypt the absence of suffering and tears coincided with death, with the stony bliss of Osiris; in Christianity the kingdom is preached to the living, not to the dead, and even of stones God may raise up children (Matth. 3, 9). Instead of Styx, Hades, Osiris, the angel of the Apocalypse shows nothing but organic things: "And he shewed me a pure river of water of life, clear as crystal, proceeding out of the throne of God and of the Lamb. In the midst of the street of it, and on either side of the river, was there the tree of life, which bare twelve manners of fruits, and yielded her fruit every month" (Rev. 22, 1f.).

No matter how saturated with Babylonian astral myths, how full of inorganic images, the Apocalypse does posit the strictest equality of the basic categories of the New Testament: *phos = zoë*, light = life. Next to the dreadful slough of hell, which later rendered such good service to the Church, stood the loftiest of all castles in the air, the pure castle of light—Paradise. Christ's ascension was thought to be the high road to it. In Christianity this Easter *muthos* became absolute as the myth of the end.

CHRIST, OR THE
UNCOVERED COUNTENANCE

First of all, the lamb here wants to shed its blood. The blood with which the doorposts were daubed once before.

To this day the Jews observe the feast of the children who were thus vicariously saved. And how familiarly the rest seems to occur all over: breaking on the wheel; nailing to the cross, which is a wheel with the frame left off to symbolize the law, but also the sun; the mourning of Baldur, and all the sacrificial touches in the profound Hercules legend. Siegfried, the founder of the old Germanic initiation, was vulnerable only in the spot marked by Kriemhild's embroidered cross, and on this same spot Jesus actually carried his cross later. It all does seem to converge, and we might think that the object of the universal quest could be the same salvation, the same solar wheel magic. We might, so to speak, think of Christianity as druidic-Germanic also, though on astral paths. Looking farther afield, however, we find that not much coincides here, after all. The sun itself, the seeming link, the vinculum that should connect even Christianity with mere *astral myths,* is particularly capricious.

To the Fiji Islanders, for instance, sun and moon used to

be man and wife; they split up, and the sun now wants to eat the moon, but the stars give it red animal skins to rest on, at least in the evening. Then there are Indian sun legends of two brothers, sons of the pine resin; they shot their arrows into the sky to make a ladder, which they climbed in order to kill the sun that had glued their father to the tree trunk. Whereupon the older son mounted the sun's throne, while the younger turned into the moon—so the first sun does not even exist any more. Wholly divergent from these are such lofty solar myths as we find in the late system of Mani, for instance. According to that, sun and moon are two vessels: the moon bark loads the souls of the departed and the light of their good works, thus becoming "full"; it then transfers these materials to the sun, and at the "Pillars of Praise" the sun delivers them to Ormuzd, the highest of gods, for the construction of his kingdom, until all light that is held captive in the world will eventually have been carried upward by the two mediating craft. Thus we see, with a certain geographical expansion, that there really is nothing congruent here, that in the astral myths everything shifts to and fro. Their realm, in which the mystery of the son of man has not occurred, falls far short of allowing an astral-mythical reduction of Christianity; the myths themselves diverge too greatly. There is but one point in which the old views go hand in hand: their idea is to bring the saint to the sun, not the sun to the Saviour, like Christianity. When Osiris is resurrected, the great falcon of dawn, his eternally calendrical divinity, always comes back to the spring, to the sun's increase in size and radiance, to the history of the natural year. In the cult of Mithras, too, the sun appears less as the god's companion than as the god himself, and even if such major figures as the Mother, Typhon, and the Son do approach from afar, they are nothing but earth, night, and sun; it is the human element which conversely symbolizes the astral one in the ponderous, mysterious parade of these nature idols and their falsely sanctified concepts. On the other hand, while the sun accompanies the life of Jesus that began with his birth at the winter solstice, while it especially surrounds his ascension with the aura of a risen god of vegetation and the year, a closer looks reveals the crucial, saving fact that all these are mere pagan legacies and dowries of a Near-Eastern mixed marriage, sharply distinct and distinguishable from the prophets and from the Gospel that announces not the sun, but the son of man—not the world, but the *exodus* from the world.

So, the main point here does seem to be that the lamb bleeds. And likewise, if man in the exodus peril of death will daub his doorposts with lamb's blood, his first-born will be passed over. Attaching the rest of the Passover feast was easy, no doubt—but do not these lines already show a pagan infection? Even the story of Esther and Mordecai was infiltrated by an astral legend, and as for this Passover, the lamb's blood was still near enough to recall, as were the kid that was killed, and Joseph, lifted up out of the pit and sold to Egypt, and the white bull, and the boy Horus. If we refer to other parts of the Scriptures, notably to Deutero-Isaiah, we find his verses on the sacrifice of the lamb (Is. 53, 4–7)—in which salvation, by the way, is credited more to the manner of dying than to the objective act itself—countered by the later Deutero-Isaiah's, if not Trito-Isaiah's, word that "he that killeth an ox is as if he slew a man; he that sacrificeth a lamb, as if he cut off a dog's neck; he that offereth an oblation, as if he offered swine's blood; he that burneth incense, as if he blessed an idol" (Is. 66, 3). Above all, they are countered by the fact that in the heydey of Moloch, when polytheistic astral cults flourished even among the Jews, the unsleeping God had refused the sacrifice of Isaac on Mount Moriah, the mountain on which the Lord sees, as the text says explicitly, and the memorial site of the three shofar blasts of the higher Day of Atonement. Unreserved yielding; moral conviction, sealed by death if need be; the use of grief for the destruction of the Adam, that true principle of grief—none of these can be removed from the life of Jesus, from his out-and-out revolutionary ethics concerning all creatures. But the dogma of the vicarious sacrificial death, of the sacrifice offered once for all *as an act of terrestrial-cosmic magic*—this was clearly added by Paul from the cults of Near-Eastern calendar gods.

Both in the Old Testament and in the New there is still plenty that is astral-mythical and "Babylonian," but as a shell, at best, and mostly as an incongruity.

What is thus mixed with the course of the year is past, a dance of the dead. It can no longer be used to circumscribe the rest, nor do we find in the inanimate realm more guidance staring us in the face than in the manifest process of our own. A "more" may look plausible if one has fully experienced that stony silence, compared with which human communication seems to contain depths indeed, but not the ultimate depth. The most perfect I would have to revert to stone, then; in the series of spheres of mystic vision Goethe's Makarie—the woman in *Wilhelm Meister's Travels* who "not only carries the whole solar system in herself, but moves in it as an integrating mental part"—would rank far above Dostoevsky's Prince Myshkin, that most impenetrable of external souls, that massif of physical and solar nature whose silence is like God's.

An inevitable turn for man, and for the son of man, would be to serve only as a key, then, as a method to release the heaviest bolt, to unlock the one and only locked treasure and mystery, a not merely heuristic but substantial Bethlehem of physics; and the key itself needs no substance. For all of that, however, the circle of problems cannot be closed astrally and mythically any more, from the outside. It can only be closed soteriologically, by the end—and there is no doubt that this conclusion rests purely on the homogeneous topics of the subject and the philosophy of history, on the parousias of music and ethics.

The lamp of the son of man has burned through both the crystal dome and the calendrical scaffolding, and the calendar has occupied a place where it does not belong. As the Apocalypt says of the New Jerusalem: "And the city had no need of the sun, neither of the moon, to shine in it; for the glory of God did lighten it, and the Lamb is the light thereof" (Rev. 21, 23). This, then—however necessary *the elaboration of all the profound correspondences in nature* may be, as nature seemed to be unconsciously joining in the observance of the Christian mysteries—this, then, is why Mithras and the entire myth of the sun god's descent and of his assured and, for us, saving ascent has to be kept far from Jesus even on purely metaphysical grounds. If Jesus' death is to tell us anything at all, it is this, for one: that two links in the Jesus story—men and God—have failed; that they were deaf and delivered the prophet, who might have been the Messiah, to death at Satan's hand; and that this did nothing at all to defeat Satan, that the innocent blood was not poured into the hatreds of the world at all, that mankind was not at all ransomed from Satan. It was absolutely not so amiable a matter as one scholastic thought it had been: "What did the Saviour do to our jailer? He set his cross as a trap, and baited it with his blood." It was absolutely not so contentedly panlogistical as Gregory of Nyssa's explanation that Satan, unable to see more than man in the God-man, had swallowed not only the human bait but the divine hook as well. In fact, nothing in the world was ever more futile—and at the same time, as a pagan analogy to the dying and resurrected god of the year, more apologizing for this customary sort of mundane government—then the vicarious satisfaction furnished by the cross-and-sacrifice magic.

More important and more fruitful, therefore, is what we get out of Jesus' life and words—not just morally but also, and without Paul, as a promise of the most profound contents of the *logos*. Even as a matter of the *logos,* the semi-astral sacrifice text which replaced the gospel of Christ with a second one, the gospel about Christ, can be disregarded in the pure Christianity that has not yet been uncovered, in the Christianity of cognition as well as of ethics. Whether this can ever be "unadorned" is a permanent question, of course, but here, too, there is something like an unconstructive ontology. There is the eternal rank of the human soul, distinct from everything else; there is the power of goodness and of prayer, the deeply based moral good as the seed grain, the life principle of the spirit; there is the message of possible salvation by serving one another, by yielding oneself, by becoming the other, by filling oneself with love as the spirit of gathering and of the most universal self-encounter;

108

there is the message, above all, of the new aeon of a deity that has so far remained unknown. A deity of which the heretic Marcion, with his gospel of the strange God, and even more the heretic Joachim di Fiore later, had a better understanding than the masters' church with its paternal God, its masters' God not unlike Ammon, or Marduk, or Jupiter. This is the only way our hot, wounded day can come to a close, can prepare itself to accept all the longing to be like God and to fulfill them in an *omega* that equals the *alpha* which has at last been made up for—without dominion, with community, without this world. with the kingdom.

But it must happen inside us. Here alone do men become free and can meet each other. "And it doth not yet appear what we shall be; but we know that, when he shall appear, we shall be like him; for we shall see him as he is," writes John in the First Epistle. The fruitful, historic hours move in ourselves alone; the flower that is the key must bloom in the depth of the soul. "Behold, I show you a mystery: We shall not all sleep, but we shall all be changed. For ye are dead, and your life is hid with Christ in God. When Christ, who is your life, shall appear, then shall ye also appear with him in glory," writes the other Paul—the one who was not baptized to preach the sacrificial death but to conjure—in his epistles to the Corinthians and Colossians. But there is in us not only the dim Adam whose thirst to know good and evil was indeed quenched by Jesus, the Saviour and Aesculapius, the white, whitened, returned serpent of paradise. Standing above Adam is the dim Lucifer, and for his longing to *be like God,* for his truly divine parentage and heritage, not even Jesus himself has brought a recurrence, a clarifying justification, and the triumph of his essence that would clarify God himself.

This is what in Jesus remained a mystery, what was kept secret for later, for the end when this very countenance may be uncovered. But it has been restless ever since it was forsaken for the second time, since the cry on the cross fell on deaf ears, since the head of the crucified serpent of paradise was crushed for the second time. And only in the hidden, out-and-

109

out *anti-demiurgic* side of Christ can the really theurgic side of the rebelling son of man be understood. So it is in the "Our Father," in his *kiddush ha-shem,* in the hallowing of the name that is not praise but a challenge: Wake up, let thy name be hallowed, let thy kingdom come at last, "and forgive us our debts *as we forgive our debtors.* And lead us not into temptation, but deliver us from evil"—nothing but pleas to God, imploring him at long last to abandon the dark ground of Moloch within himself. He could say, "Light," and now the other word in him begins to glow: he himself, his name, the name of "truth," the end to which all things are born and moving; for here Son and Father and even Holy Spirit are nothing but the sign and the direction in which it moves, the great cue that solves the first beginning—*kiddush ha-shem,* the transfiguration, sanctification of the divine name, the most hidden *verbum mirificum* of absolute cognition. The Greeks had discovered in tragedy that man is better than his gods. And not infrequently Christian mysticism had its own *kiddush ha-shem* that made the Christian God, too, like a bushel under which the Jesus-Lucifer-type light is hidden. He breaks and is absorbed; God and his book are eaten up and the creative space of gathering sets in—so this is the meaning of the "uncovered countenance," a flatly eschatological, not theological, meaning. It lies in a downward reversal of the motion, not of love but of transcendence itself: downward to mankind, so that in the utmost novum of this New Testament its heavenly Jerusalem will "come down out of heaven," and will do so "prepared as a bride," not as a sacrificial altar, nor a throne of mercy.

110

RELIGIOUS TRUTH*

As far as religion is concerned there is now no need to point to the clouds in the heavens above. They are familiar enough, and have been convicted of humbug more often than any literary fiction. However sanctimonious the ways of the world, the fables of the sanctuary still awaken scorn and distaste.

It must be admitted: "priestcraft" has always been more obviously acceptable as a cliché than the proposition that all poets are liars: in any case a contention that only the leisured intellect could bite on, and hardly as influential, as politically definite and mandatory as the anti-religious struggle—unmistakably (it appeared) truth on crusade against darkness visible. Epicurus, Lucretius, the French Encyclopaedists, Marx and Engels are the salients of a portrayal of religion as little more than the product of ignorance and fear: scarcely (in view of the many Hate-lights in religion) a wholly false picture. Hence Marx called religion the opium of the people; and, as the decking of man's chains with imaginary flowers, the best way to keep him in chains: hardly (in view of the relation between

* Translated by John Cumming.

baptism and sword, altar and throne, and despite Thomas Münzer and the Peasants' War for Jesus' sake) a complete misrepresentation. Of course Marx did extend the metaphor of flowers and chains, for he said the desired end was that man might "throw off the chains and pluck the living flower." But in practice the Church so often denied this *religious* end (no poppy of oblivion, no opiate haze, no empty promise), that in Marx it remained a perceptive judgment, became in Social Democracy a matter of private opinion, and in Bolshevism was all but put out.

The question of truth in religion involves a strict inquiry into religious myth as well as practice, and therefore contrasts acutely with the imperceptible shrug evoked by make-believe and illusion in art. Even antagonism to art (although Plato, himself an artist, would have banished artists from his commonwealth) never did and never could approach Voltaire's intense animosity to religion, or Nietzsche's Anti-Christ. Yet this difference must be referred not to the ecclesiastical power of religion as set against the powerlessness of art (a vassal of power, at most), but to the distinctive seriousness of purpose in the modes characteristic of religion and art. The iconoclasts' attacks on art during the Reformation (and, with a semi-Islamic force, during the great Iconoclastic Controversy in Byzantium) arose not from any hatred of fictive images, but from the thoroughly biblical pathos of the invisible world.

Recognition of this unremitting earnestness, most clearly evident in the Bible, demands the addition of a *new* and certainly *paradoxical* element to the almost wholly anti-religious inquiry into the truth of religion: nothing less than a questioning that is present *within religion itself*—in other words, a religious critique of religion.

Such a critique could not arise from what is proper to works of art, as art, for they do not possess this element of unremitting, straightforward protestation. Artistic structures do not assert in this way; they are *pluralistic,* not *centralistic* like all non-polytheistic religions (pre-eminently those based on the Bible, but also—with their distinct emphases—Buddhism and

Taoism). This is immediately and decisively clear in the dominant form of expression: *allegory,* with its circuitous ambiguities, is the form of representation characteristic of an artistic utterance, despite its straightforward content (for art is pluralistic); whereas *symbolism,* unambiguous in tendency and ultimately convergent, is the form of representation characteristic of religious understanding, despite all its use of transparent poetry (for religion is centralistic).

Therefore the religion of the Bible engenders its own refusal of any mythical phenomena—in so far as they refer to the "gods of the heathen." Of course a long time passed before the existence of these local deities was called in question, but to have any part in it was blasphemy; above all, their power was as nothing against the unique power of Yahweh. The prophet Elijah (I Kings 18, 27) mocks the prophets of Baal and their god with a wit that seems almost Voltairean: they must cry aloud, for perhaps their god is asleep and must be awakened, or is musing, or on a journey. Indeed, if Elijah had been a biologist like Haeckel (and just as conspicuously lacking in taste) he might well have mocked on—to the point of opining that Baal was a gaseous vertebrate.

But later with the great prophets, pagan, mythical and kindred elements in the religion of Yahweh were out. An attack was mounted on the practice of making burnt offerings, on cultic externalism, and on many other features which until then were as permissible in Yahweh's service as in polytheistic religion and idol-worship. Isaiah hardly refers to the creation myth; instead, the Yahweh who laboured for six days is wholly obscured in favour of the God of the Exodus from *this* known land of Egypt, and the creation of a new heaven and a new earth in which no worldly power will maintain the idols, and justice will flow like the waters: until a son of man himself replaces the image of Yahweh ("I and the Father are one"), without any myths of an awful deity, a pantheon, and suprahuman imperatives (Hegel remarked of this *Cur deus homo* that the Greeks made their gods not too human, but not human enough).

113

Precisely here, that first criticism, that essentially humane religious questioning of the truth of religion, comes from *within religion* to abolish at least the hypostasis of the lord and master mythologized as Yahweh. *Aut Christus aut Caesar*—either Christ or Caesar—is now the clear alternative underlying the very idea and image of Yahweh. And so the good news and its essential content turn atheist with regard to everything that smacks of a power deity; with regard to every myth or mythical element of lordship and mastery that reflects power and effects an ideology of power: whether Yahweh as Baal, as Marduk, as Ptah, or (finally) as Jupiter. Therefore the reflex projected by tyranny and fear into that heaven far above is abolished within the myth (though indeed not seen through); and abolition offers a certain freedom. The replacement is not any myth chosen at random, but a radiant myth whose concern is none other than light; enlightenment without chains, but with the living flower; illumination as fulfillment. Of course, as a reflection of and defence against domination, darkness is a constant of myth; its prevailing archetype is and remains (as Adorno rightly remarks) in antiquity the unarrested and inexorable course of fate, and in Christianity, hell.

But there is more, much more. Protest, exodus, Christ-impetus: all these urgings produced within the myth itself an explosive anti-myth of freedom, far removed from the impotent species to which both Bultmann's neo-bourgeois "demythologization" and Bonhoeffer's "religionless Christianity" belong. A paradox then: an increase within religion of the inquiry after its truth; made by existing antitheses to the myth (for it was an alien myth); made so that religion itself can be not opium but protest, central though not dominant: the purposive, symbolic expression of a One, a True, and a Good without superstition. In *The Principle of Hope* I called this: "a religious protestation in which the self (the buried self) is no longer treated as undisclosed, and *sursum corda* is no longer conceived of as a lifting up of hearts to a hypostatized transcendence in which man has no part: for the good news of Christian salvation is *Eritis sicut Deus* ('you will be like God')."

114

This *Eritis* is clearly the most subversive word in all myths open to an anthropocentric interpretation—from the serpent up to Prometheus, and on to the resolution of all longings and thoughts under God in the "third Gospel" of the Christlike community. Because the anthropological critique of religion involved in "you will be like God" needs no demythologization, a light that can be preserved from the shadow of superstition will (ultimately) also disclose the only possible legitimate form of religious truth. But this (much more than in the case of the immanent resolutions of art) remains a clearly utopian and indeed eschatological enlightenment; taking the form of a proclamation of that which is believed in hope, and that which is to come: the uncovered face of the essence of human salvation. The end of the world as it exists is presented in the prophetic books, in Jesus' words (Mark 13), and especially in Revelation, as the truth of the existing world; this is quite, quite different from the wholly non-apocalyptic drive towards resolution found in the pre-visions of art.

Truth need not fight shy of elevating thoughts, which must certainly not be restricted to mere rhetorical uplift, or to reveries in which this world has no part. The most important emphasis laid on the world by the Bible is that of the future in which present things of falsehood, of darkness and of death will break and be changed. But what of *philosophical* truth? What can and may, indeed must it learn from hope (and allow itself to learn) of the nature of this great revelation? It can discover that art, because of the sensuous particularity in which it exhibits its very nature, can be an instrument of philosophical inquiry. Not only the implications of perception for aesthetics, but those of aesthetics for perception in Kant, Schelling and Hegel, indicate the critical, non-illusionary kind of experience to be obtained from this type of pre-vision (i.e., in art).

The case is quite different with religion, on account of the enormous number of superstitions, reactionary myths, absurd claims to substitute for science and scholarship. "I believe it because it's absurd" (the *"credo quia absurdum"* syndrome that began with Tertullian's *"credibile quia ineptum est"*) has

115

not merely served to express the paradox of Christianity and the genuine mystery (the *absconditum*), but has stressed the irrational, and played the supra-rational off against the limited understanding of the subject masses. More than any deception in art, this sublime obscurantism is inconsistent with the operation of philosophical truth.

Nevertheless, the total expansion of hope that we find in humanism came into the world only in one form—that of the Bible. What basic manual of hope could be more important philosophically for a transcending without any transcendence—without a transcendence posited as existing, and packed and substantial in content? The Bible first presented philosophy with the consciousness of *evil* as part of its concept of life; and contributed it to every notion of enlightenment as illumination from Augustine on. Therefore it was the source also of precision in the *concept of postulating* the Right; for this kind of hypothesizing is properly concerned with the dark and arduous terrain of this earth, and reads its instructions for the campaign ahead in the lines of that which is not, but ought to be. And the source above all from which, against impending nothingness, there arose the philosophical *concept of hazard*—an experimental notion entirely concerned with constructing a model of the objective ahead. Of course an experimental rig will never allow us, even at best, more than test runs for an incursion into the *true truth* as yet unrealized in the process of the world on its way; yet the continuing guidance it receives at least preserves it from all forms of relativism. The world is filled with a variety of test-models, and continually and late-maturing evidences and works of a moral-aesthetic and religious pre-sentiment: the shining forth in advance of the "uncovered face" which, as such, has in a very few instances developed into the existence in the present of no more and no less than—pre-sentiment.

An unswerving and essentially utopian direction always saves these testimonies from any mere transient "attraction," and clearly marks them out as actual experimental manifestations of the real thing. "Whoever is bound to a star," says Leonardo, "does not turn back." Starting from a religious base, this is

116

indeed universally true, in a meta-religious sense as well. There is always an unvarying course set for the most practical of all things: the power to have an ideal and to hold it in this very world, the form of which, not being yet the true form, is—as the Bible says—passing away (1 Cor. 7, 31). This is a religious metaphor for the coming of the "better aeon," or the "messianic omega" (another religious trope for the *optimum maximum*). Nevertheless, when we gaze at this world of ours (even after the Cross, still in a very bad way, ever and again devising new means of staying as it is), we see that to add any "present" eschatology to this best of all possible directions is unrealistic; not only in the empirical sense, but in view of that which itself (to a degree of being that, even in a metaphysical sense, must be called "not-yet-being") truly *is*.

But there is something wholly present to us: the world's instability to stay in its desperate state; and its possession of a critical, anti-static element that, in its very restlessness, reveals the truth.

And so, driving and dialectical, latent and as yet unsuccessful, truth is apparent in process. Not in motionless objective facts, not—as true truth—in a hypostatized ascension, but in process.

CHRISTIAN SOCIAL UTOPIAS

1. The Bible and the Kingdom of Neighborly Love

What does Scripture tell us as soon as it turns historical? It tells of the suffering of an enslaved people. They have to carry bricks, to toil in the fields, and their lives are "made bitter." Moses appears, and kills an overseer; it is the first act of the founder-to-be; he must leave the country. From the outset, the God he imagines while abroad is not a masters' god, but one of free Bedouins in the Sinai region of the nomad tribe Moses has married into. Yahweh begins as a threat to the Pharaoh; the Sinaitic volcano god becomes Moses' God of liberation, of the exodus from slavery. Thereafter, this kind of exodus gives to the Bible a basic tone it has not lost since. There is no other book in which the memory of nomadic institutions—in other words, of a primitive semi-communism—remains as strong as in the Bible. Community life without a division of labor and private property appears as God's will long after private property had come into being in Canaan and was accorded some measure of recognition by the prophets.

Jeremiah, following the older Hosea's example, referred to the years in the desert as Israel's bridal time, not only because of Yahweh's greater proximity, but because of economic innocence. Once in the Promised Land, of course, and settled, the communal life ended fast. Farming and wine-growing were taken over from the conquered Canaanites who had long reached the agrarian and city-dwelling stage; crafts and trades evolved, as well as wealth and poverty and glaring class distinctions; creditors would sell their debtors abroad as slaves. The two Books of Kings are as full of famine as of the rich splendor that produced it. On the one hand, "there was a sore famine in Samaria" (I Kings 18); on the other hand, King Solomon "made silver to be in Jerusalem as stones" (I Kings 10, 27). Amidst this exploitation the *prophets* appeared, thundering against it, projecting the judgment and along with it the *very first plans for a social utopia.* And as if to demonstrate continuity with the semi-communistic Bedouin times, they did it in league with a semi-nomadic opposition that was still close to the Bedouins: with the rough, unsociable types called Nazarites.

There were ties also to the Rechabites, a southern tribe that had held aloof from the luxury and from the money economy of Canaan, keeping faith with the old desert God. The Nazarites retained even the outward habit of the desert; they wore cloaks made of hair, let their own hair grow, and abstained from wine. Their Yahweh was still a stranger to private property, a God of the poor. Samson, Samuel, and Elijah were Nazarites (I Sam. 1, 11; II Kings 1, 8), but so was John the Baptist—all of them hostile to the Golden Calf and to the sumptuous masters' Church derived from the Canaanite Baal. A single line, full of curves but recognizable as one and the same, runs from the Nazarites' memories of primitive semi-communism to the prophets' preaching against wealth and tyranny and on to the early Christian communism of love. In its background the line is almost unbroken; the famed prophetic depictions of a future kingdom of social peace reflect a Golden Age which in this case was no mere legend.

The denunciation of "apostasy" from Yahweh likewise took its bearings from Nazaritism: apostasy meant turning from a sort of pre-capitalistic Yahweh to Baal, and also to that masters' Yahweh who had conquered Baal at the price of turning himself into a God of luxury. The prophets would accordingly appear in times of great internal and external stress, as exhorters to change. Amos, who calls himself a poor herdsman and a gatherer of sycamore fruit, is the oldest (about 750 B.C.) and perhaps the greatest among them, and his Yahweh is a barn-burner. "I will send a fire upon Judah, and it shall devour the palaces of Jerusalem . . . because they sold the righteous for silver, and the poor for a pair of shoes. They pant after the dust of the earth on the head of the poor, and turn aside the way of the meek" (Amos, 2, 5–7). And further, withering the masters' church: "I hate, I despise your feast days, and I will not smell in your solemn assemblies. . . . But let judgment run down as waters, and righteousness as a mighty stream" (Amos 5, 21 and 24). It is in this same spirit that Joachim di Fiore, the great chiliast of the High Middle Ages, will later say, "Altars are trimmed, and the poor suffer the bitter pangs of hunger." This God is in no mood to discuss religion with expropriators. Baal is no colleague of his, nor is Mercury. "He looked for judgment," Isaiah exclaims, "but behold oppression; for righteousness, but behold a cry. Woe unto them that join house to house, that lay field to field, till there be no place, that they may be placed alone in the midst of the earth!" (Is. 5, 7f.).

Thus Yahweh is invoked as a foe of the expropriators of peasant holdings, and of the accumulators of capital, as an avenger and tribune of the people: "I will punish the world for their evil, and the wicked for their iniquity; and I will cause the arrogancy of the proud to cease, and will lay low the haughtiness of the terrible. I will make a man more precious than fine gold; even a man than the golden wedge of Ophir" (Is. 13, 11f.). But Deutero-Isaiah, the great unknown, adds, "This is a people robbed and spoiled; they are all of them snared in holes, and they are hid in prison houses; they are for a prey, and none delivereth; for a spoil, and none saith, Restore" (Is. 42, 22). Until the time of universal happiness and wealth, characterized as socialist wealth: "Ho, every one that thirsteth, come ye to the waters, and he that hath no money: come ye, buy and eat; yea, come, buy wine and milk without money and without price" (Is. 55, 1). Surely the day of awakening will come for the spirit of liberation, for Yahweh the exodus God. He is the topic of the famed utopia that occurs in Isaiah and the slightly younger Micah in almost identical language and may even have been taken from a prophet older yet: "For the law shall go forth of Zion, and the word of the Lord from Jerusalem. And he shall judge among many people, and rebuke strong nations afar off; and they shall beat their swords into plowshares, and their spears into pruninghooks; nation shall not lift up a sword against nation, neither shall they learn war any more. But they shall sit every man under his vine and under his fig tree; and none shall make them afraid" (Micah 4, 2–4; Is. 2, 3f.). Here is the original model of the pacified international that forms the core of the Stoic utopia; the verse from Isaiah furnished the real, influential basis for all Christian utopias.

It is questionable, of course, whether the old Israelite prophets (and, in a broader context, the old East as a whole) had a concept of the future, and thus of time, coincident with the concept that has evolved since Augustine. The experience of time is bound to have undergone a good many changes; above all, it is only in more recent times that the future has been augmented by the *novum* and has charged itself with it. But the content of the biblically-intended future has remained intelligible in all social utopias: Israel became poverty as such, and Sion became Utopia. Misery makes messianical: "O thou afflicted, tossed with tempest, and not comforted, behold, I will lay thy stones with fair colours, and lay thy foundations with sapphires. . . . In righteousness shalt thou be established; thou shalt be far from oppression, for thou shalt not fear; and from terror, for it shall not come near thee" (Is. 54, 11 and 14). Time and again, down to Weitling, an aura of this light in darkness surrounds the social utopias.

The Roman came into the Promised Land that had become less and less as promised. The rich got along quite well with the foreign occupation; it provided protection from desperate peasants and patriotic resistance fighters. It provided protection from prophets who could be labeled "agitators" now, without any qualms. The Nazarite John the Baptist preached among the

lowest of the low and promised an end to their misery. "Now
also the axe is laid unto the root of the trees; therefore every
tree which bringeth not forth good fruit is hewn down, and cast
into the fire" (Matth. 3, 10). There was more than ample room
in those days for glad tidings, whether social-revolutionary or
national-revolutionary; the turn seemed near. "He that cometh
after me," said the Baptist; "his winnowing fan is in his hand;
and he will thoroughly purge his floor, and gather his wheat
into the garner; but he will burn up the chaff with unquenchable
fire" (Matth. 3, 12).

And Jesus' own coming was by no means so introverted and
other-worldly as a Pauline reinterpretation—always welcome to
the ruling class—would have it. His message to the laboring and
heavy-laden was not the cross; this they had to bear anyway,
and the fearful outcry "My God, why hast thou forsaken me?"
shows that Jesus experienced the crucifixion as a catastrophe,
not in the sense of St. Paul. The great saying in Matthew 11,
25–30, is of this world, not of the other; it is an edict of the
Messiah-King who terminates all forms of suffering and does so
on earth, as one into whose hands all things are given to be
changed: "My yoke is easy, and my burden is light." Jesus never
said, "The kingdom of God is within you." Literally, this portentous line (Luke 17, 21) reads "The kingdom of God is
among you"—and it was said to the Pharisees, not to the disciples. It means: "The kingdom is living among you Pharisees
now, in the chosen community of these disciples"; its meaning is
a social one, not an invisibly internal one. Jesus never said, "My
kingdom is not of this world." That verse was interpolated by
John (18, 36) and intended to help Christians before Roman
tribunals: Jesus himself did not try with a cowardly pathos of
the beyond to give himself an alibi before Pilate. Such an attempt would have run counter to the demonstrated courage and
dignity of Christianity's founder; above all, it would contradict
the meaning which the words "this world" and "the other world"
had in Jesus' day. That timebound meaning was derived from
the astral-religious speculations of the old East—in other words,
from the doctrine of world periods. "This world" meant the

122

same as the one now existing, the "present aeon," while "the other world" meant the "future aeon" (thus Matth. 12, 32; 24, 3).

These concepts were not contrasted to suggest a geographical division of this world from the beyond, but a *succession in time on the same stage, here on earth.* The "other world" was the utopian earth with a utopian heaven above, in accordance with Isaiah 65, 17: "For, behold, I create new heavens and a new earth; and the former shall not be remembered, nor come into mind." The goal was not a beyond after death, where the angels sing; it was the terrestrial as well as supraterrestrial kingdom of love, with its first enclave already constituted by the original community. Not until after the catastrophe of the cross was the kingdom of the other world interpreted as lying in the beyond. Above all, it would be so interpreted once the Pilates (and especially the Neros) had become Christians themselves; what was all-important to the ruling class was that the love communism be relaxed as spiritually as possible. To Jesus, the kingdom of this world was that of the devil (John 8, 44). This is why he never suggested allowing it to go on; he did not conclude a non-aggression pact with it. He rejected armed force—not always, by the way: "I came not to send peace, but a sword" (Matth. 10, 34)—but significantly, when such force is rejected in the Sermon on the Mount, the kingdom of heaven in each of the Beatitudes is placed at the imminent end (Matth. 5, 3–10). Arms are rejected because to the *apocalypt* Jesus they are already obsolete, hence superfluous. He expects an upheaval that will leave no stone unturned anyway, and he expects it at any moment, from nature, from the superweapon of a cosmic catastrophe.

With Jesus, eschatological preaching has primacy over moral preaching and determines it. Not only the money-changers will be driven from the temple with a whip, as they were by Jesus; the whole state and temple will be brought down by a catastrophe, most thoroughly and in short order. The great eschatological chapter (Mark 13) is one of the best-attested in the New Testament; without this utopia, the Sermon on the Mount cannot be understood at all. Since the old fortress would be so soon and so thoroughly leveled, economic questions also seemed senseless to Jesus, who regarded the "present aeon" as finished in any event and believed in the immediately impending cosmic disaster. Hence the line of the lilies in the field is far less naïve than it seems, or at least baffling and disparate on a quite different level. And as for the directive to "render unto Caesar the things which are Caesar's, and to God the things that are God's," this was something Jesus said out of contempt for the state, and in view of its imminent downfall; he did not say it as a compromise, as Paul would have it. A natural disaster is an ersatz revolution, of course, but an extremely comprehensive one; Jesus does remove the tension of any real revolt, but he does not therefore sign an armistice with the existing world or forget the "future aeon." According to Jesus, the cataclysm of the kingdom of this world will indeed be cruelly executed; at the Last Judgment there is not much talk any more of loving one's enemies.

The new troops were bound by oath to Jesus alone; he was the ground, the way, the goal of the new social community that had been extricated from the present aeon. "I am the vine, ye are the branches," the founder laid down (John 15, 5), dissolving himself in the community to the same extent to which he encompassed it. "Inasmuch as ye have done it unto one of the least of these my brethren, ye have done it unto me" (Matth. 25, 40)—by this line, the social utopia intended in original Christianity is set upon a foundation of its love communism and of the international of whatever bears human features, especially if they are poor. The line adds also, in a way that was to have great consequences, what was completely lacking in the Stoa: a social mission from below, and a mythical personal authority to watch over it. Even where the social mission had all but vanished, as in the case of Augustine, the contrast to the power of this existing world and to its anti-human contents remained overwhelming throughout, through all Church-building and every compromise—and how much more so in the Christian revolutions, with the slain Egyptian overseer, the exodus, thundering prophets, expelled money-changers, and the promise to the laboring and heavy laden in mind.

124

No social utopia was worked out in the Bible, and its utopianism certainly does not exhaust it or give it its decisive value; to think so would be to overestimate the Bible in a way both false and shallow. Christianity is no mere outcry against want; it is an outcry against death and the void, and what it inserts in both of these is the Son of man. But even though the Bible contains no detailed social utopia, it does most strongly, in negation as well as in affirmation, point to this sort of exodus and to this sort of kingdom. And when the scouts brought back their report of the land flowing with milk and honey, there was no dearth of warriors eager to conquer it; nor was there later, when the land proved to be no Canaan, a dearth of hard, burning dreamers who would keep searching for it, finding more and more stirring superlatives for it, trying to bring it closer and closer to mankind. The great Babylon was shown no quarter: "Babylon the great is fallen, is fallen . . . and the kings of the earth shall bewail her, and lament for her . . . and the merchants of the earth shall weep and mourn over her; for no man buyeth their merchandise any more" (Rev. 18, 2 and 9–11). But nowhere in the Bible is the kingdom viewed as a baptized Babylon, nor —as Augustine later viewed the millennium—as a Church.

2. *Augustine's* Civitas Dei

The Greek dreams of things to come were almost always rooted firmly in this world. Life itself was to be improved in them, without any alien increment, in rational, albeit motley, fashion. The most remote isles of Greek wish-fulfillment were still located in a contiguous world, and so was their happiness. Happiness, along with its institutions, was immanently inserted into existing life and held up to that life as an example. But to the Rome that was now breaking up no immanent model could be shown any more. What men longed for was something totally different, something totally new, and the eventual victor in the competition of salvations—victorious by making political use of the new—was *Pauline* Christianity.

125

Jesus had called for the leap, although we have seen that his real demand was by no means a leap from this world to inwardness, to a beyond, but a fresh start on a new earth. Around his nucleus, however, the Christian-utopian wish for community evolved now more and more in the direction of the beyond, of inwardly transcendent concentration and of future consolation. Instead of a radical renewal of this world, an institute of the beyond appeared—the Church—and interpreted the Christian social utopia as referring to itself. Links with the Stoic utopia were added, in the form of the "superior State" already taught by Chrysippus; his *oikoumene,* along with the Roman empire, supplied the framework. But the Stoic utopia lacked the leap into the new: the general world appeared conclusive in itself, unable —and also unwilling, in line with the entire disposition of Antiquity—to produce new dispositions, new tasks, let alone new breakthroughs, out of its own substance. This took an exodus impulse not found on pagan soil. It took the impulse of Jesus to sublimate the complete and posit the explosive: with Zeus, the rational State in the world turned into the divine State against the world, with Christ. In Augustine's utopia *De civitate Dei* (about 425) the new earth as an earthly beyond found its most vigorous, even though Church-building, utopian expression.

Here, earthly desires can be considered only by the way; they can never be fulfilled. They are the bad desires that have so far prevailed and kept man away from the right life. Their location is the worldly State, and the will to that State is evil. It can therefore not be improved but has to be changed, the previous will as well as the previous State.

The goal of the change is Jesus, with Augustine initially still admitting the necessity that compels the good to live together with the wicked. Their two States are still intertwined, and for the time being the holy and desired one has to put up with the evil of the unholy one. At this point the Father of the Church (here still a faithful disciple of the Pauline social compromise) goes so far as to approve slavery, which was rejected by almost all the Stoics. He enjoins renunciation, on the ground that serving another is always better than serving one's own lusts. Augustine further vests the right to punish in the existing authority as being—no one knows why—a good *pater familias,* and he even puts this in the context of a so-called history of salvation. For the worldly State, while bad, is not the worst; ranging beneath the *civitas terrena* is the wholly diabolical primal condition of anarchy. Thus, if the states that exist on earth have no saving history, they have at least a salving one, with the first refuge offered by home and family, the second by clan and city State (*civitas* as *urbs*), and the third by the international State of peoples (*civitas* as *orbis*). This international State is easily recognizable as the same Roman one for which, from the utopian viewpoint of a *civitas Dei,* Augustine has nothing but contempt. Unlike other Fathers of the Church, Tertullian in particular, Augustine does not yearn for a Golden Age of the beginning; to him the beginning antedates any kind of *civitas* and is thus never described otherwise than as a diabolical animal kingdom. However, as a practical prince of the Church—and against every antithesis of *civitas terrena* and *civitas Dei,* which remains to be discussed—he did accept the Roman empire as the *soil* of the ecclesiastic *oikoumene,* much as the late Stoics identified Rome with their "superior State." The difference was that in Rome the "superior State" was politically powerless, while Augustine only did in theory what by then could almost be done in practice: he subordinated the empire to the Church, the dubious *salving institution* to the superior *saving institution* that had allegedly been established by Christ. This was the end of his relative recognition of the earthly State; conditions were not yet ripe for more extensive compromises. The relations of State and Church were still so little consolidated that as executor of the Christian utopia Augustine came to take a position contrary to that of the practical prince of the Church. Later in *De civitate Dei* his prudent, albeit slightly nauseated, admiration for Rome yields to a wholly dualistic hatred, to a form of the night versus light, Ormazd versus Ahriman tension of his Manichaean youth. If Jesus and Jesus alone is the goal of the change, if there is only saving history, no salving history, then the historical States, Rome included, are exclusively hostile to Christ. They themselves, not

127

just the anarchy from which they spring, are the kingdom of the devil.

This is the decisive idea in Augustine's work, beyond his compromise, and it is shown as a process: for the first time a political utopia appears as history. In fact, it produces history; history comes to be as *saving history in the direction of the kingdom,* as a single unbroken process extending from Adam to Jesus on the basis of the Stoic unity of mankind and the Christian salvation it is destined for. Two states have thus always been waging an irreconcilable struggle in mankind, *civitas terrena* and *civitas Dei,* the community of sinners hostile to God and the community of the elect (chosen by divine grace). Augustine's philosophy of history is offered as the record of this struggle: the *self-corruption of the earthly states* and the *germinating triumph of Christ's kingdom* are made antithetically plain in forceful examples. The first part of the work (which Augustine himself calls a *"magnum opus et strenuum"*) contains a critique of polytheistic paganism: the pagan gods are evil spirits and as such ruling the community of the damned already, here on earth. But the second part unfolds history's antithetical process of salvation, and it does so by splitting it up into periods whose dividing lines—as well as the horizon in which the contents of history are seen—come mainly from the Old Testament. Mankind from the Fall to the Judgment appears as one single concentrated person, and the historical periodicity is carried through in analogy to the ages of life; it is a believing philosophy of biblical history. The childhood lasts from Adam to Noah, boyhood from Noah to Abraham, youth from Abraham to David, manhood from David to the Babylonian captivity; the last two periods extend to the birth of Christ and from that to the Last Judgment. For the kingdom of God, and for the story of its breakthrough, this means that *civitas terrena,* the sinful state, perished in the flood; *civitas Dei* was preserved in Noah and his sons, but their children already renewed the curse of the false state. The Jews reassembled under the canopy—"Ye shall be unto me a kingdom of priests, and an holy nation"—while all other nations, the Assyrians worst of all, fell under the sway

128

of evil, of the power State which is the devil's. Throughout the book, summing up its philosophy of history, runs the criticism of force, the criticism of the political State as a crime. Once again there is prophetic ire thundering at Babylon and Assyria, at Egypt, Athens, and Rome (although in Rome Christianity was now the "official state religion"): "The first City and the first State were founded by a man who slew his brother; fratricide also stains the origins of Rome—stains them so one may call it a general rule that blood must have been spilled wherever a State shall rise" (*De civ. Dei* XV). And there is another famous line to the same effect, a model of realistic political criticism on the ground of so unrealistic a utopia: "With justice gone, what else are kingdoms but immense robbers' dens? *Remota igitur justitia quid sunt regna nisi magna latrocinia?*" (*De civ. Dei* IV). Justice must be understood here in a Pauline sense, of course: it is justification by yielding to, and concurring with, the saving will of God. But the political state abounds in nothing but quarrels over earthly goods, in domestic and foreign strife, in the power struggle that is far from God; the very essence of pride and the Fall is what it abounds in.

So little regard for the existing State has Augustine, as a thinker concerned with salvation (*"Deum et animam scire cupio; nihilne plus? nihil omnino*—I want to know about God and the soul. Nothing else? Nothing whatever"). So strong is the residue of the Manichaean convictions of his youth, the continuing political effect of the tension between the gods of the light and the night, between Ormazd and Ahriman. *Civitas Dei* is an ark and often a mere catacomb, hiding over and over; it will not be revealed till the end of what has been history thus far. Which is why even the Church is not wholly identical with the City of God, at least not since its right to forgive sins has been extended to mortal sins, including (since the Decian persecution) even apostasy, and it has thus come to comprise a rather mixed group. Only as *corpus verum,* as the number of the elect, is the Church entirely *civitas Dei;* the existing Church, the *corpus permixtum* of elect and of sinners, is not identical with it, only bordering upon it as a preparatory stage. The existing Church is identical, however, with Augustine's millennium, as the first awakening, the first resurrection before the second, definitive one (Rev. 20, 5f.). This first awakening is introduced and held fast by the ecclesiastic means of grace. While the chiliastic tension is thus relaxed, the City of God is not handed over to the existing Church. From Abel on, it is built up for heaven, rather, in fragments, and will not be completely revealed until the kingdom appears. It is an institution like Plato's ideal *polis,* but more consistent inasmuch as its perfect order is conceived as instituted, not by men, but by divine order. Any pure utopian order presupposes—lest it lapse into the opposite, into the mere disposition or disorder of chance or fate, *tyche* or *moira*—that there be an economy of salvation on which to found the order and the utopia itself. This fundament of transcendently communicated or inspired order, without any admixture of chance or *moira,* was not to be found either in Plato's or in the Stoic ideas of the *polis* and of the god of the *polis;* it was found only in the Christian concept of God. It is not in the existing world, nor beyond it, but after this world that the City of God appears in full, as the highest, timeless form of a *polis,* one that has escaped from time. And the basic utopian goal of society, the goal in whose direction only the Church can lead, remains *man's acquisition of the divine image* (*De civ. Dei* XXII). This is the radically supra-temporal directive, the ordering principle of the one and only best State against all others, against the systems of sin.

Civitas Dei was conceived quite literally as a part of heaven on earth, in the sense of bliss and above all in the sense of purity, the purity that does not make angels of men but does make them saints—which is more, according to Catholic doctrine. Against the dark pessimism of Augustine's view of the mundane body politic stands his optimism about the *civitas Dei,* based upon the fact that saints exist and grow in the Church— an ardently priestlike and yet space-making kind of optimism, subsequently capable of abundant secularization. The dismissal of the works of the old Adam, the putting on of Christ—in short, the hope for a spiritual rebirth of more and more human beings —turns Augustine's City of God into a political utopia.

130

And yet, it is odd how these dreams are not aimed squarely at things to come. They plunge farther ahead than any others, but the future seems garbed in existing things. It thus becomes possible to ask: is *civitas Dei* a utopia, strictly speaking? Or is it the phenomenon of a transcendence that exists already and is current in this world? Is that which really unfolds here the daydream of what socially has not yet come into being, or is a completed transcendence, an *"ecclesia perennis,"* infused into the world? The City of God often seems to be a mere germ in Augustine's history—in other words, a utopian future. But it looks just as often like an extant great power, a great anti-power, come into existence not unlike the other *dramatis persona,* the devil's State. In Augustine's book, *civitas Dei* is hailed as virtually present in the Jewish Levite State and in the Church of Christ. So vast a dream as that of the millennium is sacrificed to the Church, supposed to be fulfilled in it already. And a main point: *civitas Dei* is ultimately said to exist as a fixed structure of grace, made up of those predestined for election—whether or not they wish that citizenship, whether or not they strive, dream, work for God's kingdom.

In Augustine's theology one can no more work for the kingdom of God than for any other good; it comes from grace and exists by grace, not by the merit of works. By divine predestination, the outcome of the historical difference between *civitas terrena* and *civitas Dei* has been decided also; like grace, the side containing light and heaven conquers irresistibly. All this does indeed remove Augustine's ideal State from the properly utopian will and planning thought—*and yet the City of God is a utopia.* It is not one that implies a will to change things, but the soul, according to Augustine, has only the freedom of willing to will, anyway; since Adam's fall it is not free to be morally able to will (*non possumus non peccare*). But as grace stirs man not only to be good but to be ready for goodness, *civitas Dei* is also ahead of man and lives within him in utopian fashion: as the grace of the expectancy which the elect are predestined for. And another essential point: as we recall, the community of the perfect and saintly on earth will not appear until the end of what

131

has so far been history. The City of God will not fully succeed until the worldly state goes where it belongs: to the devil. Thus *civitas Dei* is not just historically current as a decisive *dramatis persona;* it is also produced—or, to use a more cautious word, elaborated—by history as the "acquisition of the divine image." And it hovers above the historical process as a whole; it is "the eternal body where none are born because none die, where true and strong happiness reigns, where the sun does not rise over good and evil, but the sun of justice shines upon the good alone" (*De civ. Dei* V). This is certainly transcendence, but not a firmly extant one that would contradict the utopian character. *Socialis vita sanctorum* is a historic-utopian transcendence, for unlike St. Paul's it is back on earth. Paul also speaks of "God's State," but he—characteristically, for the distance between Jesus and him—speaks of it in the purely transcendent sense of a "State in the heavens," segregated on high, while Augustine posits something like a new earth. This is why his transcendence can be utopian: because it is entwined with the productive hope of *human history.* In history it associates, runs risks, triumphs; unlike pure transcendence, it is not all settled and fixed.

To Augustine, *civitas Dei* is therefore present only as a stumbling block and an ever-jeopardized advance appearance; not till the end of what has so far been history will it be a utopia. Indeed, Augustine gives even the perfect City of God a new goal, a goal to which it is a mere preliminary. For *civitas Dei* is not the kingdom asked for in the Lord's prayer; that kingdom is what Augustine calls *regnum Christi.* Now and then, of course, and with apologetic adornments, he gives that name to *civitas Dei* as well, but the *regnum* proper is never called *civitas,* for it no longer stands in time. So, as the earthly Sabbath is to Augustine a utopian festival in expectation of the heavenly one, *civitas Dei,* only seemingly complete and extant, carries its utopia in itself: the kingdom of Christ as the last, heavenly Sabbath. The seventh day of Creation is still vacant, and Augustine marks it with his most centrally utopian word: "We ourselves shall be the seventh day—*Dies septimus nos ipsi erimus*" (*De civ. Dei* XXII). This is a kind of transcendence which, once it has broken through in a man, makes him want to have achieved the break-through himself, Augustine to the contrary notwithstanding. Our alleged "inability not to sin" (*non possumus non peccare*) proved no great obstacle there, especially as the radical moral unfreedom of the will did not prevail even ecclesiastically. Nor was the relaxation of the millennium into the Church an obstacle, especially as *civitas Dei,* that lofty dream, constantly gave the lie to the Church's claim to be the millennium. Chiliasm kept erupt-ing in all periods of unrest. "God's kingdom on earth" came to be the revolutionary magic formula throughout the Middle Ages and the early modern age, down to the pious radicalism of the English Revolution under Cromwell. Augustine's own City of God proved more lasting in its definition of the power States than in its apologia for the Church, more lasting in its fraternal utopianism than in its theology of the Father. Henceforth the brotherhood of man was part of utopia even where no Father was any longer believed in—*civitas Dei* remained a picture of political wish fulfillment even without God.

3. Joachim di Fiore, the Third Gospel, and Its Kingdom

The question was whether the expectations would be taken seri-ously. The revolutionary movements were in a position to do so, and they created a new image of the kingdom. They also taught a new kind of history, one that breathed life into the image and held out a promise of its incarnation. The most portentous social utopia of the Middle Ages was designed by a Calabrian abbot, Joachim di Fiore (about 1200 A.D.). The point, to him, was not to cleanse Church and State of their horrors; they were abolished instead. And the extinct Gospel was rekindled, or rather, a *lux nova* was kindled in it—the "Third Kingdom," as the Joachim-ites called it.

There are three stages of history, Joachim taught, each one closer to the attainable breakthrough of the kingdom. The first stage is the Father's, the Old Testament's, the stage of fear and of known law. The second is the Son's or the New Testament's, the stage of love and of a Church divided into clerks and laymen. The third, the coming stage is that of the Holy Spirit or the illumination of all men in a mystical democracy, without masters and without a Church. The first Testament brought the grass, the second brought the sheaves, and the third will bring the wheat. There are various elaborations of this sequence by Joachim, most of them referring directly to his own time, as the time believed to be that of the end, and with the political prognosis that the nobles and priests cannot and the "laymen" will not go on living as before. Thus, in a pre-bourgeois romanticist vein, Joachim preached on the curse of the corrupt feudal and ecclesiastic rule and on its radical termination, and he preached with a hope-filled wrath, on a note of "*Satis est*—that's enough!" such as had not been heard since John the Baptist. It invigorated the slogans in his three categories: age of dominion and fear = Old Testament; age of grace = New Testament; age of mental perfection and love = forthcoming final kingdom ("*Tres denique mundi status: primum in quo fuimus sub lege, secundum in quo sumus sub gratia, tertium quod e vicino expectamus sub ampliori gratia. . . . Primus ergo status in scientia fuit, secundus in proprietate sapientiae, tertius in plenitudine intellectus*"—"We come down to three states of the world: a first in which we were under the law, a second in which we are by grace, and a third, which we expect from the near future, by a broader grace. . . . The first state lay in knowledge, the second lies in the possession of wisdom, and the third in the fullness of the mind"). Two persons of the Trinity have shown themselves; the third, the Holy Spirit, may be expected at an absolute Pentecost.

In its foundations—though not in its social-utopian force—the idea of the Third Testament which Joachim presented in his treatise *De concordia utriusque testamenti* goes back to the third century A.D., when Origen, that strictly un-canonized Father of the Church, had taught three possible *conceptions* of the Christian texts: one of the body, one of the soul, and one of the mind. The physical conception is literal, the psychical one, moral-allegorical, but the mental one (*pneumato intus docente*) reveals the "eternal Gospel" meant in Scripture. To Origen, of course, the third Gospel also was a mere form of conception, even though the highest; it did not have to evolve by itself, in time. Nor did Origen's third Gospel step outside the New Testament which was complete as given, to the end of time. Joachim's greatness is that he transformed the traditional trinity of mere *standpoints* into a threefold gradation *in history itself*. Linked with this, and even richer in consequences, was his complete transfer of the kingdom of light *from the beyond, from the consolation of hoping for the beyond, into history*—even though into a terminal state of history. Jamboulos (like More, Campanella, and many others later) had located the ideal community on a distant isle, and Augustine in transcendence; but Joachim's utopia, like that of the prophets, appears exclusively in the mode of a historic future, as the status of such a future. Joachim's elect are the poor, and they are to enter paradise in the flesh, not only as spirits.

There are no more "estates" in the society of the Third Gospel. It will be an "age of monks"—that is, of a universal convent-type consumer communism—and an "age of the free spirit," that is, of spiritual illumination without segregation, without sin and the world of sin. The body, too, will thus be guiltlessly gladdened as in the primal paradisiacal condition, and the frozen earth will be filled with the phenomena of a spiritual May. There is a hymn written by a Joachimite named Telesphorus (at the end of the fourteenth century) that begins, "*O vita vitalis, dulcis et amabilis, semper memorabilis*"—"O Life, quick, sweet, lovable, ever memorable Life!" The *libertas amicorum* was not Puritanical. Their theme was exodus, an exodus from fear and servitude or from the law and its state, from clerical rule and tutelage over the laity, or from the Church as a dispenser of the grace of love; Joachim's doctrine with its band of brothers was not an escape from the world, to heaven or to a beyond. On the contrary: as he preached it, the kingdom of Christ was as strictly of this world as it had not been since primitive Christianity. Jesus was the Messiah of a new earth again, and Christianity happened in reality, not just in the cult and in future consolations. It happened without masters or property, in a mystical democracy. This is what the Third Gospel was for, what was to come with its kingdom. Even Jesus ceased being a head and dissolved in the "society of friends."

It is virtually impossible to trace all of the courses taken by this quite historically intended dream. It kept moving for long times and to far distant countries; for centuries, genuine and forged writings of Joachim's remained in circulation. They appeared in Bohemia and in Germany, even in Russia, where sects aspiring to original Christianity were clearly influenced by the Calabrian preaching. The Hussites' "kingdom of God in Bohemia"—repeated a hundred years later in Germany by the Anabaptists—meant Joachim's *civitas Christi*. Behind it lay the misery that had come long since; in it lay the millennium whose coming was due, so men struck a blow of welcome. Special attention was paid to the abolition of wealth and poverty; the preaching of those seeming romantics took brotherly love literally and interpreted it financially. "During its journey on earth," Augustine had written, "the City of God attracts citizens and gathers friendly pilgrims from all nations, regardless of differences due to customs, laws, and institutions that serve material gain and assure the earthly peace" (*De civ. Dei* XIX). The Joachimites' coming *civitas Dei,* on the other hand, kept a sharp eye on institutions that served material gain and exploitation, and the tolerance it practiced—namely, toward Jews and heathens—could not but be alien to international ecclesiasticism. Its criterion for citizenship was not whether a man had been baptized, but whether he heard the fraternal spirit in himself.

According to Thomas Münzer's great supra-Christian definition, the future kingdom would be formed "by all the elect out of all the dispersions or generations of all kinds of faith." Here the impact of Joachim's Third Kingdom is clear: "You should know," wrote Münzer, praising a true Christian's witness against princely lackeys and priestly scribes, "you should know that they attribute this doctrine to the abbot Joachim and call it an eternal gospel, with much mocking." The German Peasant War put a stop to the mocking, and the radicals of the English Commonwealth, the agrarian communists called "Diggers," the Millenarians and Quintomonarchists, all inherited from the Anabaptists and Joachim. It took Menno Simons' purge of the Joachimite-Taborite spirit to turn the Western Baptist sects—not Mennonites alone—into quiet (peculiarly quiet) evangelical communities. Also deserting the millennium was the other *irredenta* that detached itself from Baptism, the modern utopianism that was no longer irrational but beginning to be rationalistic.

Plato and the Stoics triumphed over Joachim di Fiore, even over Augustine. The result was greater precision of institutional detail in the utopias, a joining of forces with bourgeois emancipation—already utopianized into socialist tendencies—but the final goal, the ultimate end which in Joachim's utopia had been of the essence, was enfeebled as the rational utopians, the Thomas Mores and Campanellas, translated it as social harmony. A liberal or authoritarian State of the future took the place of the millennium. In the medieval Christian utopias with their mythologizing ways of thought the final goal had never been precisely put, but neither had it ever been lost sight of. It lasted all through the fermenting, dream-laden, red dawn that filled the Joachimites' and Anabaptists' utopia to the brim and turned its whole sky into an eastern horizon. This way of thinking had less social detail in its utopia than Plato or the Stoics, let alone the rational constructions of the modern age, but it had more of a utopian conscience. For this conscience and the problem of a final goal we are indebted to the chiliastic utopias, quite irrespective of the untenably mythological designations of their content. And Joachim was cogently the spirit of *revolutionary Christian social utopianism;* this is what he taught and what remained effective of his teaching. He was the first to set a date for the kingdom of God, for the communist kingdom, and to demand its observance. He deposed the theology of the Father, relegated it to the age of fear and servitude, and dissolved Christ in a commune. More than any other man, he was in earnest about the social expectancy which Jesus had assigned to the new aeon, and the Church had reduced to hypocrisy and cant. Or, as Marx correctly observes on the Christianity of the ecclesiastic centuries: "The social principles of Christianity have

137

now had eighteen hundred years time to develop. . . . The social principles of Christianity have justified slavery in Antiquity, have glorified serfdom in the Middle Ages, and are prepared, if necessary, to defend the oppression of the proletariat, even though with slightly piteous mien. The social principles of Christianity preach the necessity of a ruling class and an oppressed one, and their only pious wish for the latter is that the former may be charitable. The social principles of Christianity raise the Church-bureaucratic compromise of all infamies to heaven, and thereby justify the continuation of those infamies on earth. The social principles of Christianity hold any viciousness committed by the oppressor to be either just punishment for sin, original and otherwise, or a trial which the Lord in his wisdom has imposed on the redeemed. The social principles of Christianity preach cowardice, self-contempt, humiliation, humility, submissiveness —in short, all the qualities of scum; and the proletariat that will not be treated as scum has far more need of courage, of self-confidence, of pride, and of a sense of independence than it has of bread. The social principles of Christianity are craven, and the proletariat is revolutionary; so much for the social principles of Christianity."

All of this fits the Church, or what for eighteen hundred years has been, *ex cathedra* or *ex encyclica,* defined as Christianity; and if Joachim di Fiore were to return together with Albigenses, Hussites, and militant Anabaptists, they would understand this sort of criticism very well. They would understand it even though on their part they would apply it to the centuries of ecclesiasticism, and above all, would derive it from the very Christianity that brought about the Albigensian, Hussite, and Anabaptist interruptions of the ecclesiastic centuries. All Joachimism was an active struggle against the social principles of a Christianity which from St. Paul on would ally itself with the class society in a thousand compromises, a Christianity whose earthly salvation practice is itself a single catalog of sins, down—or up —to the last link: the understanding which Fascism was shown by the Vatican. Down to the mortal enmity which the "second kingdom" in Joachim's sense, the clerical one, feels for the third, the one now beginning to begin in the Soviet Union and not understood—or perhaps understood only too well, and slandered —by the forces of darkness. The so-called natural law, or indeed the "sanctity," of private property is the social principle at the heart of this Christianity.

And the pyx which priests of this Christianity exhibit to the laboring and heavy laden indicates no new aeon but gilds the old, along with the cowardice and submissiveness required of its victims, but without the day of judgment and the triumph over Babylon, without the aim of a new heaven and a new earth. Resigning oneself to fear and servitude, being consoled with promises for the beyond—these are the social principles of Christianity which Marx despised and Joachim consigned to the pit; but they are not the principles of a long-abandoned original Christianity and of the social-revolutionary heretical history it spawned. What Joachim di Fiore expressed by his expectation of the kingdom is simply what the centuries had left intact of the eschatological preaching of Christ; what he had said of a future "spirit of truth" (John 16, 13); what seemed not concluded with the "outpouring of the Holy Spirit" at the first Pentecost (Acts 2, 1–4).

The Western Church saw this sort of thing as concluded, leaving open only the compromise with the class society; the Eastern Church left at least a continuance of this outpouring open. The Wester Church, after the Lateran Council of 1215, put all monasteries under the spiritual control of their diocesan bishops; the Eastern Church adopted the Western order of the sacraments, but left to monks, even to sects, a charismatic and often heretical sort of independence. To deprive adventism of any kind of sanction, the Western Church confined all enthusiasm to Apostles and to the old martyrs; the far less thoroughly organized Eastern Church, on the other hand, teaches a continuing presence of the Spirit outside the priestly Church, among monks as well as among laymen. The East knows no monopoly on administering the host, none of the hard and fast, jurisdictionally locked and bolted salvation business; Russian Orthodoxy under the Czars was too ignorant for this, anyway, having no scholasticism, much less the legal acuities and dogmatic formulations of scholasticism. What lived in Russian Christianity instead, impervious to the hindrance of the Holy Synod, was a constant, unwritten Joachimite essence; it lived in the ease of kindling a sense of brotherhood, in the adventism of the sects (one of which, the Chlysts, holds that there have been Russian Christs, seven in number), in the unconcluded revelation that is the basic motif of it all. It thus remained possible for some great oddities of a Christ-romantic nature to arise even on bolshevist soil. An indication, thoroughly Joachimite in spirit, came from that undeniable Bolshevik and equally undeniable chiliast, Alexander Blok, in his hymn-like poem "The Twelve" (they are twelve Red Army men) when a pale Christ walks ahead of the Revolution and leads it.

Western ecclesiastic concerns are as far from such spiritual presence as the Eastern Church is at least theologically open to it. In the West it was only the heretical sects that would allow revelation to well up anew and would accordingly celebrate astounding Pentecosts on the advice of the Holy Spirit. This advice included social principles of Christianity which—as shown by Thomas Münzer's example—were not craven and did not treat the proletariat as scum. This was a heretical Christianity, and finally a revolutionary-adventist utopianism; the social principles of Baal would have produced neither one. They flowered in Joachim's preaching, where a single antithesis exposed the masters' Church: "Altars are trimmed, and the poor suffer the bitter pangs of hunger." We have seen that this antithesis sounds as if it had come from the Bible, from Amos, from Isaiah, from Jesus as quoted by Münzer. Even the State constructions of pure reason that have been preparing for socialism from the sixteenth century on are fitted into the third aeon, despite their *ratio*. They do not occupy this ground any more, but basically, although silent about its finality, they still hold it: no such utopias are possible without unconditionality. The will to happiness speaks for itself, but the language of the plans, the period pictures of a "New Moral World," is a different language: it is chiliastic. No matter how social utopianism may be secularized and finally, at last, put on its feet, since Joachim it always implies a *societas amicorum,* something Christlike that has become society. Happiness, freedom, order, the whole *regnum hominis* reverberates in it, in utopian use.

What the young Engels said in 1842, only a few years before the Communist Manifesto, has a distinctly Joachimite ring to it: "The self-assurance of mankind, the new Grail about whose throne exultant nations gather . . . This is our vocation: to become the Templars of this Grail, to gird the sword about our loins on its behalf, and joyfully to risk our lives in this last holy war that will be followed by the millennium of freedom."

Utopian unconditionality comes from the Bible, and from the idea of the kingdom that remained the apse of each New Moral World.

THE NATIONALIZED GOD
AND THE RIGHT
TO COMMUNITY

Even if a thing has ceased entirely it does not vanish at once. A gap remains, keeping the form of the former fullness. The house that has been torn down and become a thing of the past will plainly occupy the place in which it stood. The same is true of the State—but there another power, standing in a quite dissimilar place, is glad to fill whatever gap the State may leave. This power is the Church, whose demise along with property and classes is not so manageable, at least, or so necessary as the State's.

A future world management of productive processes in accordance with needs will not undertake any kind of State business, but it is quite conceivable that something like centralized counseling will remain, something like an administration of what life is all about. Something to keep the emotions of men in order and, churchlike, to teach their minds how to keep living in readiness and with a direction. This is why, in the same society in which the processes of production and distribution will go on far out at the circumference, the essential human concerns will move to the center, to the end, into the teleological questions of "where to" and "what for."

Instead of the shabbiest of all worries, the worry about gain

142

that used to shroud as well as to preoccupy the final stage of most men's lives—instead of this, our true, worthwhile, proper worries will then stand out more clearly than ever, the questions of what is really wrong with life. A society that is no longer antagonistic will, of course, keep all mundane fates firmly in hand. Its members are not in economic-political situations, and they have no economic-political fate. But this is just what makes them more sensitive to the indignities involved in being human, from the jaws of death down to such ebb tides of life as boredom and surfeit. The heralds of nothingness are not mere shadings any more, as in the class society; they wear new features, largely inconceivable as yet, but the train of purposes they rupture has a new way of gnawing too. The Church had tied such things to the allegedly ineradicable earthly vale of tears, justifying the very aspects of it which men have merely brought upon themselves. To the metaphysical need that is so very complex, the Church would advance mythological answers in which the powers that be, our earthly masters, occurred once more and the State that is given on earth was reinforced by one in heaven.

And yet—no matter how transparent the ideology behind this has become—the really metaphysical question will outlast the mythological-transcendent answers handed out by the power churches. The question will not go away with those churches; in its own fashion it lives even in the adventures and obscurities of unadulterated immanence, in the objectively real obscurities, and precisely in those. If culture has a strategy against the seclusions of existence, it is not quite unthinkable to have a general staff for this campaign, and to have it long after the five-year-plans of socialist construction are completed, even after all possible insights have been gained into the *écrasez l'infâme* concerning the Church, its auto-da-fés, its stultifying effects, and the blessings which, never by accident, it would bestow on every type of "White Guard." Because this is not all there is to it, the natural law of the revolutionary sects has never damned the Church in the same total sense in which it damned the State power. The sects condemned the State because, *a limine,* there is too much of Nimrod, of Ahab, of Nero about the State; but

143

they condemned the Church because, having allied itself with the Neros, it has too little, if anything, of Christ—because it is no longer the community of Christ. And because of this metaphysical (not mythological) need, which can hardly be satisfied in a social manner, ecclesiasticism is not going to be quite as rootless as the State once the society of property and classes is abolished. Instead of "governing persons" we shall be "administering things," managing processes of production and exchange; but where is the place for the *organism* of persons, for the *apse* and, above all, for the *apse window of solidarity* that will cast a transcending light without transcendence?

The gates of hell will not overwhelm the Church; it has opened its own gates to hell too often. But it is one thing for the power Church to pass, the Church of superstitions, and it would be quite another thing if a power-free force of conscience should be on guard, should undertake to stand guard and to teach whither and why. In the future ship of state (said Bebel), the teacher, not the officer, will be Number One; and the same could be the case in a Church embarked on a voyage without superstitions. It could be thoroughly religious, but not in the sense of a *re-ligio* or reconnection with dominion and its mythologies, but as the forward reconnection of a whole dream with our deficient makeshifts.

Now to get back to our given Church: it lives almost entirely for modesty and moneyed piety. It zealously inveighs against the harm done to Joseph and the sheep, but it has made its arrangements with the upper classes and serves as their spiritual defender. It bristles at see-through blouses, but not at slums in which half-naked children starve, and not, above all, at the conditions that keep three quarters of mankind in misery. It condemns desperate girls who abort a foetus, but it consecrates war, which aborts millions. It has nationalized its God, nationalized him into ecclesiastic organization, and has inherited the Roman empire under the mask of the Crucified. It preserves misery and injustice, having first tolerated and then approved the class power that causes them; it prevents any seriousness about deliverance by postponing it to St. Never-Ever's Day or shifting it to the beyond. The Church had conquered as a means

144

of mollifying the *proles* of Antiquity, and as a feudal, subsequently capitalistic (and sometimes even frankly fascist) world power it has splendidly prepared the "coming of Christ's kingdom." Finally, the concatenation with the bourgeois State interest—a new Constantinian state of affairs—is uniting the Roman Catholic Church with the Protestant ones in anti-communism. After all, the anti-Ghibelline tension between Rome and the State was profoundly co-conspiratorial anyway; it concerned only the competitive shares in profit and dominion, not a negation of both on grounds of the Gospel.

In Spain—and mostly also in the France of the *ancien régime,* where the Church was the largest landowner and received tithes —the State had no trouble with the Church, and the rights of both were as inseparable as Castor and Pollux. Similarly, it became the patron of the fascist attempts at a so-called corporate state; Leo XIII's prescription for this was not the first, but it was the first whose aim was anti-socialistic. Under the given finance-capitalistic circumstances the clerical idea of a guide State has nothing in common with the medieval reality. It is modern class struggle ideology from above, the fantasy of a vertical "occupational link" between the worker and the owner of a shoe factory; this verticalism is supposed, by means of a plant community and an integral edifice of such communities, to overcome the horizontal chasm between capital and labor—and in that, of all things, the Church sees an element of the *corpus Christi* idea. Gone are the competitive anomalies that had Jesuits like Bellarmine and Mariana teach the right to resist a bad authority to the point of tyrannicide; what the Vatican advertizes to the capitalist States now is a cure of souls providing for obedient citizens. It will consecrate only a pronouncedly capitalistic authority, not the legal one of Spain when it was fighting the fascists, and of course not the bolshevist one. Here there are no possible transitions whatsoever, for all the "honorable past" of Papism (the strictest form of churchly organization).

Too much of this past, not to mention the present, seems scarcely worth honoring. It is indeed a culpable simplification and mere journalistic jargon to call the Church "a Roman branch of Wall Street"; but a structure of compromise is what it has been from the outset, and only against socialism are there rock-ribbed limits to its elasticity. A separation of ecclesiastic Christianity from capitalism is therefore hard to visualize, although the young clergy has never been quite like the old and is not so today, and although socialists need not much longer discuss religion in terms of the dishwater of the Enlightenment either. Still, the authoritarian administration of vine and branches has almost always run more along Caesar's line than along Christ's —and so will any clericalism, even one that shrinks from bureaucratizing, centralizing, dogmatizing itself. The Roman Church's own past provides an example whose instructiveness is not confined to Catholicism. Intellectual life in Italy died down after her Hispanization; the trial of Galileo made wavering segments of the Lutheran intelligentsia immune again, indifferent or embittered against Marianism as against standstill and chains. There is an encyclical issued by Gregory XVI in 1830, a prelude to the 1870 proclamation of infallibility, with reference to the "madness that everyone is entitled to freedom of conscience." *Ergo vestigia terrent. Aut Caesar aut Christus* applies in every respect, and Caesarian touches discredit. And yet—so far as we can see in a long-lasting dawn—*catholicity,* without any parallels to a materialized institutional Church and an absolutized shepherd's role, may well be implied in *solidarity.* The new ecumenism is part of a society that is no longer essentially antagonistic, part of a community that can grow without hindrance. And the *oikoumene,* to live not just for the day but beyond the day, needs an institution that does more than administer things, an institution that is very much in earnest about the amity that goes deep and the fraternity that is difficult. Socialism is the road to it, the new finally realizable inheritance of what was meant by emancipation within and peace without. The red faith has always been more than a private matter. There is a basic right to community, to humanism, that extends to politics and to purposes. This is what the demanding right was en route to: the eunomia of walking upright in community. Art is not alone in holding mankind's dignity in its hands.

146

MAN'S INCREASING ENTRY INTO RELIGIOUS MYSTERY

1. Introduction

CHIEF, MEDICINE MAN AND RELIGIOUS FOUNDER

It is not the individual child who paints, but something universally childlike in him. And it is not the common man who sings, but common needs or a common spring sing out of him. What lives here in individuals and uses them to express itself is a *group,* whether childlike or national. It does not take a "gifted I," so to speak, to produce children's paintings or folk songs; in fact, these forms of expression will subside or vanish altogether once puberty, in one case, and individual economic activity, in the other, dim the group light that would burn about the heads with such universal effectiveness.

The difference between the ways in which puberty and individual economic activity bring an "I" into being is certainly very great; and yet, in both the physiological and economic cases, something self-willed and self-segregated is drawing apart from the previously collective soul. This collective soul is no doubt at work in religious movements and formations also; but in those a kind of personality *sui generis* emerges long before the so-called advanced social differentiation. Frequently, if not indeed as a rule, movements of faith have been linked with impulses beneath or outside the "I": with spasms, with panic, with obsession; nevertheless, here the group puts forth a distinct individual, a leader. Primitives who have attained only rudiments of a division of labor, who have no nobility at all, whose chieftains scarcely outrank the rest of the tribe, do worship the *medicine man.* Among the primeval *gentes* the chief has authority, but no nimbus; he is *primus inter pares.* But the wizard, even in a society that is still wholly cooperative, is viewed as different in kind. The mysterious powers attributed to him, the uncommon and often very strenuous schooling he has undergone as a disciple of the spirit world—these make him look like a separate individual even before there is any social gradation. The separateness of the wizard, and then of the teacher of magic, is independent of all other social differentiation; hence the very early appearance of the magical individual, the man whose acknowledged "charisma" has relieved him of the need to wait for the place to which a personality in other occupations has access only in a developed class society, notably in the incipient and still ascending capitalistic one.

The result is another pecularity of importance: no religion has begun in total anonymity, without a more or less strongly emphasized founder. Folk songs can originate anonymously, and so can heroic epics, even without the Romanticist exaggerations of the occurrence; but religions are at least regulated and, if new, established by a named individual. Holy men are placed at the beginning of the faith; they are now not merely charismatic, like primitive wizards or later miracle men, but *productive.* This is true also of the older, primarily regulating types. They are founders in lesser degree, even without a new god. As profound an expert as Frazer can find no exception to the rule that all major religions have been founded by exceptional men (s. *The Golden Bough,* 1935, IV 2, pp, 159ff.). There are, of course, notable degrees of this charismatic quality, of the greater or

148

smaller, more blurred or more sharply profiled density with which legend has conveyed a *genius religiosus*. Cadmus, for example, seems lackluster, Orpheus nebulous, Numa Pompilius overly sacral; none of them shows much *gestalt*. They mark a beginning, and that beginning is attached to them, but they stand beside their visions, which are not entirely human. And the mythical originators of the Egyptian or Babylonian religions are incomparably more intangible than Moses or Jesus. As mere signs of a religious beginning they can almost dispense with a historical core, whereas Moses or Jesus have features, and what comes down from them through all legend is a real attitude that cannot have been invented. They themselves have entered into the faith that bears their names; a past substance of faith has been changed by their appearance as historical persons. That the more regulating originators of the Egyptian and Babylonian religions, as of the old Chinese and Indian ones, do not emerge half as strongly as Lao-tse or Buddha, let alone Moses or Jesus—this does not refute the rule that religion, unlike folk songs and original epics, has founders.

There are three reasons why some founders are more obscure, why they are even described in tradition as more obscure, and the same reasons indicate why the founding of religions did not become fully free until Moses and Jesus. First, the indistinct founders mostly lie *far back in time*. Legend names and shrouds them simultaneously. There are no written texts going back to Cadmus, Orpheus, or Numa Pompilius, not even any dating unquestionably from their times. Without such records the original teachers tended to turn into figures of itinerant tales shifting from place to place, blurring even local features that had initially been quite pronounced. Secondly, a founder remains indistinct if his mainly regulating and formulating activity kept him essentially within traditional custom, if he marked no breaking point in a wave of the past, no point of opposition to the cult as it had been—in short, no point of preaching a new god.

The Egyptians, to cite an example, distinguished two very solemn founders of their faith: Imhotep, a priest of the dead at the beginning of the Third Dynasty, and above all, the divine

149

scribe, Thoth. Both remained legendary, Thoth all but completely mythical; neither one stands out from the religious tradition they both signify. On the other hand, if the Pharaoh Amenophis IV—who preached the Sun God as the one and only deity—had succeeded with his solar monotheism, there would be a breaking point and Egypt would have a profiled religious founder, not just a mythical or enfeebled one. Of course, even the heretic Amenophis would hardly have acquired the clear profile of Moses or Jesus, and that for the third and last reason: that a *nature religion* as it existed in Egypt, in Babylon, and even in the Vedic books, will *eo ipso make the founder's figure less manifest*. For where the gods appear as natural beings, where nothing significantly human has registered in heaven, man as a teacher of salvation cannot clearly enter heaven either. Nature-mythical definitions will conceal him or even take his place—as Oannes, the prophet of the Babylonian gods, appears only as a fish-man from the sea, and Thoth, the legendary original teacher of Egypt, coincides with Thoth the moon god. And if Lao-tse and even Buddha, for all the clarity of his profile and the power of his appearance in his glad tidings, seem somewhat more mythical or more mythologized than Moses and Jesus, the reason is this same not wholly dispelled nature-religious background or, in Buddha's case, the great acosmism that takes the place of the cosmos.

There are founders everywhere, but they are not fully manifest unless they have pitted their new god against traditional custom and a manless nature religion. Above all, they are manifest where they and their believers zealously attach themselves to the new god. Moses and Jesus are the first to arise in this sense, the first men who were meant to be saviours themselves, not only mythical teachers, not mere signposts to salvation. Orpheus is named along with the gods, and so are the nature-mythical regulator-founders, including the cosmomorphic Confucius and Zoroaster, the Messiah of the astral light; but their names lag behind the gods, and their relation to them is external. The Dionysiac founder *foams* away before his nature god; the astral-mythical one *plunges* away before his, like a shooting star; and even Buddha, the great self-redemption, *finally sinks* away in the acosmos of Nirvana. *Moses, on the other hand, compels his God to go with him: he turns God into the exodus light of a people. And Jesus pervades transcendence as a human tribune and makes it the utopia of the kingdom.*

Yet whether distinct or not, whether penetrating nature and transcendence or not, it is always men who speak the words of salvation. And what the divinely hypostasized ones spoke was never anything but a *longed-for future.* In these illusionary hypostases, of course, that future itself could be grasped only in illusionary forms, and in some pleas to the gods—and even more to the divine kingdom: to come, at last—the illusion could be one which, instead of reconciling with the given situation and its ideology, would show this situation and ideology to be delusive and would not let men make their peace with it. But this protestation, this pleading, radically utopian, and humane protestation took prophets, not formulators of a custom, even if the prophets were merely putting a new kind of divine illusion in the place of the old. In the cases of Moses and Jesus this new illusion also contained unrealities, but not the downright mythical ones alone. Besides, now and then, it contained a very different sort of unreality, a possible representation of what might be—what ought to be, at least—which could be understood as pointing to utopian reality. There is thus a functional link between *the founders' increasing self-injection into the religious mystery* on the one side, and the real message, the incarnated abyss of the miracle, on the other side, the side of the glad tidings. And the increasing self-injection ultimately rests on that specific transcending which is the start of every religious act, and in which the productive act leaves all other exits or presemblances behind. The more mature the appearance of religions, the more will this specific transcending prove to be that of a most powerful hope, of the *totum of a hope that relates the whole world to a whole perfection.*

If the founder stands forth only slightly or disappears in the cosmos, and if the mode of perfection has an external and essentially astral-mythical structure, it may indeed—just as it

originated on despotic orders, as an ideology and actual con-
secration of dominion—find it peculiarly easy to combine even
its structure with social despotism and patriarchalism, in other
words, with thoroughgoing dependencies exacted from without
and from above. No ecclesiastic compromise is then required;
instead, as in Egypt and Babylon, the genuine establishment of
the faith itself will lead back to, and culminate in, an ideology
of dominion. However radical and total the utopia of perfection
may be as a religious one, here its own substance turns it into
no more than a supreme ideology. But where plebeian movements, protestations, and hopes, where prophetic, utterly non-
conforming, contrasting founders carried their decisive transcending into the future and into the *totum* of a community—
if there the ensuing religion was to be turned into a conformist
ideology, it could be done only by subsequent Church compromises (or exegetical wiles).

The preaching of Jesus, being eschatological in character, was
the least conciliatory toward the "existing aeon," which was
why it caused the greatest sensitivity to mere lip service and
ecclesiastic compromise. Presenting a contrast was vital to it,
far more than to other religions, since it began as a thoroughly
social movement among the laboring and heavy laden; at the
same time, it gave to those who labored and were heavy laden
an impulse, a sense of values, and a hope they could never have
found in the mere fact of their oppression—or have not found
there, at least, in four thousand years. But the source of the
impulse was the strongest *secessio plebis in montem sacrum;*
here, at long last, transcending *in toto* became "orthodox."

If the line "Where there is hope there is religion" applies at
all, Christianity with its vigorous starting point and its rich
heretical history seems like a final emergence of what religion
is—namely, *not a static and thus apologetic mythus, but a
human-eschatological and thus explosively posited messianism.*
Therein alone—detached from illusion, from divine hypostasis,
from any kind of masters' taboo—lives the *sole hereditary
substrate religion can signify:* to be a *total hope,* and an explosive
one.

152

Aut Caesar aut Christus: this battle cry evokes a kingdom other than that of dominion, and a kingdom unlike that of the oppressive enormities in which a mythical, especially an astral-mythical religion would put its apologetic assuagements, its not yet explosive hopes. It is precisely the force of an explosive perfection that has been increasing and rich, and has thus undeniably been the depth of the projected wishful deification that corresponds to the intensity of injecting the human factor. The fact that all religion has founders, means at the same time that in its conjuring, and sometimes even under the cover and under the prevailing ideologies of masters' and astral myths, religion has been one of the most seriously tempting-attempting invocations of encompassing perfection, a conglomerate of intoxicating or thoughtful elements, of anthropomorphic or cosmic ones, of Promethean revolt or hypostasized peace—and with the religions of protestation constituting at least the most human of all those projections and hypostases into enormity.

THE NUMINOUS
IN THE HUMAN ASPECT OF RELIGION

There is a pious sense of the uncanniness of many things. This feeling can make us blind, but it can also let us see around the corner, where there may be other, unwonted sorts of life. Even the non-pious, unless he is a dolt, will not posit his own being and his accustomed sights as the measure of what is and what is not. Religious feeling in particular stands squarely against swagger, and against that cozy liberalism that serves as its own edification and thinks even of the beyond as being rather sensible and sociable. The Bible counters by reflecting on the nothingness of man, and the Bible is not misanthropic. And the biblical God counters that his ways are not our ways, that his thoughts are not our thoughts, and he is not represented as a demon. This distance, this horror of the *threshold,* marks every religious relationship, or it is not religious. From this standpoint —and note well, only in this one respect—Rudolf Otto is right

153

to define the mark of the religious object as "total Otherness," and the aura of sanctity as a "numinous shudder." From this standpoint—and *only* as this antidote—the early Karl Barth is right to defend the outrageously illiberal proposition that "the divine speaks a constant 'No' into the world." And to teach that "the reality of religion is man's horror of himself," and that "we humans may be capable of conceiving infinity, but measured by our finiteness, and thus in itself, it is nothing but an infinite finiteness" (*Der Römerbrief,* 1940).

What is here believed as God is indeed an utterly uncompromising despotism far removed from human participation (which is derided as "federation theology"), but what is purchased at this grotesque price is protection of the *humanum,* the *cur Deus homo,* from the triviality to which an all too companionable liberalism has reduced it. The Church, says Barth, has kept betraying God to man—in other words, to the designs and thought movements of the unperforated, untranscended creature; and against this Barth calls upon a *Deus absconditus* who does not coincide with the despotic God after all. Religion, and the Christian one in particular, shakes up the subject, rather, and gives subjectivity a share in the object of the cult, even though Barth's extreme-heteronomous creed does look as if he meant to remove the son of man as a mediator and thus to rid Christianity of Christianity itself.

Yet despite this a-humane grotesquerie which would not have hindered and might indeed have confirmed even a Moloch priest in his vocation—despite this abuse of Tertullian's originally by no means obscurantist or irrationalistic version of the *credo quia absurdum*—Barth's theology contains an important warning. What it defends fanatically is awe, a sphere so easily lost in the very subjectivity of religion, down to the insipid psychologism or the ersatz moralizing of the cultural philistine. The illiberal element of taboo theology can and must—after powerful detoxication, with power over its *humanum*—be brought around to a religious or meta-religious humanism, not in order to make the latter irrational, but, on the contrary, to keep it from growing obtuse. The idea of *Deus absconditus* alone helps to maintain the *problem* of the legitimate mystery called *homo absconditus:* what the community in its ultimately proper sphere, in an unpsychologized, not secularized sphere, contains of the kingdom. It is true that the so-called *mysterium tremendum* may serve authoritarian reaction as an ideology suitable for its infamous *irratio;* but it is equally certain that the nontransferability of categories to which we are accustomed in immanence constitutes one of the first criteria of the religious stratum. How little reactionary *irratio* need be connected with this criterion shows in the fact that it is by no means confined to obscurantism, nor to a despotic theism—quite the contrary. Hence Spinoza, that dependably rational pantheist: "Moreover —to say a word on the intellect and will usually attributed to God—if intellect and will pertain to God's eternal essence, these traits must certainly be understood in a sense altogether different from that in which men generally understand them; for the intellect and will that might constitute God's essence would have to be worlds away from our intellect and will [*a nostro intellectu et voluntate toto coelo differe deberent*] and could be like ours in name only, as the Dog, the celestial constellation, and the dog, the barking animal, are alike" (*Ethics* I, Proposition XVII, Note). The crux remains that *"total Otherness" applies to the eventual human projections of religion also.* It takes total Otherness to give the appropriate measure of depth to everything that has been longed for in deifying man. It is total Otherness that lends to the *hubris* of Prometheus—that really heaven-storming quality whereby the Promethean is distinguished from the flatness of mere individuality, and from the scanty humanization of taboos.

The abyss of total Otherness invades the *hubris* of Thomas Münzer and makes it mysticism, an unruly, kingdom-inheriting mysticism: "As it must occur to us all in the advent of faith, that we fleshly humans shall become gods by the incarnation of Christ, and shall be God's disciples with him, taught and deified by him." So, what this numinous element in the *regnum humanum* itself contains in place of the emasculating capitulation to a flatly heteronomous majesty and its Above—deemed an Above because man does not occur in it—is the opposite: that wholly other Otherness which will not let us think greatly, overwhelmingly enough of what is human. Therefore, when so powerful a surprise invades the religiously designated contents that hold it open, it will not let them approach as oppressive but, conversely, as wonderful. The non-transferability of immanently accustomed categories to the religious sphere—this is the leap that becomes recognizable as the highest human utopia in the words of St. Paul: "Eye hath not seen, nor ear heard, neither have entered into the heart of man, the things which God hath prepared for them that love him" (I Cor. 2, 9). Wonder, as the Wholly Other regarding the objective world of religion, is here plainly man's *very own joyous mystery,* exulting in the religious content of man's hope, that is, in the hope content that is still due to explode itself into the Wholly Other. And between the world of religious subjects and the taboo of the previous religious objective aspect, Christianity has emphasized the link that is here called kingdom, the kingdom of God. But this makes the subjective side only more aware of something *Wholly Other* in its object, namely, of the mystery of spatiality surrounding the supreme object: the religious subject side receives this too, now, as the mystery of the kingdom. God becomes the kingdom of God, and the kingdom of God ceases to contain a God.

In other words, this religious heteronomy and its materialized hypostasis dissolve completely in the theology of the community—but of a community that *has passed beyond the threshold of the creature as it used to be, anthropologically and sociologically.* This is why the very religion that proclaimed the kingdom of God in the midst of mankind (cf. Luke 17, 21) has most strictly maintained total Otherness against the old Adam and the old world that has come to be: subjectively as rebirth, objectively as a new heaven and a new earth, as a transfiguration of nature.

It is this boundary content of wonder, of total detachment, which makes even the best of human societies a means to an ultimate end, to the ultimate end of total detachment which

156

has been religiously conceived in the kingdom. And whose unattainability also becomes perceptible in the best of societies —as the uneliminated frailty of the creature, as the uneliminated irrelation of the natural environment—and accordingly contradicts any partial optimism on the part of several social utopias that have dropped out of the *utopian totality.* The wishful image in all religions, and most especially in those involving a messianic homecoming, is certainly a livable existence, but one not limited to such trains of purposes as are already surveyable and, so to speak, locally patriotic.

Religion, *with constant final reference to the last leap and the utopian totum,* is not exhausted with all its ethicizations and smoother rationalizations. Morality and surveyability do not exhaust it even in the case of Confucius, its strongest ethicizer. The wish content of religion remains livability in the *mystery* of existence, a mystery conveyed in man and inclined to man's deepest wish, to the point where wishing comes to rest. *And the farther the subject, with its religious founders, invades and overwhelms the objective mystery of a God conceived as the supreme Without or the supreme Above, the more powerfully will man be charged, in an earthly heaven or on a heavenly earth, with the awe of depth and infinity.* The increasing humanization of religion is not matched by a relaxation of its shudders; on the contrary, the *humanum* gains the added mystery of something divine, something deifiable, and it gains this as the future establishment of the kingdom, the right kingdom. Even the majesty of a *Without* and *Above* (as designated mainly in Egypt and Babylon) has been and is being used in these projections—despite the heartless, salvationless masters' ideology of its static astral-mythical vault—to educate for the depth of a universe that contains man. In fact, an awe that includes the *humanum* and culminates in it needs the *numinosum* that was once so loftily experienced in star worship, in the grandeurs of nature; it needs the numinous as a corrective, to preserve its own religious objectivity—in other words, precisely lest man be not conceived grandly and mysteriously enough. Thus this estrangement goes with religion everywhere, even with one viewed

157

in utopian terms and quite without obscurantism. Its *obscurum* —"The Lord said that he would dwell in the thick darkness" (I Kings 8, 12)—is not one of superstitions that have devoted too little knowledge to fate; it is the darkness of conscientious knowledge, of seeing the uncanny always in the depths around us and having no hope for its dissolution, its sublimation, except in wonders. The *Phoebus post nubila* that furnished the messianic faith in particular with a fighting, a truly red-flaring illumination does not now exist as a consonance and is no flatly cloud-dispelling consonance at all; it has only made the clouds less homeless. Such conscientious knowledge as the indicated hereditary substrate of religion—in other words, as the remembrance of being *hope in totality*—simultaneously grasps the world's being in enormous suspension, in suspension toward an enormity of which hope believes that it will be a good one, and active hope works to that end. To the end that religion will mark the sphere in which man's fear—of the uncanny in himself and in worldly being—can echo from the depths, nearby or distant, as awe.

On this premiss, piety has always penetrated its *Above*. Man wants to be with the powers he believes in, however subject to them he may feel. The more so if he feels related to them, made of kindred stuff as in the Greek faith or, more mysteriously, in the same image as in the Judaeo-Christian one. Increasingly the religious founders inject themselves into their total *Otherness,* forging it into the mystery of a human content or of one conveyed by men. Also at work is the force, the call of this free, this devout *importuning:* "I will not let thee go, except thou bless me" (Gen. 32, 26). How often has this importuning made man see that he is better than his gods—how powerful a source has it been, not of humdrum complacency, not of an emancipated philistine substituting for Prometheus, but of the very founding drive of a new *mystery!* And the crux: even in the broadest astral-mythical visions, in estrangements that had all but fully turned into apologetic alienations and into ideologies of a despotically static Above—even in those an unknown *humanum* has spoken at the utopian end and can thus be pointed out, has foretold itself and the unknown within and before it.

Numen, *numinosum,* mystery, even a No to the existing world: none of these is ever anything but the *secret human element* itself. The secret one, to be sure—that which still hides from itself and is distinguished by the leap of total Otherness from the known *humanum* and its immanently accustomed environment. In the religious *ineffabile* the never manifested contents of the existential abyss receive a sign that they are not buried, not forgotten. They receive, most decidedly in the Bible, a hope that they are not foreclosed: that in utopia they have an adequate time and space of their own, conceived as the kingdom. There is no complete coincidence in intent, extent, and content between the religious idea of the kingdom and any idea of social utopianism, no more than the religious self coincides with the extant human creature, and no more than the shelter of religion coincides with the empirical cocoon which a complacent positivism spins around itself. In the chiliasts, the idea of the kingdom has posited, acknowledged, and required the paths of utopianism as preparing for the final leap; in the Gospels the idea appears, not as a heavenly beyond, but as a new heaven and a new earth. But what it contains in its anticipations is something absolute in which antitheses other than the social ones shall cease, an *absolutum* that will change the understanding of all previous contexts.

What Engels, in an early critique of Carlyle, says of the kingdom as an internal clerical construction, remains true, of course: "Once again it was the Christians, by setting up a peculiar 'history of the kingdom of God,' who denied all inner essentiality to real history, claiming this essentiality solely for their transcendental history that is abstract and fictional to boot. It is their perfection of the human species in their Christ that brings history to an imaginary goal and so interrupts it in mid-course." But this indictment is also true from a religious standpoint, so true that a Joachim di Fiore would have been the first to agree with it, and more passionately than anyone else. Yet this is why, exactly why social history, social utopianism, and even an accomplished classless society are set apart, by that leap which

159

the explosive intentionality of rebirth and transfiguration posits, from the kingdom as the *summum bonum* of religious utopianism.

The kingdom remains the central religious concept—in the astral faiths as crystal, and in the Bible, where the intention erupts totally, as glory. In all these unconditionalities lies a boundless desire whose *hubris* expands even on the Promethean one, and whose "I will not let thee go, except thou bless me," does not perish in the humility of the concept of grace. For while grace is to be far removed from the domain of the human will, while it is not to be earned by works, the concept of it still derives from hope for the leap, and for the dignity of being able to stay ready for the utmost perfection. Hence that non-passiveness we cannot fail to hear even in the thickest divine forms of religion; hence the super-additum of tremendous immoderation in each pious shudder, even when it seems wafted down from above. Hence the eventual transformation of the alien astral-mythical mystery, the chance to crack it into the mystery of a *citoyen* of the kingdom and of his paradoxical relation to what has come to be. Hence, finally and above all, the greatest paradox in the religious sphere that is so rich in paradoxes: *the elimination of the deity itself,* so that religious mindfulness and total hope may have an open space ahead, rather than a ghost throne of hypostasis. Which means no less than this very paradox: the religious intention of the kingdom as such *involves atheism, one that has at least been understood.*

For atheism does not dispel superstition only to replace it with as paltry a negative as superstition was a windy positive. What atheism does, rather, is to remove from the world's beginning and process what had been conceived as God, that is, as an *ens perfectissimum,* and to redefine it as not a fact but the one thing it can be: the supreme utopian problem, the problem of the end. The place held in the religions by the concept of God, the place filled with seeming reality by the thing hypostasized as God, this place itself has not vanished with the disappearance of what seemed to fill it. For it always remains the place of projection at the focal point of radical utopian intentionality; and the metaphysical correlative of this projection remains what is hidden, what is still undefined and undefinitive, what is really possible in a mystery sense. The place marked by the former God is thus not nothing; it would be nothing only if atheism were nihilism, and not just one of theoretical hopelessness but a nihilism universally, materially destructive of any possible substantial goal and perfection. Materialism, the world's explanation by itself, has only as mechanical materialism omitted the marginal space of the former God hypostasis as well; but it has also omitted life, consciousness, the process, the recoil of quantity into quality, the novum, and all dialectics. And even mechanical materialism, at least in the form advanced by Feuerbach, must leave in anthropology a special storage space for the religious projections, as their "origin and object."

In Feuerbach's case, as remains to be shown, it was a flat, fixed anthropology, not just an abstract and general one without history or society, but one derived from a scarcely expanded occurrence of man; even so, Feuerbach's anthropological critique of religion treats religious contents by no means as if they were nothing, as in nihilism. And the true materialism, the dialectical one, while voiding the transcendence and reality of any divine hypostasis, does so without stripping the final qualitative contents of the process, the real utopia of a realm of freedom, of that which had been meant by an *ens perfectissimum*. Something attainable, something to be expected from the process, is not at all denied in dialectical materialism; a place for it is maintained, rather, and kept open as nowhere else. What this amounts to is that even in secularized form, and much more in utopian totality, the kingdom *remains a messianic frontal space without any theism;* indeed, as increasingly demonstrated by every "anthropologization of heaven" from Prometheus down to the belief in a Messiah, it is only without theism that the kingdom remains at all.

Where there is a great master of the world there is no room for freedom, not even for the freedom of God's children. Nor is there any room for the figure of the kingdom, for the mystical democracy of chiliastic hope. The utopia of the kingdom wipes out the fiction of a divine creator and the hypostasis of a God in heaven, but precisely does not wipe out the final space in which *ens perfectissimum* has the abyss of its yet unthwarted latency. The existence of God—indeed God as such, as a distinct being —is superstition; faith is solely the belief in a messianic kingdom of God, without God. Therefore, far from being an enemy of religious utopianism, atheism is its premiss: *without atheism there is no room for messianism.*

Religion is superstition where it is not what its historic phenomenal growth in line with its valid intentional substance enabled it to mean: the most absolute utopia, the utopia of the absolute. Not to exist, not to have become—this is the real basic definition of *ens perfectissimum,* and if it had become, it would not be one different from its kingdom, not one hypostasized as God. In the religions that posit it (Taoism and especially Buddhism do not) the God hypostasis in the sense of a world creator or world ruler is simply unscientific, indeed anti-scientific, and to a sense of faith that deems itself too good or too profound to offer a retarded sense of science, if not nonsense, the hypostasis is at most the mythologized vice-reign of a hope that is an All Hallows of mankind—without the Lord.

The history of men's consciousness of God is thus by no means the history of God's consciousness of himself; but it is the history of the currently highest possible frontal content of existential openness on all sides—forward, upward, and inward. All higher religions feed on the frontal intensity of radical longing, and on the search for anticipations of an *ens perfectissimum* that constitutes the substantial goal of this longing. In art the anticipation posits sheer presemblance, but in religion, where the element of detached enjoyment is wholly lacking, it ultimately posits our own totally concerned pre-existentiality. And in line with the gravity of the *transcendere* is an existential transformation: to the endeavor, through the founder and through his God, to be reborn as a new man. Nature itself is transformed in the Christian Apocalypse; unlike every ideal landscape of aesthetic presemblance, it must perish to be transfigured. So it is *metamorphosis* which in the atheism of religion,

above religion, makes out the final criterion of the religious
sphere, a criterion which also flows from the pious invasion of
the Above, from the will to become like that which is meant by
God. Judaism and Christianity, as the highest religions, show the
full intentional gravity of this transformation, but the only thing
that can do justice to it is a concept of knowledge augmented
by religious conscience. And the end of religion in this knowledge, in this comprehended total hope, is not simply no religion,
but—carrying Marxism further—the inheriting of religion, a
meta-religious conscientious knowledge of the last problem of
whither and why: *ens perfectissimum.*

For a will aimed upward at this problem lives on in the very
will that aims forward. In running after a founder, the people
were ultimately running after a will to be as in heaven. This
sursum corda applies especially when the total Otherness of
heaven is not an existing one at all, when it is posited as utopian,
as a new heaven and a new earth; it is then that *sursum corda*
carries the specifically religious hereditary substrate, to wit, the
messianic one. Religious founders would go in for messianism
long before the Jews took it literally and made it the basic reduction of religiousness, the pursuit of the kingdom pure and
simple. *Messianism is the salt of the earth—and that of heaven,
lest not only the earth lose its savor but the intended heaven, too.*
What the *numinosum* promised, messianism aims to keep; its
humanum and the world that fits it are not merely what is
unaccustomed, what is thoroughly unbanal, but the far shore at
dawn. And it was a long road till the founders, with human
latency, betook themselves into their God's name. Till the history of divine concepts from fetish to star, to exodus light, to
the spirit of the kingdom, was run through and ran out; till faith
has—or will—come closer, from projections of divine obscurity
and a throne in heaven to the incognito and the "Tarry awhile"
of Goethe's Faust.

All religion has been a thing of desire, more intermingled with
superstitions and illusions than anything else, but it has not been
a thing of splintered or limited desire. It has been total, and its
illusions have not been void but experimental, mindful of a per-

163

fection that does not exist. Every religion, even the astral-mythical ones, found the invisible easier to believe in than the visible, and the divine substance of each would no more coincide with the tangible sort of reality than the religious break-throughs coincided with what man had been thus far, and with his world, whose wretchedness the prophets were deploring.

What is conceived and longed for as God is so superior to existing realities that despite all hypostases of the realities it turns increasingly into a utopian ideal whose non-being does not refute it. Not-yet-being, the mode of reality of concrete ideals, is of course never a not-yet-being of God; the world is not a machine for manufacturing such a supreme person, such a "gaseous vertebrate" (as Haeckel rightly called it). Rilke, Berg-son—even the early Gorki—have variously failed to achieve distinction by such God-making, and Lenin rightly described efforts of the sort as "necrophilia." An atheist who knows what the word means will not try a poor imitation of the founders and go back to God-making. *Once the God hypostasis has gone once for all, he will proceed to the unconditional and total content of hope* that has served for so many and varied experiments under the name of God—experiments full of superstition and illusion, of ignorance and, as we all know, of uncomprehended social and natural forces being hypostatized into man's fate in the beyond. But then there have been men in equally desperate need who would protest this fate, would seek in magical-mythical ways to turn it or to conjure it for the better.

So religious imagination cannot be dismissed *in toto* even after a successful disenchantment of the world image; it can be overcome only by a specific philosophical concept that will do justice to the ultimate intended substance of the imagination. For what was alive and is rising in the midst of all is this sighing, this conjuring, this preaching at the red dawn; and even amid the mythical nonsense that is so easy to note there lived and rises the unfinished question that has been burning only in religions, the question of the sense we cannot make out, of the meaning of life. It is the true realism that will be stirred by this question, one so far removed from mythical nonsense as to be responsible, rather, for every bit of sense. Needed, therefore—because of the particularly total pull of desire from this sphere—is a new *anthropology of religion*. And overdue—because of the particularly totally intended essence of perfection in this sphere—is a new *eschatology of religion*. Both without religion, but both with the corrected, unfinished problem of mankind's growing such enormous wings, such changing and at times incompatible wings, including some that adjoin obvious fool's paradises and yet keep tempting, attempting the uncommon sense—according to the human-social horizon. This is why Cadmus, Orpheus, and the Olympian gods of Homer, why Egypt's sun of the dead and Babylon's astral mythology, why the Chinese *tao*, Moses or the Exodus, and the clearly distinct god-men, Zoroaster, Buddha, and Jesus, mark *the founders' increasing injection into the experimental glad tidings of an ens perfectissimum*, with the social mission of the injection and the human content of its *perfectum* always corresponding to each other. In the astral myth the founder fades out; his god is complete, starlit externality. In Christianity the founder becomes the glad tidings itself, and eventually his God fades out in a single human All Hallows. . . .

2. *Founders, Glad Tidings, and* Cur Deus Homo

THE FOUNDER AS PART OF THE GLAD TIDINGS: MOSES AND HIS EXODUS GOD

Myths cannot hide a particularly forceful, zealous speaker. His traditional picture shows him in the flesh; the sound of a real voice rings through the fables. So it is with *Moses,* the earliest leader of a people out of servitude. In point of time Moses is the first founder with a profile, and he has remained the most visible one as a man, a human being. Attempts to turn him into a legend like Abraham, Isaac, and Jacob—who do represent mere Israelite tribal names and perhaps even predated Canaanite gods

—have been futile. After all, it was never quite possible to dissolve even the Joseph story into legend, the prologue to Moses' work, as by tying Joseph to an itinerant fable of the youngest brother envied by the older ones, or by making him out to be a variant of Tammuz, the Babylonian god of light, who goes down in the West Country. It now appears that the Joseph story and the person of that royal chancellor have a good deal of historical probability. For Joseph knows more about Egypt than can be known to a legendary figure that has been invented or merely superimposed on a West Country. His story, centuries before the Exodus, shows a strikingly Egyptian local color: the rites of investiture (Gen. 41, 42) are described not only in detail but with complete accuracy, and equally accurate are the statements on the mortmain of the Egyptian Church (Gen. 47, 22 and 26). So, however fragmentary and questionable the Egyptian testimony thus far known on its events, not even the Joseph story which lies so far back provides a precedent for dissolving Moses and the Exodus into a fable. There were Egyptian chancellors of Semitic stock, and the clay tablets of Tel El Amarna, found as late as 1887, prove that Canaanite kings sought the Pharaoh's help against invading "Ibri."

Moses, of course, was even more lavishly festooned than Joseph with that wreath of legends which mythological research, the Babylonian one in particular, has itself been weaving. And that although there has not been a nation yet which in the absence of some historical reason would, so to speak, volunteer a report on its days of slavery and humiliation—although no nation yet has simply concocted details of its liberation, its way out of slavery, or confused its own struggle with that between spring and winter. But mythological researchers, notably the pan-Babylonian brand, have been imputing these practices to the old Israelite history, just as they imputed even more fanciful forms of them to the story of Jesus. The reed box in which Moses was saved from the Pharaoh's wrath predisposed him to impress these scholars as analogous to a whole mythical group of young sun or spring gods. Like him, the little Adonis or Horus or Jesus was pursued by the winter giant; like him, each

166

of the various young sun gods was sheltered in some narrow hideout, in a trunk or in a cave. Moses' work, the Exodus, was similarly vaporized into a solar myth of Babylonian origin: "The deliverance from Egypt is deliverance from the dragon of winter in the sense of the world year myth" (Jeremias, *Babylonisches im Neuen Testament,* 1905). In pan-Babylonian ears, even the Egyptian disaster in the Red Sea evoked memories: of Marduk's battle with the dragon, the nether-world demon Tiamat. Different from this pan-Babylon, incomparably more serious and involving major philological achievements, were the attempts of radical Bible critics to delete Moses from history—not always as a living person, but as the preacher of a new God, the originator of a faith. According to a so-called Kenite hypothesis (cf. Budde, *Die Religion des Volkes Israel bis zur Verbannung,* 1900) Moses borrowed Yahweh from the Kenites, the tribe he married into after his flight. They had their pastures on Mount Sinai (perhaps on the volcano that is now extinct), and Yahweh (probably the Wafter or Blower) had been worshiped by them as a volcano god from time immemorial. With Yahweh himself thus a plagiarism, it is no wonder that the Ten Commandments are not supposed to belong to Moses and the children of Israel either. According to Wellhausen, a radically barbed, anti-semitic epigone of Bible criticism, the Decalogue comes from the Canaanites; the Jewish priests adopted it in Canaan, along with the ritual laws; the Commandments were credited to Moses only much later, after Cyrus, and their entire substance, not just the phrasing, was interpolated (cf. Wellhausen, *Israelitische und jüdische Geschichte,* 1901). What an all too radically dissolving Bible criticism finally leaves of Moses and ancient Israel is nothing but a wild batch of religions without any center, of sacred stones and trees, of wholly diverse local deities, of ancestor worship, human sacrifice, Canaanite customs, and late Babylonian myths. The Jewish faiths, we hear, were founded by the prophets, and Moses, Yahweh, the Exodus, the Decalogue and its locale—all these are no more historical than Cain and Abel. But then a strange thing happens: it is precisely where the Bible critics void the late adjustments and predatings of the priestly

167

code, where they have uncovered really alien elements in Mo-saicism, that the originality of Moses becomes clearer than it had been before the critical triumphs and extravaganzas.

As the theory of evolution does not blur man's difference from the animal but makes it rather more notable than before, so does the Bible appear even more original and unique since its extra-biblical sources and elements have become fairly well known. It is possible and even probable that Moses took the Sinai god from the Kenites, but that god did not remain what he had been. There is no doubt that the Decalogue, not to mention the ritual code, contains late insertions from Canaan, but the concise basic stock has no parallel in Canaan or anywhere else in the world. What happened with Moses was a leap in religious consciousness, and the ground for it was laid by an event that is the greatest antithesis to the earlier religions, those of mundane piety or astral-mythical fate: by *rebellion,* by the Exodus from Egypt. It was thus, not as Nimrod or as a gigantically prominent medicine man, that Moses became the first *heros eponymos,* the first *name-giving originator of a religion, and of a self-antithesiz-ing one*. Other, later antithetical religions such as Zoroaster's warlike and Buddha's acosmic one would be utterly incompre-hensible for Europeans except for the archetype of the Exodus —just as the founding figure of Moses constitutes the prototype for all those who stand not beside their doctrines but messiani-cally within the doctrine itself.

An enslaved people—this is here the need that makes men pray. And a founder appears who starts out by killing an over-seer. *Suffering* and *revolt* mark this beginning, and from the first they turn faith into a way out. Due to Moses, the Sinai god adopted from the Kenites did not remain the local god of a volcano; he became the *spirit of the Exodus.* The volcano god is set in motion, and except for certain choleric-eruptive traits his character is changed. The local god is detached from his soil; his theurge Moses makes him a cloud and a pillar of fire travel-ing away from Sinai, accompanying what had been a people of strangers, moving on to the untrodden, to untrodden splendor. And just as the Exodus God is Mosaic, not Kenite, the *basic stock of the Decalogues* preserves a creation of Moses, not a moral code of the Canaanites or—still more far-fetched—of Hammurabi, the old Babylonian potentate whose legal code of around 2100 B.C. has about as much in common with the Ten Commandments as the Corpus Iuris has with the ethics of Kant. No doubt the Decalogue contains interpolations; the commandment not to covet your neighbor's house is senseless among nomads, as is the commandment to rest on the Sabbath. Both presuppose the settled life and ordered work days of a Canaanite tiller of the soil; in fact, the hallowing of the seventh day occurred especially late, during the Babylonian exile, and has Chaldaean roots. Not found in Canaan, however, was the unbroken communal ethics which Moses put into words: for this came from primitive communist conditions, which among nomads were not yet quite extinct but were extinct in the agrarian culture of the Canaanites, who had long reached the class-establishing stage. A line such as "Thou shalt love thy neighbor as thyself" (Lev. 19, 18), this condensation of the Ten Commandments into one, has no more than a still unconscious inception even in the primitive commune; to have made it conscious and stated it in all but glaring terms was Moses' work. In Israel, too, it was remembered as such—not only in the midst of Canaan, but in opposition to the very Canaan-type economy which the Israelite conquerors had now taken over. The kulak morality and Baal's religion they found there was invaded by a different essence, by one that would never quite capitulate, despite all receptions. The Nazarites from Samuel to John the Baptist, in their nomad habit made of hair; their close allies, the prophets, with their view of the desert years as "Israel's bridal time," as the time "when Israel was a child" (Hosea 11, 1)— these drew their memories as well as their strength from the founding by Moses, from the Decalogue and from the Exodus God. Without Moses the prophets would have had no ground to stand on; however lofty and universalistic prophetic ethics becomes, it still shows the lasting impulse of the Exodus leader and his idea of the holy people. The injection of Moses changed the substance of the salvation that had made up the external, wholly completed goal of the pagan religions, the astral-mythical ones in particular. *Now, instead of the finished goal, a promised one appears, one yet to be acquired, and instead of the visible nature god there appears an invisible one of justice, of a kingdom of justice.*

This brings up another question, of course: if not propheticism, has the Book of Job (after so little good in Canaan, after so much unfulfilled promise) not dealt the Mosaic faith another kind of blow, namely, its own denial? A rejection of its glad tidings, an insurrection—and now not just against Pharaoh, or Baal, or Belial, but against the Yahweh of pseudo-justice himself? This is indeed the substance of Job's revolt; neither the lame accuracies and traditional harmonies of his friends nor the thunderstorm in which Yahweh manifests his disparate majesty can save the faith in the justice of the once so grandly proclaimed and proclaiming God. Against a subjects' intelligence that will no longer be limited, a theocracy that has become inhumane can no longer prevail. And yet, even the Book of Job that was so late in coming, that came to be even geographically on the outer limits of Judaea, even this book remains genuine Old Testament, a Moses in the anti-Moses.

Long before Job, the priestly editing of the Bible text failed equally to suppress its subversive features or to consign them to oblivion—features such as the grumbling of the children of Israel, the measuring of Yahweh's deeds by his promise, by that highest definition which Isaiah gave him in the end: that he was the Holy One in Israel. The grumbling was a comparison of God with his ideal, and suggestions of it are found in Moses himself, in the man of the Water of Contradiction (Num. 20, 13), of the doubt that Yahweh would deliver his people (Ex. 5, 23), of the plea that Yahweh himself, not just an imperfect angel, lead the way into the Promised Land (Ex. 33, 15). Instead of the angel, Moses insists on Yahweh, and he does so with *kiddush hashem,* the hallowing of the name; he insists upon him who has become "countenance." "Where not thy [face] goeth, lead us not up hence." But Yahweh's countenance is far above his justice, which Job denies in terms that leave God looking scarcely better than the old demon of Sinai. Significantly, "Prince of the Countenance" is a later title of the Messiah, the intended guide to the last Yahweh, to the definitive substance of the belief in Yahweh.

No religion has gone through so many strata of sublimation and indeed utopianization of its God as that of Moses, but all of them are suggested by the concept of his *Exodus God* himself. The God of Moses is the promise of Canaan, or he is not God. Even the revolt of Job, the Hebrew Prometheus, goes back to this promise and has therefore a very different acuity, a very different substantiation from quarrels with the deity in other faiths. In Job the exodus grows radical: Yahweh is not only measured by the ideal of his justice, of the realm of justice, but there is an *exodus from Yahweh himself,* to the unknown Canaan that was his broken promise. "I know that my avenger lives, and at the last will rise above my dust. The witness of my guiltlessness will be with me, and I shall see him who frees me from my guilt; with my own eyes I see it, not another" (Job 19, 25–27, according to Bertholet's translation). The messianic faith of this text, which tradition probably corrupted not without cause, is a departure from Yahweh as well—for the sake of his utopia. But had Moses not preached God in Canaan, and Canaan in God, Job would have had neither a language for his indictment nor a light for his rebellious hope. The impulse of Moses holds the whole Old Testament together, including the messianism that appears so late in it, or rather is uttered so late. This messianism in particular is latent in a glad tidings whose herald fills it with himself and his people, with the exodus spirit and with the promise of the land, the land of promise.

MOSES; OR UTOPIANISM IN RELIGION, AND RELIGIOUSNESS IN UTOPIANISM

Scripture has accumulated much that oppresses, much that tends to cower. But this is just what has been added, what has been imposed on a dissatisfied, lastingly creative faith. The children of Israel themselves cast off a yoke, and they followed the man who said to Pharaoh, "Let my people go." The *law,* which about 450 B.C., after the return from Persian exile, served the first rabbis to segregate a people and to hold it together—this law is not part of the impulse of Moses. Even less a part of it is the *Lord God* throning on high, the one whose cult the Israelites had adopted in Canaan and who is Baal. He is the same Baal whose religion must be preserved for the people, according to the prescription of any master class, along with the triviality and bombastic traditionality in which Job's friends, those prototypes of every opium clergy, dispense their kind of trust in God. The Exodus God is of another sort; in the prophets he proved his hostility to masters and opiates. Above all, his sort is not the static one of all past pagan gods. For at the very start the Yahweh of Moses gives a definition of himself that takes our breath away time and again, a definition that makes all static thinking senseless: "God said unto Moses, I Shall Be Who I Shall Be" (Ex. 3, 14). Here, as distinct from the interpolation of legalistic and Baal-type material, it does not matter how late such a highly messianic definition was inserted into the original text. For however complicated it appears in both language and thought, its meaning does not spring from any priestly code but from the original exodus spirit itself. *Eh'ye asher eh'ye,* I shall be who I shall be—despite its ambiguity, despite its being interpolated, this name reveals Moses' intention and does not conceal it. Yahweh's self-description is ambiguous because the verb *haya,* on which *eh'ye* is based, can mean "being" as well as "becoming." And it is interpolated because only a late theology could substitute such a mystery word for the word "Yahweh," the utterance of which was forbidden. The addition is here autochthonous nonetheless, the exegesis of a real intention—of the same intention which caused the local god of Mount Sinai to move to the future, to Canaan, as to his distant home.

To appreciate the uniqueness of this line, it should be compared with another interpretation, or rather, with the late commentary on another divine name, that of Apollo. Plutarch reports (*De EI apud Delphos, Moralia* III) that the sign EI was chiseled above the gate of Apollo's temple in Delphi. He tries to interpret the two letters as mystical numbers, but ultimately comes to the conclusion that the EI means the same grammatically and metaphysically—namely: Thou Art, in the sense of a timelessly immutable divine existence. *Eh'ye asher eh'ye,* on the other hand, put a God from the end of days, one whose being was the quality of the future, on the very threshold of Yahweh's appearance. This god of the end, this *Omega* god, would have been folly in Delphi, as in any religion whose god is not one of exodus.

There is, of course, a tension between God as time and God as the beginning or origin, the starting point of the Egyptian- and Babylonian-influenced biblical doctrine of creation. The complete identification of the *Deus Creator* of a world represented as finished and very good with the *Deus Spes* whom Moses preached to his people, this identification was reserved for rabbinical theology (and later for the Credo of the Christian church). But the prophets—which is so important and so essentially in keeping with the conception of the *Exodus God*—the prophets rarely mention the God of Creation, and if he is mentioned it is almost exclusively as intending to prepare the ground for man: "For thus saith the Lord that created the heavens; God himself that formed the earth and made it; he hath established it, he created it not in vain, he formed it to be inhabited" (Is. 45, 18). Though this designation of the goal as a kingdom of God among men is already inherent in the Mosaic story of the Creation, the prophets provided it with a unique reinforcement, turning reminiscence entirely into anticipation: "Remember the former things of old; for I am God, and there is none else . . . Declaring the end from the beginning, and from ancient times the things that are not yet done" (Is. 46, 9f.). Even in the later, extensive mysticism of Creation—which in the Cabbala became a Gnostic mysticism of emanation—the God of exodus and promise never lost the final power. His power pervaded the Gnostic mysticism of the world's beginning and of the divine throne carriage (*merkaba*), aiming both at the messianic omega. The Cabbala even has God create several worlds, only to smash them again because man does not occur in them; it is toward

173

man alone that the Creator is active. At this point, in fact, the tie to man as the substantial purpose of Creation becomes so inevitable that when the Lord of heaven and earth wishes to dwell among his people (Ex. 25, 8) he must, as *Eh'ye asher eh'ye,* share their entire fate to the end. Exile clothed the *Deus Spes* in the most painful radiance as Yahweh himself seemed to have been exiled with his people.

To the Cabbala, God as *Shechina,* that is, as the presence of his light, is now homeless himself in a world in which man does occur, but as a prisoner. *Shechina* shines not from the beginning of the world, but as a messianic light of hope and comfort. One of the greatest Cabbalists, Isaac Lurya (1534–1582), went so far as to introduce the idea of exile into the doctrine of the Creation itself, altering it altogether: *bereshith,* the beginning, the word with which the Bible starts, became not the beginning of a creation but that of a captivity. The world, said Lurya, has come into being as a contraction (*tsimtsum*) of God and is thus a prison from the outset; it is not only the prison of Israel but that of the sparks of all souls, and finally Yahweh's own. Coming to the fore, instead of the glory of Alpha, the dawn of Creation, is the dream of the end, of the day of deliverance, whose only link with the beginning is dialectical, as with a primal Egypt that has to be voided. However inconsistent with the solemn hymn of Genesis, such amplifications of Mosaicism correspond exactly to the original Exodus God and to *Eh'ye asher eh'ye,* the God of the goal. The suggestion of *Deus Spes* in Moses remains even though the picture of a last guide out of Egypt—in other words, of the Messiah—appears only a thousand years later; messianism is older than this faith in the Messiah. For there seemed to be no need for a new saviour while the people's fate was bearable, or while they believed that their sins alone had caused calamity to strike.

But despite the God-pleasing conduct prevailing in the Jewish ecclesiastic state after 450 B.C., conditions kept getting more hellish. As a result the picture of a last leader moved into the foreground, becoming clear-cut since the second century B.C., since the oppression by Antiochus and the Maccabean War.

The dream culminates in the Roman period: the Messiah is the secret king, the Lord's anointed, the restorer of the kingdom of David. As such he is a national-revolutionary leader with romantic luster, but at the same time, in the sense of the universal Zion of the prophets, he rules over a whole new *time span,* a kingdom of God. Rising thus in the messianic faith, besides the hope for a king from the house of David, is the hope for a superior Moses. The ten plagues and the Egyptians' destruction in the Red Sea become apocalyptic: a prerequisite of the advent of God's reign is destruction of the power now ruling on earth. And the national revolution itself, however little, entwines with the turn of the world, with the new heaven and the new earth. Even more powerful, far exceeding this sort of cosmic Moses, was the augmentation of the Messiah picture by that of a heavenly primal man, according to an idea shared in those days by Persians and Jews.

This heavenly human figure full of wisdom, mighty as a cherub in God's pleasure garden, makes its first appearance in the Book of Ezekiel, a contemporary of Zoroaster (about 600 B.C.) — (Ez. 28, 12ff.). In the famed vision of Daniel (about 160 B.C.) the inherited messianism receives such an incarnation: "One like the Son of man came with the clouds of heaven, and came to the Ancient of days, and they brought him near before him. And there was given him dominion, and glory, and a kingdom, that all people, nations, and languages should serve him" (Dan. 7, 13f.). And the learned formula for the deification of the messianic idea was found by Philo, the Alexandrian contemporary of Jesus: the heavenly original man—the first-created Adam, made in God's image (Gen. 1, 27) rather than out of dust (Gen. 2, 7)—is the *logos,* God's first-born son, indeed the "second God." This is no longer merely the Lord's anointed, but an intramundane or *human God.* The other God, the unknowable one of heaven, cedes more and more of the pillar of fire and clouds, of the powers of exodus and salvation. These powers go to the Messiah figure; despite his subordination to Yahweh, the Messiah virtually becomes God's equal—but as the good God, the helper, the good in God. This is a theological change far exceeding the sublimation of Yahweh that had occurred so far; for in the form of the son of man as a second God it goes against the sole trust in Yahweh himself. Even if unknowability and absolutized transcendence move Yahweh higher and higher, the very disparateness of such distance deprives the needy of a being to pray to. There is a qualitative recoil involved in excessive exaltation: it makes the faithful turn away, since to this transcendence they can no longer relate at all. In the God they believe in, absolute transcendence becomes tantamount to abdication. Eventually, such loftiness comes to be just another way of saying that God has forsaken his people ("Heaven is high, and the Czar is far," said a Russian proverb corresponding to that loftiness in whose eye man is too small to be thought of).

In late Judaism, in Job (about 300 B.C.) and also in Ecclesiastes (about 200 B.C.), we have seen the actual outbreaks of a consummate anti-Yahweh feeling that the world is evilly ruled; and then transcendence, God's complete separation from the world, could at best be useful as a shield against this feeling. It became only a negative shield, of course, not one that would keep men from looking more and more passionately to the heavenly original of man for Yahweh's previously praised saving function. In the end there is virtually no concealing the fact that the idea of the Messiah comes as a no-confidence vote in Yahweh, indeed as apostasy from Yahweh—in spite, and because, of the exaltation of Yahweh that is proclaimed in the late Psalms in particular. But what is crucial here, too, what Moses founded, is not broken even by this strongest leap. Messianism is not broken even by a Messiah who is the antithesis of Yahweh; for he is not the antithesis of the old Exodus God who had declared that he would be Israel's healer.

Although it took all the despair in Judaea to raise the Messiah to Yahweh's side and even pit him against Yahweh; although the idea of the Messiah did not arise on Jewish soil alone but simultaneously, with manifold interchanges, in Zoroastrian Persia —for all that, the Exodus God was by then so constituted that he could not remain God if, instead of crushing Pharaoh and his oppressive empire, he appeared as Pharaoh himself. It does

176

not matter to what extent alien influences have assisted; it matters even less to what extent philological anti-Semitism would seek to rob the Jews not only of the Decalogue but of the idea of the Messiah.

This exodus idea which has now burst forth is without any analogies in the Egyptian-Babylonian court-style panegyrics that acclaim each currently reigning ruler as a saviour-king. There are, as will be seen in more detail, indubitable analogies in Zoroastrianism: this also knows a heavenly original man, Gayomard by name, and Zoroaster's final appearance, the Saoshyant who brings the end of the world, corresponds to the Jewish Messiah (as to the Paraclete of the Gospel according to St. John). But first of all, while the Jews may have been influenced by these parallel Persian ideas during the Babylonian exile, from 586 to 538 B.C., and may have preserved them after their return to Palestine, it is by no means certain whether these ideas had not previously radiated from Palestine to the Iranian region. The ancient Persian religion, a nature religion largely coinciding with ancient Hinduism, strictly excluded messianism—as strictly as that eminently historic faith was intended by Moses and emerged tangibly in the first Isaiah, more than a hundred years before Zoroaster: "And there shall come forth a rod out of the stem of Jesse, and a branch shall grow out of his roots" (Is. 11, 1). This verse, which is not interpolated, and the ones that follow, are messianic throughout, even though as yet they have no recourse to a heavenly primal man and his return. Secondly, however, while the properly apocalyptic elaborations of the faith in the Messiah begin simultaneously among Persians, Jews, and, last but not least, Chaldaeans, it does appear that even if the work was a collaboration, the Jews alone had all the necessary strength of suffering and therefore all the seriousness of hope. The Persians of Cyrus and the Chaldaeans of Nebuchadnezzar were ruling a world, and their gods did not need any future to be victorious. There is a significant document, the ornately thankful Behistun hymn of Darius, which shows how one could do without the Saoshyant. Judaea, on the other hand, was so badly off even after the Jews' return that there alone could the faith in the Messiah become wholly *explosive,* not just a faith in a *crowning apotheosis.*

Philological anti-Semitism succeeds here even less than with the Kenite Yahweh and the Decalogue. Reitzenstein, as an expert on Iranian mythology, is neutral, at least: "It cannot simply be a matter of borrowing the Jewish concept of a Messiah; hopes for a saving king and a blissful time of limitless duration arise independently in the most varied nations and influence each other's specific features in literary commerce" (*Das iranische Erlösungsmysterium,* 1921). And Max Weber strikes a balance that discards neutrality and views messianism accurately, as inherent in Moses and the prophets themselves: "The peculiarity of the Israelite expectation is the rising intensity of its projections into the future, whether of paradise or of the saviour-king, the first from the past, the second from the present. This happened not only in Israel; but nowhere has the expectation moved to the center of religiousness with such evidently, constantly increasing force. What made it possible was the old *berith* (covenant) of Yahweh with Israel, his promise in connection with the criticism of the wretched present; but it took the force of the prophets to turn Israel so singularly into a nation of expectancy and of waiting" (*Gesammelte Aufsätze zur Religionssoziologie* III, 1923). Consistent with this is the fact that the idea of the Messiah endured only in its biblical form; in this form alone has it been experienced by suffering peoples with a sense of mission.

In expressing what makes out the essence of religious longing, in voiding the static astral myths, in fully maturing the concept of the Exodus God—in all this the idea of the Messiah is indeed plagiarized, but not simply from Persia. It is plagiarized from the central utopia of the religions themselves. Every religious founder appeared in an aura that *belongs to the Messiah,* and any founding of a religion lies as a glad tidings within the *horizon of a new heaven and a new earth.* It retains this horizon even if both perfections have been abused by the master churches for idealizing the conditions of an existing order—in other words, as apologetics for that order—and that, of course, was much easier for the astral myths of perfection with their decidedly old heavens and old earths than for religions with a prominent founder, a pathos of the new, and a human center. Any founder's appearance posits a messianic element, and every glad tidings involves a Canaan-type experiment. Judaism has made the Messiah and Canaan particularly plain, but in more or less truncated or remembered form these definitions lie in all religions. All are grouped around them; every religion is a hybrid of transient mythology and invariantly intended messianism.

Messianism is the utopia that permits the total Otherness of religious contents to be expressed in a form posing no threat of theocracy or of anointing masters: in the form of Canaan with its unexplored splendor, in the form of the miraculous. Judaism congealed in the armor of its ritual laws, but messianism survived all codified epigonism; what kept it alive was misery and, above all, the promise in Moses and the prophets—a promise not to be refuted by experience. "To deny messianism is to deny the entire Torah," says Maimonides, the greatest Jewish teacher of the law, and he was a rationalist, not a mystic. The glad tidings of the Old Testament goes against Pharaoh, and the antithesis sharpens its constant utopia of liberation. What was meant by Pharaoh, by Egypt, by the kingdom of Edom, is as much the negative pole of the glad tidings of Moses as Canaan is its positive one. Without Egypt there could be neither an exodus nor any such evident messianism; but the road to the holy dwelling opens when Egypt drowns in the sea—and so even the Apocalypse is latent in Moses. . . .

THE FOUNDER AS ONE WITH HIS GLAD TIDINGS: JESUS; APOCALYPSE; KINGDOM

> Yes, to countless folk it seems a vastly great fantasy. They cannot hold it to be other than impossible for such a game to be set forth and carried through, knocking the godless off the seat of judgment and raising up the lowly churls . . . As it must occur to us all in the advent of faith, that we fleshly,

179

earthly humans shall become gods by the incarnation of Christ, and shall be God's disciples with
him, taught and deified by him, nay more, changed
into him altogether, so that this life on earth may
turn into heaven. Phil. 3.

THOMAS MÜNZER, *Ausgedrückte Entblös-
sung des falschen Glaubens* [An Emphatic
Exposure of the False Faith], 1524

Men pray to a child born in a stable. No eye can be turned
upward in a closer, lowlier, more secretive way. At the same
time the stable is true; so mean an origin is not invented for a
founder. Myths do not paint misery, and surely not a misery that
lasts a lifetime. The stable, the carpenter's son, the fantast among
little people, the gallows at the end—this is historical stuff, not
the golden tapestry beloved of legend. And yet there have been
attempts to dissolve *Jesus,* like Moses, into sheer legend with
no one behind it. Jesus lived no more than William Tell, then,
and Herod need not have bothered with infanticide, and Pilate is
washing his hands not in innocence but in air.

No doubt Jesus is surrounded by myths, but those are merely
the frame a man stepped into, the frame a man filled. The frame
was one of expectations, and as such it is important to Christ's
personal existence also, to his entrance into unrest, into prophecy, into the myth of the year-god. The *unrest* was the political
one in a Jewish nation longing for a leader, for a strong king, a
descendant of David capable of chasing out the Roman occu-
piers. Hence the first following of Jesus, his entrance into
Jerusalem, and the readiness to intone the Hosanna with which
the old Israelite kings had been hailed. *Prophecy* provides the
second, far broader element of expectation, one spread all over
the Roman empire. Hellenistic kings had long been assuming
the title of *soter* (saviour) which came from the old Oriental
court ceremonial. It was exactly about the time of Christ's birth
that the title passed to Augustus, the hoped-for emperor of
peace, and that the Egyptian Horus myth of the divine child
converged with the saviour image. Then there was the connec-

tion—genuinely Roman, though interlaced with messianic infusions from the Roman Jewish community that may have included Horace—of the emperor with memories of the Golden Age, the age of Saturn. Augustus was referred to in the famous prophecy of Virgil's fourth Eclogue: "Returning are the virgin and the reign of Saturn, and from high heaven a new progeny is sent to earth. The child with whom the Iron Age is ending and a new Golden one dawns for the world—favor his birth, chaste Lucina! Your Apollo is reigning . . . Behold the world atremble on its shaken axis, the land, the endless oceans, the deep sky—behold all things rejoicing in the hope of times to come!"

The very word *evangelium,* in the new sense of an all-converting glad tidings, occurs outside Judaea with reference to the emperor, not to the King of the Jews. Thus on an altar in Priene in Asia Minor, in an inscription hailing the birth of Augustus, not of Christ Jesus: "This day has changed the aspects of the world; it would have perished, had felicity for all men not appeared in the one born this day. To date your own life and your vital forces from this birthday shows good judgment; gone at last are the days when you had to rue being born. Providence, which so showered this man with gifts, has sent him to us and to coming generations as a *soter;* he will end strife and gloriously fashion all things. To the world this god's birthday brought the *evangelia* that go with him; his birth launches a new count of time."

These odd raptures in observing an imperial birthday show how much faith in miracles and salvation was abroad in the Roman empire of Christ's day, and how great a need for such faith. The tranquillity and public safety brought by Caesarism, that spawn of anarchy, are not enough to explain such extravagant homage, especially considering how greatly it differed from the later emperor cult. It was a strange sense of an imminent turning point, rather, of an end to the Iron Age, that ran through the Roman empire in those days; this feeling as much as the Mandaean prophecy of John the Baptist echoed in the liturgical formula of Luke 2, 14: "Glory to God in the highest, and on earth peace, good will toward men." And finally, however astral-mythically tinged, there was the third element of expectation, the *year-god myth,* to round out Christ's eternal, purely general frame. It was not the life of Jesus but his death that entered into the frame of a god of the year, of the seasons, of vegetation—of a god who goes down now and will rise again.

At the time of Christ the cult of such gods was widespread in Asia Minor, largely mixed with Orphic-Dionysiac images of the "die-and-become" idea. There was mourning and rejoicing over the Phrygian Attis and the Babylonian-Phoenician Tammuz (the same who earlier was supposed to reduce Joseph in the pit to a myth). Both are nature gods who bloom and vanish. A fir tree was cut and raised to Attis at the coming of spring, wreathed in violets, adorned with the god's picture, and swathed in bandages like a corpse; in the Roman Attis cult the fir was carried ahead of a procession on the twenty-second of March. In the Attis cult as well as in that of Tammuz (Hellenized into Adonis) the vernal equinox and the summer solstice were combined or shifted into each other: the death rites were held on the first day of spring, and the resurrection was celebrated two days later. And the god's misfortune was not only bewailed but ridiculed: about a Persian festival linked with the calendar cult of Asia Minor we have reports indicating that the dying year-god's role was played by a slave in royal garb under the title Zoganes, or by a criminal who had been condemned to death and was mockingly paid royal homage. What may have come from this is Christ's mocking by the Roman soldiers (Matth. 27, 28f.): he is hailed as a fool's king with scarlet robe, reed, and crown of thorns.

The year-god mystery produced a mythical pattern into which the dying of Christ, his Good Friday, would fit in large part; the crucifixion, a real event of an even less imposing sort than the birth in the stable, could in this case be shrouded or linked with the ceremonies of a calendar god. And yet, as noted before: with all these pictures of expectation, with Jewish unrest, Roman prophecies, and year-god myths from Asia Minor, the historical Jesus himself could still not be successfully dissolved into a legend. On the contrary, the general expectations of the frame, and indeed the later *cult-picture gospel about him,* are the very things that make *Christ's own life and gospel* especially striking and concrete by contrast. Christianity was thus prevented from being a pneumaticists' and theosophists' religion in the sense in which the neo-Docetism of the so-called "Jesus myth" turns it into a mythologists' religion.

And finally, more even than birth in a stable and death on the gallows, Christ's *personal effect* on his disciples furnishes proof of reality. If he were an invention, if his person had been *ex post facto* interpolated into the myth, the early Gospels would be fanciful and speculative, and the later ones historicizing; but the opposite is the case. No doubt, Jesus did appear against a sky ablaze with mythical sheet-lightning, and some of it issued from himself, with the *Mandaean apocalyptics* which no Christ legend mentions contributing more than the three expectations listed here. But a religious founder who animates and fulfills what has roundabout been converging eschatologically, toward the "fullness of time," from myths—such a founder cannot himself be confused with nature gods. Least of all, if his gospel is as alien to natural mythology as Moses had been, if vegetation does no more than furnish parables for a quite different seed, if the vault of heaven has no more room for anything but the clouds on which the son of man returns. Above all, it is the founder's *life story,* drawn from the recollection of so many witnesses, that has no parallel in any of the legends and holy adventures of Attis, Mithras, or Osiris.

The real figure of Jesus exhibits a trait less inventable than any other because it was less to be expected than any other: shyness. It shows in his early view of himself as just a preacher (Mark 1, 38) and in his dismissal of, his command to keep silent about, the event of Caesarea Philippi (Mark 8, 27ff.) that turned the preacher into the Messiah. The stable at the outset and the gallows at the end were merely incongruous in the legendary saviour image, but this shyness is utterly incompatible with it. Equally impossible to construe are the temptations and despondencies of Christ; they bespeak *ecce homo,* not Attis-Adonis. *The anxiety-ridden last supper, the despair in Gethse-*

183

mane, the forsakenness on the cross, and its outcry—these do not jibe with any legend of the Messiah-King, or even of the suffering Messiah. The latter would not have experienced the agony of doubt; he would have drawn a sense of fulfillment from his suffering, as did so many later martyrs. Finally, the Gnostic-Docetist dissolution of Christ into pure *logos,* light, life, and other hypostases, an endeavor of which mere rudiments show in the Gospel according to St. John, would no doubt have fully succeeded without the resistance encountered from the historic reality of a person; a vegetation god would not have put up this resistance.

Thus *Christian faith lives by the historical reality of its founder as no other faith;* essentially it means to follow a way of life, not a cult image and its cognition. This real recollection worked throughout the centuries: however internalized and spiritualized, *imitatio Christi* remained primarily a historic experience, and a metaphysical one on that basis only. This concrete being of Christ mattered to believers; it gave them in intoxicating simplicity what no cult image or picture of heaven could give. The very heaven, in the sense of a mere baptized astral myth, grew empty and stale. A *mystes* of Attis, no matter how accomplished in the exercises of visualizing his god, could never have spoken like Thomas à Kempis: "I would rather roam the earth as a beggar with thee than possess heaven without thee. Where thou art there is heaven, and where thou art not there is hell and death" (*De imitatione Christi,* III). And a last, most crucial point that leads entirely from the general, mythical frame to the *novum* of religious philosophy: if Christianity is not a baptized natural or astral heaven, *neither is it heaven as Yahweh's throne room.* As the son of man, Jesus injected himself into this Above: he is more exactly present in this super-humanization of his God than either Zoroaster or Buddha. He injected not the extant human being, but the utopia of a human possibility whose core and eschatological brotherhood he lived as an example. God had been a mythical periphery; now he has become the humanly adequate, humanly ideal center, the *center of the community wherever* it may be gathering in his name.

184

This required a convincing founder in whom the word had become flesh, tangible flesh, *crucifixus sub Pontio Pilato*. It required the unfeignable delicacy of a *hubris* so calmly stated that it was, and is, not even felt to be *hubris*.

A man seemed downright good here; that had not happened before. With a *downward trend* of his own, to the poor and despised, but without patting them on the back. With *rebellion upward*—nobody can fail to hear the whiplashes against the money-changers and all those who trouble the flock. It will not be long till the table is turned and the last shall be first. Poverty stands nearest to salvation; wealth impedes it, inwardly and outwardly. But poverty, to Jesus, is by no means part of salvation in the sense that it need not be wiped out. Nowhere is the usual, enforced, wretched poverty defended; only voluntary poverty is advised, and the advice is given only to the luxury-loving, to the rich youth of Matthew 19, 21. For himself, after all, the son of man did not praise the condition of not having where to lay his head. Nor is voluntary poverty viewed as an end in itself—not, at least, regarding the advice rather than the loving choice of the poor, of which more later. Keeping poor is considered a means to keep the heart from hardening, to advance the community of brethren. This community, built on the communism of love, wants no rich members, but neither does it want poor ones in the sense of being forced to want. "Neither said any of them that ought of the things which he possessed was his own; but they had all things common" (Acts 4, 32), and the possessions were gathered from gifts that would suffice for the short period of time the old earth was granted by Jesus. The passage on the lilies in the field and the fowls in the air is by no means naïvely economic, for when the gravediggers of the world and its worries can be heard at the door, providing economically for the day after tomorrow is silly.

Similarly, the advice to give Caesar that which is Caesar's (Mark 12, 17) does not teach getting along with the world, as Paul does later, but disdaining the world: soon there will be nothing any more that is Caesar's. The pound that is to gain by usury is exclusively goodness, the inner treasure. The way to

185

raise it is the *imitation of a love* that made a man cease to want anything for himself, that made him ready to lay down his life for his brethren. The Eros of Antiquity was love of beauty and splendor; Christian love embraces instead not only the lost and oppressed, but especially the inconspicuous. The motion of ancient love is reversed, and this alone does make partiality to the poor an end in itself, now—the end that follows from their election, from the sojourn among the little people. Jesus himself is present among the helpless, as an element of their low estate. He stands in obscurity, not in splendor: "Inasmuch as ye have done it unto one of the least of these my brethren, ye have done it unto me" (Matth. 25, 40).

Christian love contains this inclination to inconspicuousness in the world, to the encounter with it and to the effect of the encounter; it contains the pathos and the mystery of little things. Hence the importance of the child in the manger, together with the meanness of all circumstances in the cramped, out-of-the-way stable. The surprise of finding the Saviour in a helpless child became an enduring part of Christian love, most assuredly in its Franciscan form; it regards the helpless as important and the outcasts in the world as called. It always has the adoration of the child in mind, and the search for the chief stone of the corner which the builders had thrown away. Reverence for inconspicuousness is the final key to this reversal of the motion of love, and to its hearkening, gripping, waiting for a turnabout at *the asides, the silences, the anti-greatnesses* of the world. This love has no parallel, therefore, in any previous moral faith, not even in the Jewish one, despite the "Love thy neighbour as thyself" (Lev. 19, 18) that was received in Matthew 22, 39. Buddha leaps into the fire as a rabbit, to give a beggar a meal, but his love does not lead to the beggar, does not seek divinity in impotence. If the three wise men from the East who came to the manger had been Confucius, Lao-tse, and Buddha, only one, Lao-tse, would have noticed—though not adored—this inconspicuousness of the very greatest of all. But even he would have failed to notice the *stumbling block* which Christian love represents in the world, in its old contexts and hierarchies graduated according to the power of dominion.

186

Jesus is the sign that contradicts this very power, and the world contradicted that sign with the gallows; the cross is the world's reply to Christian love, to the love of the last that shall be first, of the outcast in which the true light gathers, of the joy which in Chesterton's acid phrase was the great publicity of a few heathens and became, or will become, the little secret of all Christians.

To justify itself, the same world later used its heathen myths to turn the crucifixion into a voluntary sacrifice, as if it had been Christ's idea, not the world's. As if this death itself had been a work of love and, as St. Paul phrased it, the price which Jesus paid to God to redeem mankind from sin. Jesus is the Messiah, not although he died on the cross, but because he died on the cross—this is how Paul, who had not known Jesus, dialecticized the "white terror." The result is that Yahweh also wanted Golgotha; he is not Satan but a creditor, only so horribly loving as no creditor has ever been: giving his own son in payment of a debt which the heavenly laws governing such obligations would not have allowed him to remit otherwise. But the real Jesus died as a rebel and a martyr, not as a paymaster. In keeping faith with his own unto death he never willed this death. He hoped that the cup would pass from him, and of his sayings previous to the fearful pre-death night in Gethsemane only interpolated ones point to the cross and to death, much less to baptism in death. He prophesied to the disciples: "There be some standing here, which shall not taste of death, till they see the Son of man coming into his kingdom" (Matth. 16, 28)— was the Son of man himself not far more certain to ascend alive, like Enoch and Elias? Both subjectively and objectively the crucifixion came from without and not from within, from Christian love. It was the loving rebel's reward and his catastrophe, the catastrophe of one who had preached a new heaven and a new earth for the living, not a beyond for the dead. A rebel against custom and ruling power died on the cross, a troublemaker and dissolver of family bonds (Matth. 10, 34–37; 12, 48), a tribune of the last, apocalyptically shielded exodus from Egypt.

This is Christian love, an all but micrological love that gathers its own in their obscurity, in their incognito before the world, in their discordance with the world—gathers them *for the kingdom where they will be in accord*. The particles and seeds of the new aeon contradict the old one of Herod and Rome, the power of the whole existing creation. Thus the rebellion, in the end, was even more monstrous than either the Jews or the Romans of the day suspected. What was ultimately in Jesus' mind was not a restoration of David's glory, not even a national revolution on the narrow given stage—the world as a whole was due to collapse in accordance with the Mandaean preaching of John the Baptist (Matth. 3, 2–12), the man who had called Jesus. And Jesus took up the call: *the best-attested of his words are escha-tological*. The thirteenth chapter of Mark shows how he really spoke, about the destruction of Jerusalem, of the temple, of the world of the old aeon. If he had merely proclaimed himself the Messiah or the son of God in the traditional, restoring sense, the priestly caste would have protected him from denunciation to the Romans, and least of all would Caiaphas, the high priest, have insisted on his death against the governor's will. For nei-ther before nor after Jesus was claiming messianic rank consid-ered a crime that merited the death penalty; his was the only case in which Leviticus 24, 16 was interpreted to mean that the son of God was a blasphemer and had to die (John 19, 7). Previously even Cyrus was hailed as the Messiah-King, and so was Zerubbabel, a leader of the Jews returning from Persia (Haggai 2, 5ff.); so the messianic pretension as such was not unheard of. And after Jesus—though at a completely desperate time, of course—the great national hero Bar Kochba was pro-claimed Messiah by Rabbi Akiba, the highest priestly authority; so the messianic title as such was not always blasphemy. Only when the Messiah did not remain strictly national or failed, as a universal one, to conform with the Church of the law was he handed over to the Romans. Only when he appeared as the Son of man in the pre-cosmic as well as in the apocalyptic sense of this title, when a natural disaster destroying even Jerusalem and the temple was proclaimed as the instrument and the proof of his triumph—only then was he considered a blasphemer who deserved to die. In fact, Caiaphas understood Jesus well when he understood him eschatologically, better than the uninitiated Pilate, and better than all the later gently-living ones who saw in Christ's love only peace, not the sword.

In fact, Jesus is wholly *eschatological,* and like his love, his ethics can be comprehended only in relation to the kingdom. The advice he gives—to take no thought for the morrow, to render unto Caesar that which is Caesar's—is just the start of the quite positive gist of his moral commandments: of a dismantling, an extrication, of the morality of an advent world. It is a morality of getting ready for the kingdom, a preparatory function of its early coming; with the ethics of Christ, in the strict sense of the Sermon on the Mount, there can be no adjusting in time, in continuing history, in secular society. The Sermon on the Mount itself is one of a time that had become purely adventist, and only on a threshold viewed as reached, at the dawn of something imminent, do these seeming quietisms make sense. This is why each of the nonforcibly forceful Beatitudes concludes by citing the kingdom of heaven as the direct reason for it (Matth. 5, 3–12). Yet it is not as decreed in an extreme-dualistic Lutheranism: as if the ethics of Christ were not temporal at all and *thus not adventist either,* as if it were wholly outside history. As if Christ's kingdom were an absolute leap, something not born anywhere in time but happening abruptly at the end of time, quite disconnected from history, after the whole ocean of reality has run its course. Rather, Jesus preached of the time that is fulfilled and has, in consequence, been fulfilled by and through history; else there would be no room at all for ethics in an earthly context, not even for an ethics of immediate eschatology.

The utterly paradoxical one of the Sermon on the Mount bears no relation to any other, however deeply immersed in religiousness; for it is an ethics of the world's end. As such it has not only vanished in the compromise moralities of Churches designed for permanence; it has been weakened even in the social doctrine of the heretical Christian sects—unless these, though enfeebled, would still move in a state of expectancy or renewed belief in a directly impending Apocalypse. For every other, every temporal imitation of Christ the advent ethics as one of the world boundary became a boundary ideal. It became that even to St. Paul: "And they that use this world, as not abusing it; for the fashion of this world passeth away" (I Cor. 7, 31). Jesus, on the other hand, represents absolute extrication from the world, and the morality he teaches is solely that of final wakefulness: "Watch ye therefore: for ye know not when the master of the house cometh, at even, or at midnight, or at the cockcrowing, or in the morning" (Mark 13, 35). Here every seed relates to the dread harvest festival of the Apocalypse; this is the end to which the grain of commitment and the fruit of works are stored. Downward trend, imitation of a love focused on the laboring and heavy laden, on the downtrodden as a whole —all of Jesus' teachings and parables serve to create a community shortly before that day. And what comes home here is precisely what is inconspicuous in the world: "The kingdom of heaven is like to a grain of mustard seed, which a man took, and sowed in his field; which indeed is the least of all seeds; but when it is grown, it is the greatest among herbs, and becometh a tree, so that the birds of the air come and lodge in the branches thereof" (Matth. 13, 31f.). Jesus and his mankind alone will enter the kingdom, as all that which has been saved and left over—nobody and nothing else. So, *totally equating the founding act with the substance founded,* this vine and these branches alone form the kingdom of God. Neither the worshipped cosmos nor the negatively omitted one: the collapsing one becomes the instrument, indeed the stage of the kingdom; only as room for the indwellers will nature continue to exist. Or, as the Apocalypt puts it, close to Jesus' sense: "And the city had no need of the sun, neither of the moon, to shine in it; for the glory of God did lighten it, and the Lamb is the light thereof" (Rev. 21, 23). Thus the glad tidings of Christ had the social effect of a Noah's ark, and the soteriological one of the advent of the *Son of man* who was with God before the Creation and will at last accomplish a new creation. Theologically the effect of the glad tidings was the voiding of

190

God's absolute transcendence by *homousia,* Christ's *equality with God.* And its democratic-mystical effect was *the Exodus God's perfection into the God of the kingdom, Yahweh's dissolution in this glory.* The Creator—not to mention the Pharaoh —in Yahweh was dropped; he remained solely as a goal, and the last Christ called solely on the community to serve as the goal's building material and its city.

JESUS AND THE FATHER; THE SERPENT OF PARADISE AS SAVIOUR; THE THREE WISH-MYSTERIES: RESURRECTION, ASCENSION AND RETURN

When a child runs so far ahead the father has a hard time keeping up with it. The physical father is treated as of no consequence; the carpenter Joseph was soon denied; light fecundates from above. But the heavenly father also looks strange beside this son. He is no longer enthroned in solitude. Once Jesus is believed to be Yahweh's mediator, he is closer than Yahweh; he even pushes him aside. The divinely sent one becomes the sender himself: "I and the Father are one"; "he who seeth me seeth the Father"; "all things are delivered to me of the Father" (Luke 10, 22). The dissociations—"Why callest thou me good? there is none good but one, that is, God" —are infrequent. Not until death draws near, in the garden of Gethsemane and on the cross, does the Father re-emerge as the Other, and duality is restored by surrender and forsakenness. But the very death on the cross, the very bitterness of this dying, has given Jesus something additional that makes Yahweh, the only good one, incompetent. What makes him incompetent, in the consciousness of the disciples, is not the sacrifice doctrine but Jesus' demonstrated loyalty and devotion unto death. For the Yahweh of Moses and the prophets could never suffer death; among the infinite qualities of his infinite goodness one was missing after all: devotion to the end. This, by definition, only a mortal *man* could have and show, not an immensely distant God whom neither torture nor the fear of death could touch.

At this point the sacrifice doctrine itself recoiled against Yahweh, quite against its purpose of explaining the cross away as a catastrophe—a catastrophe not just for Christ but for the Father, who as master of the world that caused this death might seem not unlike Satan. In itself, the sacrifice doctrine belongs to theodicy rather than to Christianity; in fact, as said here before, its construction of Christ's death as the discharge of a debt in the sense of Roman contract law puts it into the realm of a demonic jurisprudence, not of religion. But if God Father gave his son in payment, it was still the son alone who offered himself, as high priest and as butchered beast at once. He performed the utmost act of love, something of which Yahweh, for all his omnipotence—not only for all his goodness—is incapable. Even with the consummate triunity of later doctrine it was solely the second person of the deity that offered itself on the cross.

A new God arises, one hitherto unheard of, who sheds his own blood for his children, a God who is the incarnate Word, capable of suffering the fate of death in its full earthly sense, not merely in the ceremonial of the Attis legend. Thus, by the *hubris* of complete surrender, a man has transcended every past idea of God; Jesus becomes a divine love such as had not been conceived in any deity. Hence the wonderful choral in Bach's *St. Matthew's Passion: "Wenn ich einmal soll scheiden, so scheide nicht von mir—wenn ich den Tod soll leiden, so tritt du dann herfür"* [When once I must depart from here, do not thou part from me—when I must suffer death, do thou step forth then, I pray thee]. Hence one of St. Paul's most beautiful sayings: "I am persuaded, that neither death, nor life, nor angels, nor principalities, nor powers, nor things present, nor things to come, nor height, nor depth, nor any other creature, shall be able to separate us from the love of God, which is in Christ Jesus our Lord" (Rom. 8, 38f.). Who is precisely not a lord like God: "Wherefore in all things it behoved him to be made like

192

unto his brethren, that he might be merciful" (Hebr. 2, 17), and far more a son of man than anyone has ever been before God: "For we have not an high priest which cannot be touched with the feeling of our infirmities; but was in all points tempted like as we are, yet without sin" (Hebr. 4, 15).

Thus the charge that Jesus was a blasphemer had some truth to it, from the high priest's point of view, and not only because Jesus foretold the destruction of the whole old aeon and agreed with it. This agreement and the underlying revolutionary incitement sufficed to condemn him, but the additional ultimate villainy was *Christ's self-injection into Yahweh*. The Church would pit him against the Old Testament only as far as the law was concerned: in line with the verse "The Son of man is Lord even of the sabbath day" (Matth. 12, 8), it held that believers in Christ are no longer subject to the harsh law of Moses. The God of vengeance no longer applies; the curtain to this temple has been ripped down the middle. Yet the antithesis is a far deeper one, and mitigated only by the fact that it is no outright antithesis to the Old Testament at all, that at the most crucial point it turns back to it, rather. Turns back, of course, to a scene which in the Old Testament itself is full of implications and concordances against Yahweh—meaning always Yahweh as *Optimus Maximus,* like other Jupiters, not Yahweh the Exodus God, the *Eh'ye asher eh'ye*.

Whereas the decisively rebellious passage comes from the Gospel according to St. John, an all but uniformly unhistorical one, the words it quotes Jesus as saying—to Nicodemus—jibe with an age-old Jewish tradition that was not simply attached to Jesus afterwards. The verse that abounds in concordances reads as follows: "And as Moses lifted up the serpent in the wilderness, even so must the Son of man be lifted up / That whosoever believeth in him should not perish, but have eternal life" (John 3, 14f.). What Moses had done was to make a serpent of brass against the fiery desert snakes which were killing the people, and he had "put it upon a pole, and it came to pass, that if a serpent had bitten any man, when he beheld the serpent of brass, he lived" (Num. 21, 9). Though the verse

193

might be interpreted along the lines of a mythical homoeopathy, there is no overlooking the contrast with that curse which the Creator Yahweh of Genesis pronounced upon the serpent and what it may stand for. Item: Jesus refers to the serpent, to that subterranean-*subversive healing creature.* He refers to the dialectical animal of the depths of the earth from which destructive gases and healing springs rise simultaneously, from which volcanoes erupt and treasures are raised. Jesus and an almost apocryphal verse of Moses both refer to the serpent cult of all nations with its inherent ambiguity: the serpent is what crawls on the ground, a devastating monster, Hydra, Python, Typhon, the Babylonian dragon of the abyss—and it is the snake of lightning, the high flame in the sky.

The serpent is both the arch-enemy fought and conquered by Apollo, by Siegfried, by Michael, and the snake of salvation twining round the staff of Aesculapius, the Egyptian Uraeus snake on diadems and on the sun, a magic sign to ward off hostile powers. Above all, the serpent cult prevailed for a long time in Israel, as evident from its abolition by Hezekiah who "brake in pieces the brazen serpent that Moses had made; for unto those days the children of Israel did burn incense to it" (II Kings 18, 4). The saviour-serpent in the desert was the only one referred to in the amazing, equating parable of Christ; but at the same time and furthermore, beyond the purely nature-mythical definitions of the pagan serpent cult, the parable touched on a well-understood, wholly different, and soon completely revaluated opponent of the Creator Yahweh: the serpent of paradise itself. It was the Naassenes or Ophites (*naas, ophis* = serpent)—doubtless a heretical Jewish sect long before their appearance as a Christian-Gnostic one about 100 A.D.—who carried out the definitive *revaluation of the serpent of paradise in regard to Jesus as the usurper of Yahweh's place.* They interpreted the serpent of Genesis as the life-giving principle in the lower world, but not only in the world-preserving, that is, evil sense. Instead, the serpent of paradise is at the same time the symbol of world-exploding reason; for it teaches man to eat of the tree of knowledge, it tells the first men of a kingdom

194

that is higher than that of their creator and the world's. It teaches them to infringe the law of the demiurge, so a knowledge of salvation will make them like that highest God who is not Yahweh, that God whom only Jesus would preach again— *eritis sicut Deus, scientes bonum et malum.*

This knowledge brought the wrath of the demiurge upon mankind, but the Ophites, and such related sects as the Cainites, crisscrossed the Bible with a whole fiery chain of descendants of the slandered serpent of paradise, that anti-Yahweh rebel. They saw it in Cain, whose sacrifice the demiurge refused even though he accepted the bloody sacrifice of Abel, for blood pleases the lord of this world. They saw the serpent in Esau, who did not get the blind Isaac's blind blessing, but when Jacob saw Esau again it seemed to him as though he "had seen the face of God" (Gen. 33, 10), the face of the true God. They saw the serpent in Moses, as the power of the rod that struck water from the rock in full accord with the grumbling of the children of Israel, and they saw it in the rod that became a serpent and destroyed the hostile serpents of the magicians— that is, of the gods of perdition—the same hostile serpents which later destroyed the children of Israel in the desert, and against which Moses raised up the white serpent, on the true God's advice.

Above all, the serpent of paradise was in Jesus, according to the Ophites. He was its last, supreme reincarnation, and again Yahweh crushed its head in the dust. A bishop named Hippolytus reports quite unequivocally on this Ophite doctrine: "None can now be saved and resurrected without the Son, who is the serpent. For as he brought down from above the paternal original images, so is he carrying up from hence the ones awakened from sleep, and those who have again assumed the character of the Father [the true God]. . . . As a magnet attracts nothing but iron, so does the serpent return from the cosmos none but the perfect generation of like essence, which has become the image of God" (cf. Leisegang, *Die Gnosis,* 1924).

That which taught men to eat of the tree of knowledge remains accordingly the first phenomenon of redeeming knowledge, of the knowledge that leads out of the garden of animals and even out of the dreadful paternal house of this world: the serpent of paradise is the larva of the goddess of reason. So Jesus frees men of the rule of the demiurge, the same of whom he says "Your father . . . was a murderer from the beginning" (John 8, 44), and he brings the revelation of the true God whom he calls "your Father in heaven." What has thus again been emphasized in the Bible is a Titanism, a Promethean revolt especially in the Old Testament itself. Priestly editing has left only traces of it, but the traces exist; in Jesus' day they must have been unforgotten in Jewish folklore and interpreted as signposts to messianism, which was an exit from Yahweh anyway. Among the Titanisms that survived the priestly editing of the Bible, besides the serpent of paradise, are Jacob's struggle with the river god he overcomes (Gen. 32, 24f.); the giants (*nephilim*) who clearly appear before the Flood (Gen. 6, 4); the tower-building motif of insurgence against Yahweh; and last, not least, the legends of the rebellious ocean (Ps. 33, 7; 65, 7; 104, 5–9; Job 38, 8–11; Prov. 8, 22–31; Jer. 5, 22; 31, 35; Ecclesiasticus 43, 23). Nor was the secret Jewish doctrine of later days, feeding on Gnosticism but also on unextinguished folklore, oblivious of the strange relationship of serpent and Messiah, for all the dilution of the revolt against the demiurge into the usual fight against Satan.

Nathan of Gaza, a disciple of the false Messiah Sabbatai Zevi (about 1650), published a "Treatise on Dragons" (*Derush hatamimim*) in the form of a commentary to a Zohar passage on the mysteries of "the great dragon that lieth in the midst of the rivers of Egypt" (Ez. 29, 3). The letters in the word *nahash,* Hebrew for serpent, have the same numerical value as the ones in *Mashiach,* Messiah, and the treatise interprets this to mean that the soul of the Messiah shone into the abyss where the demonic powers dwell, that ever since the dawn of Creation it has been a "holy serpent" among serpents. The messianic soul is chained in this prison—in other words, in Egypt, which under Pharaoh-Satan's rule is looked upon as the world prison pure and simple—and not till the coming of the kingdom of justice will the "holy serpent" be freed to appear in upper-worldly form. So great, then, is the extent of a tradition that *linked the Messiah with the saviour-serpent in the desert, and among the Ophites with the tree of knowledge itself.* And yet it was not the Ophites who carried the Christ-Yahweh antithesis to the extreme; to them, after all, the true God appeared in the Old Testament also. The radically antithetical detachment of Ophis-Jesus from the Old Testament was attempted only by the Gnostic Marcion, about 150 A.D. Jesus' word "Behold, I make all things new," was now interpreted against Yahweh in any form, the exodus form included; Yahweh became Zoroaster's *Ahriman.*

But the new was *the new God, the out-and-out strange God* of whom no word had reached mankind before Christ. This was the Marcionite interpretation of the great *logion* as a governmental decree of Christ: "No man knoweth the Son, but the Father; neither knoweth any man the Father, save the Son, and he to whomsoever the Son will reveal him" (Matth. 11, 27). Marcion, who felt he was completing the work of the antithetical St. Paul, linked this word of Christ closely with Paul's Athenian sermon on the unknown God, the *Theos agnostos*—but what the envoy of this God severed men from, in this view, was none but the very maker of the world whom Paul, and even more the later Church, identified with Christ's Father. Marcion thus represents the strongest of anti-Yahweh concepts, a flat dismissal of Yahweh in favor of Christ as the total *novum* or paradox in Yahweh's world. Of course, as he breaks off the bridge to the Old Testament, Marcion himself is standing on that bridge, together with the Ophites. Or, differently put, Marcion comes not only from Paul but just as much from Moses. The dawn of the true or unknown God occurred between Egypt and Canaan, in the Exodus God, although he never even dawned in the Creator, in that opulent mythology of the past. The Egyptian Ptah and the Babylonian Marduk were the sources on which this mythology had drawn in turning the future, the *Eh'ye asher eh'ye,* into the beginning, and into a well-contented one at that; not only Jesus but the whole utopia of messianism must oppose this. The prophets, we recall, had rarely mentioned Yahweh as the maker of the world but had emphatically cited a new heaven and a new earth. Job's entire indictment was aimed at Yahweh as the ruler of the world, and hope was voiced simultaneously, in a living "avenger" and an impending exodus. And the apocalypt Jesus sustains this exodus idea all the way through; this is why men saw him together with the serpent of paradise, not with the God of those who found everything in the world very good, as their God did.

The founder's appearance was thus by no means as humble as his later portrayals. The lowly were to be raised up; the cross was to be *smashed,* not to be borne or even to become the thing itself. Jesus' shyness, his indisputable reluctance, vanished after the transfiguration; the experience frightened only his disciples, who shared it as a hallucinatory one (Matth. 17, 2–6). After this there was no more of the outward reticence enjoined upon them at Caesarea Philippi: that they should tell no man that he was the Christ (Matth. 16, 20). The deepest human injection into heaven was now proclaimed; the subjective factor of Christlikeness fell heir to the transcendent factor; the glory of God became the apocalyptic glory of Christ and his community. And so a wholly new fabric of faith was created— not for the sacrifice doctrine, which is and remains a theodicy of the world's maker and ruler, but for the *triumphant picture of a people's tribune behind the death on the cross.* "Abide with us; for it is toward evening" (Luke 24, 29)—for the disciples, Christ's presence was not at an end on the road to Emmaus. Thus came about the *wish mysteries: resurrection, ascension, return.* The empty grave was the only logical starting point for this *second eschatology,* this Christianity of an afterglow turned foreglow; the ascension alone let the son of man fulfill eternity; his return alone would extend the first community's advent consciousness into a like consciousness of all the communities to come. As a real memory, the dead Jesus necessarily raised hope to dimensions such as no founder had inspired yet. To those who believed in him, this man, if any, had to be the *first* of the sleepers who have been wakened. He, if anyone, had to ascend to *heaven,* not like one ennobled, so to speak, as Hercules or Elias were removed and taken far away, but as an anchor of hope that takes others with it. Jesus, if anyone, had to return to complete the *kingdom of man:* "Let us hold fast the confession of our hope without wavering, for he who promised is faithful" (Hebr. 10, 23; RSV). Pending that return, however, the Evangelist inserted yet another carrier: the mysterious *Paraclete*—the only indication that while Jesus, in the minds of the disciples, covered the return, the last judgment, and the kingdom, he did not cover the entire future until the return. This continuing effect of Christ is indeed distinct from himself, but the color and direction of the effect are also due to the belief in him. *Paraclete* (as we have seen in the parallel Zoroastrian figure "Saoshyant") means 'helper,' 'comforter,' 'aid.' He occurs only in the extensively interpolating Gospel according to St. John, but there as a promise made by Christ himself: "I will pray the Father, and he shall give you another Comforter, that he may abide with you for ever" (John 14, 16).

So Jesus, by this astonishing word, declares himself to be only the first comforter, and not forever—the Evangelist has backdated the catastrophe of the cross into Jesus' own knowledge. And there comes an interpretation differing from that of the sacrificial death, one which, as it were, lifts messianism above the dying Messiah and gives a new embodiment to it, for the advent period: "I tell you the truth: It is expedient for you that I go away; for if I go not away, the Comforter will not come unto you; but if I depart, I will send him unto you. . . . Howbeit when he, the Spirit of truth, is come, he will guide you into all truth; for he shall not speak of himself; but whatsoever he shall hear, that shall he speak; and he will show you things to come" (John 16, 7 and 13).

The *novum* of the Paraclete, as the Evangelist defines it in these few dark hints, is mainly that he will not speak of himself and so will be just a herald of what he hears. Such passivity might suggest an angel, since the angels of the time of Christian belief are messengers exclusively, without a will and substance of their own. But the Paraclete is also called "Spirit of truth"

199

and described as a guide to all truth. "Spirit of truth" is not the category of an angel; but it is both the category and the exact translation of the Persian *Vohu mano* who appears with the last Zoroaster, with the Saoshyant of the world's end. So there is more to the idea of the Paraclete than the mere presence of a comforter until Christ's return: the "Spirit of truth" designates the return itself. In fact, an even stronger effect on the Paraclete than that of the Persian messianism is exerted by the continuing Jewish one: *contained within the belief in the Messiah who had appeared was a belief in one who had not yet appeared—* though always defined by, and clothed in, the appearance of Jesus and the governing category of his return. *Thus the "Spirit of truth" became the Holy Spirit, together with the Son.* Only with this coming of the Holy Spirit has the Son truly come— and accordingly, believers in the Paraclete henceforth envisioned *Christ's being* in yet another form, a definitive form. From this alone, not from the Jesus of the New Testament, comes the real word of redemption, and with it the world's irresistible turn to the kingdom. Or, in the language of the Ophites: in the Paraclete the serpent of paradise manifests its *sophia* for the third time, and this time its head will not again be crushed. Even a Father of the Church, Tertullian, considered Jesus and the New Testament a preparatory stage and just as perfectible as the Old Testament was perfectible. Tertullian's "perfecter" is the Paraclete; he is the point of reference for Adam, Moses, and Jesus, the point where the *ultima legislatio* occurs, *in libertatem perfectam.*

From this Paraclete concept it is not hard to find links to medieval millenarianisms, notably to Joachim di Fiore and his doctrine of the Third Kingdom. There Christ's return is not one of the same New Testament Christ either, for the age of the Holy Spirit is no longer that of commitment and promise. The Paraclete does not speak of himself any more; he lays down reality, in which inwardness has become outwardness of mind. He becomes the utopia of the Son of man, who is himself not utopian any more, because the kingdom is present. Yet none of this leaves the realm of nostalgia for Jesus; in fact, it is *Christ's*

200

being that is repeated, enhanced, in the comforter who has become the Holy Spirit. The disciples believed that the pneuma that came over them at Pentecost was poured by Christ, by the Christ of the ascension: "Therefore being by the right hand of God exalted, and having received of the Father the promise of the Holy Ghost, he hath shed forth this, which ye now see and hear" (Acts 2, 33). Even in this ecstatic interpretation the risen Christ has received only the *promise,* not the Holy Spirit itself—much as the pneumatic disciples' speaking in tongues is a mere unfinished hieroglyphic, compared with the truth of the kingdom. Yet with the spirit so firmly promised to the Christ up there, the fulfillment or *parousia* of the spirit, however explosively conceived, always appeared to Christianity in the measure of the stature of Christ (Eph. 4, 13). None of the chiliasts would dissociate the wish mystery of the return from the figure they viewed as having ascended to heaven. Christ, the founder, became the triumphant substance of salvation regarding the Paraclete as well: he absorbed the Paraclete of the future as he had absorbed the God of the past. And with the *eschaton of the kingdom aimed at*—not just in the teachings of the historical Jesus but even more in the three wish mysteries of the Christ of faith—believers came to see Jesus in this future phenomenon as well, as in everything touched by the kingdom. Jesus as he who returns, as he represents himself according to the pictures of the Daniel Apocalypse (Dan. 7, 13f.), as the Son of man riding the clouds of heaven, shares logically in the leap to the new. This leap made the very strengthening and magnifying function of nostalgia a turn into "total Otherness": the Christ of the wish mysteries came to live completely behind an explosion, on an eschatological plane. Which is why the kingdom—*finis ad quem omnia*—leaves no stone of the old unturned, no stone of the temple, but no stone of Sion either. Hence the change of name everywhere (in the East, the name denotes the essence): "The Lord shall call his servants by another name" (Is. 65, 15); "To him that overcometh will I give to eat of the hidden manna, and will give him a white stone, and in the stone a new name written, which no man knoweth" (Rev. 2, 17). As the Old

201

Testament—the Exodus Yahweh's, not the Creator Yahweh's—
said of Sion itself: "And thou shalt be called by a new name,
which the mouth of the Lord shall name" (Is. 62, 2).

Christ's resurrection from the dead has no analogies in religious history; but the world's apocalyptic transformation into
something as yet wholly nonexistent is not even hinted at anywhere outside the Bible. And since this *omega,* this outright
novum, relates exclusively to the human content of the faith,
the mysticism of heaven becomes that of the Son, and the glory
of God, that of the redeemed community and its location.
Christian mystics, Eckhart in particular, have therefore conceived this location as nothing but the fulfilled moment of us
all, nothing but this moment's *nunc stans* in relation to the
kingdom. This is religious protestation—no longer dealing with
the self as something unexposed, nor with *sursum corda* as a
hypostasized Above in which man does not occur. "*Eritis sicut
Deus*" is the glad tidings of Christian salvation. . . .

3. *The Earthly Core as Real Extra-Territoriality*

THE PATH OF THE NOT-YET EXISTENT GOAL

Eventually the upward drive becomes a forward drive. Making
that easy and self-evident might suffice, considering the situation
of most people. But even today the majority will be hard pushed
to know what the light is, and where. Really to pursue the right
goal, by the proper path, appears to be the most difficult thing
of all. And even that path leads astray if in thinking about the
Whither one does not constantly think of the *Why* of the overall good too.

This is in the people who take the path, and in the path's
own course. It is not extant, however, as a phenomenon or
achievement, but as a human will and a historic trend; to be
well founded, therefore, the overall good requires confidence in
it. Believing more easily in what has not appeared than in what
is visible takes a trained hope; it means that at midnight we are
confident of the dawn. Reverses (and there are a thousand times

more of those than of victories) can only correct this posture, not refute it. Our will in this posture is as much aimed theoretically at the effect on the whole of all partial movements as it is practically aimed at the whole as such, and so definitive a will is necessarily immoderate. If the goals of a man fighting for higher wages do not include the disappearance of a society that compels him to have to fight for wages at all, he will not get far in his fight for wages either. And if a man thinks he is human already, if he thinks he will be the unalienated pinnacle of his creation if only the wretched society has been changed, he is not taking seriously enough what remains to become of him—especially as the Babbitt (whom capitalist society has produced on so broad a scale) will not be removed by giving everybody an electric refrigerator.

There are communist philistines also. Men can want to be brothers without believing in the Father, but they cannot be brothers without believing in the far from banal contents and circumferences that were conceived religiously in the kingdom; and without maintaining this faith even though their knowledge —indeed, *because* their knowledge has destroyed all the illusions of the mythical faith. Not even the most obvious goal in the restlessly proceeding context of an incipient classless society can be attained, however, if the subject does not aim beyond the goal. In this base of their intent—a base not exhausted by its illusionary aspects—the great religious teachers felt that man is called to do the unheard-of; everything they did related to this feeling. Only the priests would use this excess of nonexistence to defend the shortcomings of existence; but they were priests, not stumbling blocks, sleep producers, not awakeners. They were the ones who took the Christian faith and made it opium for the people, the ones who took man's infinite worth, which the Bible had taught him, and tossed it into the beyond —all the way into the beyond, where it has no more bite, and cannot hurt earthly worthlessness. They gave the just distribution of supraworldly goods as a bonus to the unjust distribution of worldly goods, thereby consoling the shorn sheep. They took the widely advertised claim of what befits us and anchored it in a beyond so as to remove it from the here and now. They made

fixed transcendent images out of faith, instead of the fermenting
immanent ones that stimulate a full existence and keep the will
to it alive. The road ahead runs right over the priests, but not
over the faith that turns men into believers. For this faith with
its courage and utmost wakefulness is part of the road. It is the
posture of not only grasping a knowledge of things to come but
willing them and carrying them out against timid or short-
sighted doubts. And the faith of those who already are believers
—faith in contents, in other words—has here the thoroughly
corrected validity of knowing about the germinal things in the
world, the things that are always still unfinished. There is no
conceivable way for this latter faith to come into conflict with
knowledge, but neither is it superfluous alongside knowledge.
What it expresses, in substance, is that the essentials have not
yet been visibly poured out. Since the best is still pending, it
must be trusted if it is to succeed.

UNAVOIDABLE AND AVOIDABLE FATE;
OR CASSANDRA AND ISAIAH

Action is surely impossible if the outside world is open in all
directions. For anything can happen then—which is the same
as to say that life becomes quite unforeseeable and uncanny, as
if haunted. Under these circumstances a man might still *take a
chance,* like the knight who felt drawn mainly to adventures
that seemed to have something of the spectral about them. Yet
even chance-taking, particularly chance-taking, becomes impossible where nothing at all can happen any more except the
inevitable, which we call fate in the proper sense of the word.
The Greeks, frank and fearless in so many things, have borne
witness to this irresistible spell. The first foundation of a sense of
fate, in any case, is the unintelligibility and indomitability of
natural forces, and then of social forces. Fatalism proper may
attach itself to a subterranean power (Tyche, the three "Fates");
but a developed fatalism mainly presupposes an astral myth,
so that man will not occur in it, so that he can make no move
of his own against the motion of the stars and the spell they

weave. In the ancient East, fate was astrally determined altogether, by the position of the planets, the sun, the zodiac. Chaldaean astrology merely carried out what spread from Babylon throughout the civilization of those days: the stars, which nothing can influence, are not only indices but elements and configurations of a fate that cannot be influenced either, only read or interpreted as Enlil, the divine administrator of the "tablets of history," pursues his course north of the celestial equator. And the Greeks, whose gods had human rather than stellar form, accordingly had fate, *Moira,* ruling the gods as well. There is a passage in Homer, of course, about Zeus defending himself against the plaints of men—"For they cry out that all evil is nobody's doing but ours / Yet in their folly they bring unfated grief on themselves" (Odyssey I, 33f.)—but the Oedipus legend shows how doom rolls on even without guilt. It rolls mechanically, not caused but simply occasioned, and hence inexorable. As far as fate is concerned, the gods' only advantage over men is that they know it; they have foreknowledge of what *Moira* decreed, but their knowledge is powerless. It lets Hermes warn Aegisthus and foretell his end, but no more, and Zeus himself becomes an impotent onlooker when Sarpedon, his own son, is slain by Patroclus in line with *Moira*'s verdict. To Cassandra, who shared the gods' gift, the fall of Troy was known as an established fact. It was settled before Paris was born, before Helen was abducted, before the war broke out; no penance done by the Trojans—who were entirely guiltless anyway—could avert their destruction. This is *Moira,* this blind, direct, gigantically heavy weight that will break any human action.

In the Greeks' view *Moira* came from an order other than that of their gods; even with the older, matriarchal order of gods, of earth and night, fate was but loosely connected, as a child of the night, and for this connection it lacked all kindness, all mercy, the womb of the grave, and the homecoming in the preordained. *Moira* is the flat, disparate inevitability that brings not only the mind to a standstill but makes the blood freeze.

Action under such circumstances is senseless even if the first step is free. The Greeks alone could bear this *Moira* of theirs, for they alone had surface strength enough to put the abyss out of their minds. Those who face it are not instruments of a divine will. Neither Oedipus nor Cassandra can do anything, much less change anything. Fate itself is not a will; it is not even that much of a *medium*. Nor does *Moira* need instruments for her enforcement, or even for her appearance—none, at least, which would be required to perform anything by themselves, or even under orders.

The very irony of the Greek fate shows how little depends here on the manner or direction of *human* acts. This wholly daemonic, or not even daemonic—this even for daemons too disinterested and mechanical character is what distinguishes *Moira* from seemingly kindred phenomena found on the soil of the Bible or in its vicinity, from Mohammed's *kismet* or Calvin's predestination. For their subject, both of these have a God who is defined as good, and both let the spell be woven to an ultimately and quite unquestionably good end. It is a decree, albeit an unfathomable one, and a guidance, though superior in the extreme. Still, the *total antithesis* to non-biblical fatalism, and to the *quietism* which that fatalism ultimately seals, is not found in doctrines of impotence.

The definitive contrast appears only *in the Bible itself:* in the relation in which the *Israelite prophets stand to Cassandra* and her implications. At the same time, the contrast shows how great a change in the God men believe in is wrought by the open space of messianism, even regarding the fate which this God imposes. For now the doom or destiny no longer tyrannizes man as do both *Moira* and the astral myth. Fate is completely capable of being changed, rather; Isaiah, above all, teaches that it depends on the *morality* of men and on their *decisions.* This is the active antithesis to the Greek seer, especially to the mere passive despair of Cassandra's vision: in the Bible fate hangs in the balance, and the weight that finally decides is man himself. Of course, not every prophet regards fate as morally modifiable, and even Isaiah does not always do so. At times, the coming calamity is viewed as definitive, already suspended from heaven by iron chains; and penance then means contrition,

206

readiness to take the punishment. But the inexorable fate that was the rule for the Greeks is the exception in the Bible; a man's very first step, his moral turnabout, may reverse his fate. This is how one should read one of the Bible's most instructive passages in this respect: *the amazement of the prophet Jonah,* who failed to grasp the difference between Cassandra and himself. For Jonah had indeed been sent to inform Ninevah of its destruction after forty days, but when the city did penance and the evil did not occur, he was wrongly but exceedingly displeased (Jonah 4, 1)—as if he had told an untruth to the people of Ninevah, whereas it was the change in them that had caused a change in Yahweh (Jer. 18, 7f.; 26, 3 and 19).

Here fate itself is still wavering. It is not categorical but hypothetical throughout, and the condition it depends upon is posited twofold. First, it lies in human freedom, which the Jonah passage plainly shows as antithetical to fate. But then this freedom flows into the open space corresponding to belief in a God of time, a God in the direction of "I shall be who I shall be." Fate looks far from static then, quite unlike *Moira;* the new is a bad habitat for the inevitable. The prophets, of course, actively believing in their God as a being that unleashes wars, overthrows empires, sends plagues, ends plagues, often made Yahweh himself look like an element of fate. No religion, however extensive its self-injection into what had been the beyond, could approach the threshold of seeing through fate as something men have brought upon themselves. Also, the purely moral causes to which the prophets laid its direction are palpably mythical and had to be strained considerably to hold up as a causality of fate; the Book of Job disposed of such explanations. And yet, this moral insert in the mode of fate opened a *countermove of freedom* noticeably different from Cassandra, from mere impotent foreknowledge, from what is called prophecy outside the Bible. In Jonah, and consciously in Isaiah, mere *prévoir* is subordinated to a *praevenire,* a chance for change rather than mere lamentation, for avoidance rather than acceptance. This sort of thing goes explicitly against fate, and tacitly against fate's master: more and more, he is being brought to justice.

207

GOD AS THE UTOPIANLY HYPOSTASIZED AND UNKNOWN HUMAN IDEAL

Distance shrinks things that have happened, but it magnifies those that are hoped for. They feed on being needed, and they grow by being placed at an end. What grows in this manner is not their extant being, for this is invisible when conceived as distant in space, and when it is conceived as distant in time it does not exist as yet. Magnified by the stress that is placed on the end, and by its location at the end, is solely what has never happened anywhere—in short, a perfection that would correspond utopically to the need of hope. From olden times the acme of the ideal has been the divine, either because the gods may and can do what man may not and cannot do, or because they are unburdened by situations, walking in bliss as such. For the ideal's mode of being it does, of course, make a decisive difference whether a religion defines its distance as an essentially spatial one or else as an essentially temporal one. If the distance is essentially spatial, the supposition of an extant being of God greatly outweighs his merely ideal being even though the latter is never quite absent. If the distance of the divine is essentially temporal, on the other hand, if the breakthrough that eliminates it will not happen till the end of days, then the ideal, the unrevealed being, decisively outweighs the being that is supposed to exist—though again the latter is not absent from any religion, however strong its sense of "I shall be who I shall be." While the God in space, the God on high, has essentially the perfection of supreme being—above the roof, so to speak, of all worldly being—the God at the end of time shows his being essentially as supreme perfection, and its difference from any kind of extant being in the world is thoroughly apocalyptical. From the space god of the astral-myth a road leads to pantheism, insofar as this is worship of the *totum* of existence; from the Exodus God, on the other hand, the *totum* makes its exit from existing mundane being, in chiliasm. Even where the being of God was so far elaborated as to have "proofs" offered for it (the astral myths

208

could not consider them necessary), even in Christian scholasticism the *ens realissimum* of its God was a quality of the *ens perfectissimum,* not the other way round. To the scholastics God was primarily the highest goal, and the divine as a superlative of being, not merely of worth, was just a consequence—due to an equation between being and perfection whose source, to be sure, was Plato rather than Christ.

In essence, however, the Exodus God was no more conceived as a *res finita* than the Exodus itself; although the epitome of perfection, he was not the epitome of being in existence. Moreover: every mythology of a being is a view of something divine; every theology as a science of reality tends in this direction; but not tending there is what is conceived as divine on the side of hope, and of a hope content that has not been estranged, has not been ceded to heaven. The deep need which brought forth this hope has remained even without any case of a *Pater noster qui es in coelis* continuing as its real, merely spatially segregated object in an allegedly existing superspace. And long before God as an existing object was dethroned by the Enlightenment, Christianity had injected man and his claim—more exactly, the *son of man* and his substitutive mystery—into the former lord of heaven. What Feuerbach, and Hegel before him, in some respects, carried to a conclusion was fully implied in the question *Cur Deus homo?* From heaven, Feuerbach returned the religious contents to man, in the sense that man is not created in God's image but God in man's, or rather in that of man's current ideal prototype. This makes God vanish completely as the world's creator, but it gains a vast creative region in man, a region of fantastic riches and fantastic illusions, in which the divine amounts to the hypostasized human wish picture of highest rank. Feuerbach equates this "wish theory of religion" with "anthropologization of religion," or with abolishing the "celestial duplication of man." Feuerbach, of course, knows man, the subject duplicated in religion, only as he has so far appeared and is now given, and he knows this form only as the abstractly stable one of the so-called human species. Lacking from his view is the historical-social ensemble of the human "type" of the moment; lacking above all is its inconclusiveness. The flatness of the "homo bourgeois," which Feuerbach absolutized, can definitely not accommodate the contents of religion, no more than the bourgeois has ever been the subject from which the wealth of divine images would come forth. Least of all can Feuerbach's statically extant subject accommodate the religious images that explode the status, the chiliastic ones of "Behold, I make all things new," and of the kingdom.

It evidently takes an *open subject and its open world to* reabsorb the anticipations of outright perfection in the way the subject has projected them out of itself. If *religion* is to be anthropologized, therefore, Feuerbach's anthropologization of it presupposes a utopian concept of man, not one that is statically settled. It also presupposes a *homo absconditus,* just as the belief in heaven always carried in itself a *Deus absconditus,* a hidden, latent God. The bourgeois à la Feuerbach, that *res finita,* is the least suitable matrix for transferring the *res infinita* of the religious ideal content, for though religion may have got on splendidly with ignorance and even with stupidity, it never got on with triviality. Mysteries are the anti-trivial as such. And not only the *subject* must be understood as utopian, the call for the return of all the wealth that has been handed to the gods; the subject's surrounding *nature* must in no event seem finished either, like the mechanical-materialistic nature of Feuerbach's. In time, the exact significance of nature has not yet appeared; like mankind's it is still in utopian latency. The kingdom is outwardness, not only inwardness; it is order, not only freedom—essentially it is the order of a subjectivity to which objectivity is no longer something extraneous, and so the objectivity that still surrounds man as nature must be understood and honored in whatever part of it has not appeared as yet. Thus hope, which has been at work in religion and has now rid itself of illusions, of hypostases, of myths, intends through the idea of the kingdom that a utopian light shine on the border of the objective possibility as it shines in the subjective one. To a religious intentionality the germ within is also on the move without. The light in the stable of Bethlehem and the light of the star that stood still above it are one and the same.

Little wishes can be forgotten, and in the long run they come to bore us. Great wishes are different; the picture of a loved one who did not come or who disappeared, for instance, will go to the grave with him who has it. In the nineteenth century, as we have seen, few men have more strongly felt and more succinctly defined the unrecompensed parts of religion than has Feuerbach, that prominent atheist. Despite his narrow, rigid, abstract concept of man he marks a turning point in religious philosophy; from him onward, the last history of Christianity begins. For he wanted not only to be a gravedigger of traditional religion—an easy job, a hundred years after Voltaire and Diderot—but what struck him, rather, was the problem of religious inheritance. He knew that there is a remainder in even the most disenchanted of the affinities that have essentially built the Christmas night, the Strasbourg cathedral, and the St. Matthew's Passion; and it was this remainder which—however inadequate his agencies and horizons—he sought by means of enlightenment to take away from the priestcraft tied to a beyond. This is why he describes himself as merely "negating so as to posit," and as "disenchanting heaven in order to give weight to man." His task in this expropriation of the beyond is defined as "giving unto man, at last, that which is man's." Hence the decisiveness—especially instructive nowadays—of Feuerbach's explanation: "He who says and knows no more about me than that I am an atheist says and knows nothing about me. Whether or not there is a God was a question for the eighteenth century or for the seventeenth. To deny God means to me to deny the denial of man; it means to replace man's illusory, fantastic, celestial position, which in real life turns necessarily into a denial of man, with his sensual, real, and thus necessarily political and social position. The question of God's being or non-being is to me the question of the being or non-being of man." There are more precise definitions, such as "Man conceives of a God, and believes in him, only because he wants to be God himself and fails," or "God is the fulfiller, that is, the realization, the fulfillment of my wishes," or "God is nothing but eternal, uninterrupted joy in the form of a being."

Feuerbach thus begins by elaborating the two opposed and yet interconnected basic motives for the altar-building of the past: the wish for our essence, and at the same time the fanciful

211

relinquishment of our essence by lending it out to heaven. More permanent than these two analyses remains the test, the effusion of the beyond upon its sources, mankind and earth. The religion-building sigh of the oppressed, joy-craving creature, the religion-filled discord in man, between his existing phenomenality and his non-existent essence—none of these psychogenic explanations and dissolutions of a transcendent illusion can fully dissolve the original source of the celestialization. Something akin to this applies even to the much more concrete research into origins that interprets the celestializations as reflecting conditions of social rule along with precarious natural relations. For in this reflex and in its very possibility lies something more, something which brought about the variegated *substantial* expansion of the reflex beyond the purely repetitive vapor glow in the sky. And even if we do succeed in abolishing the human misery which religion expressed as much as it was a protest against it; even if this first source of it, this most proximate source of its wishful motivations, should be eliminated—even then there remains the *autochthonous stock of human substance* that has been surrendered to the heavenly hypostasis by way of imagination, but also by way of anticipation.

Feuerbach's view of this stock is by no means wholly negative: "Religion is the first, indirect self-consciousness of man," and even more: "The consciousness of the infinite being is nothing but man's consciousness of the infinity of his own being, or: in the infinite being, the object of religion, man's only object is his own infinite being." A plain reference to Christ's incarnation is not missing: "Man is the God of Christianity; anthropology is the secret of Christian theology." Thus *cur Deus homo,* this question and possibility that exists in Christianity alone, remains even for Feuerbach the problem of religion and at the same time the key to it. The self-injection into transcendence is immaterialized and read backwards: as the retrieval of transcendence into the self, in a manner Hegel had already defined in his philosophy of religion: "In this entire history, man has become conscious of being an immediate, present God, with this history itself, as comprehended by the spirit, representing the process of what man is, what the spirit is." Nothing but the elimination of the spirit, in other words, radical utopianization, remained necessary to bring heaven to man's own existential front and have it encompassed by its mysteries—with the result that for anthropological atheism the religious contents are not totally chimerical but "are not what they are in the illusion of theology, not foreign mysteries but domestic ones, rather, the mysteries of human nature." This line of Feuerbach's characterizes the truth in him, a truth which as the scion of a trite age he tries in vain to block with inanities such as the following: "In the field of nature enough is still incomprehensible, but the secrets of religion originate in man, and those he can know down to their bottom ground."

Such inanities of the bourgeois subject of Feuerbach's anthropology must be acknowledged—as warnings, above all, against a shallow secularization of religion—but they bow before the Christian immanence, before the *homo homini Deus* in atheism as Feuerbach conceives it. What keeps breaking through the trivialities of pseudo-enlightenment is a humanity that is not weaker than nature, nor less mysterious. In spite of everything, it allows Feuerbach to write a true conqueror's statement in the field of religion: "The faith in the beyond is the faith in the freedom of subjectivity from the bars of nature, and consequently man's faith in himself." It must not be forgotten, this background of humanistic immanence in a thoroughly progressing, thoroughly inheriting sense. For this sense has not come to a conclusion; on the contrary. It is, as Marx put it, "the unfolding of human productive forces, and thus the unfolding of the wealth of human nature, as an end in itself." *Religion inherited* (meta-religion) comes to be the conscience of the last utopian function *in toto:* that function is the self-transcending of man, the transcending in league with the dialectically transcending tendency of man-made history, the *transcending without any heavenly transcendence, but with full understanding of that transcendence as a hypostasized anticipation of being-for-itself.* This unknown future in men, not what is already existing and given in them, is what was meant in essence throughout the changing heavenly hypostases. This is how the founders of religions have increasingly injected the *humanum* into God—

213

meaning here: they have increasingly used more and more humanly close figures of the beyond to circumscribe the human incognito. Thus all instances of naming and nominating God have been gigantic figurations and attempted interpretations of the human mystery, with the hidden human figure intended through the religious ideologies and despite them. The extant human image was visibly not covered by the wishfully, much less by the utopically hypostasized faces: they were both more weird and more familiar in an enigmatic way than the human image that existed, the human prototype that governed at a particular time. This simultaneous familiarity and total Otherness, the sign of the religious stratum from animal gods to the one god of power and to the saviour god, becomes comprehensible only as such *interpretative projection of the homo absconditus and his world*. The animal god's face was a mixture of savage, horrifying, obscure features such as no man has them. The power god with his characteristically superlative being (*nemo contra Deum nisi Deus ipse*) contributed the weirdness of infinity, the boundless, thundering heavens, something tyrannical which no man has either, and which still belongs to this consummately exaggerated form of religious projection, to this superlative, this surpassing. The saviour god finally, in the form of the Son, is sheer secrecy, but of a sort that carries with it something even more surpassing: the dissipation of fear *katexochen* for all the baptized who have added Christ's projection to their old Adam. To human hope this last form of surpassing is directly presented as the miraculous, as if the real core of the incognito had a sweet taste. Hence: "Hope does not disappoint" (Rom. 5, 5)* and "I reckon that the sufferings of this present time are not worthy to be compared with the glory which shall be revealed in us" (Rom. 8, 18), or even "Eye hath not seen, nor ear heard, neither have entered into the heart of man, the things which God hath prepared for them that love him" (I Cor. 2, 9). All these are anthropologizations of religion; as

* This rendering from the Douay Bible lacks the poetry and depth of Luther's German phrase (*Hoffnung lässt nicht zu Schanden werden*), but it conveys the same meaning. The King James Version's "maketh not ashamed" does not. —Translator.

214

depth increases, they are equally religions of the unknown *anthropos* rising from his unknown state: "Till we all come in the unity of the faith, and of the knowledge of the Son of God, unto a perfect man, unto the measure of the stature of the fullness of Christ" (Eph. 4, 13). Item: the Christian hope was that all things be redeemed humanity, including a transfigured nature in which neither sun nor moon need shine any more, since "the Lamb is the light thereof." And no anthropological criticism of religion takes away the hope on which Christianity has been superimposed. All that it withdraws from this hope is what would void it as a hope, what would make a superstitious confidence of it: the mythology of its fulfillment that is definitively depicted, absurdly unreal, but hypostasized as real.

The criticism reduces the religious substance to the human wish, but to the greatest, most thoroughgoing of wishes, to the wish which in the long run can never become unessential, because it is nothing but the intention to achieve the essence. The essence may be frustrated—mythologically this frustration is conceived as hell—but its nonfrustration was mythologically conceived as becoming divine. Thus God appears as the *hypostasized ideal of the human essence which in reality has not yet come to be;* he appears as the utopian entelechy of the soul, just as paradise was imagined as the utopian entelechy of the divine world. It is scientific untidiness to posit this idea of God as real; it is poorly disenchanted fantasizing if this mythology of God, because it is not real, is now placed as a real product at the end of days by a God-making ersatz religion in the lyrical sense of the early Gorki, or in Rilke's, or in the sense of Bergson's philosophy of nature that regards the world as a machine for producing gods.

Neither does salvation lie in a disenchantment which strips the idea of gods of reality but lets it stand in its wholly mythological form: as a fixed ideal posited in a postulate. This is Kant's doctrine; it does contain the strongest utopian conscience, stated in the moral form of the postulate, but it does not interfere with the God of the catechism. He remains as the "unity of all reality," posited as a regulative idea. What Feuerbach's anthropology has done for religion instead is to put *cur Deus homo* on

215

its feet once more—and what can be brought to earth from heaven makes for profound immanence. If we are *in earnest about its transcendent irreality in past and future,* the idea of God is fulfilled as an ideal solely by its anthropological dissolution—although by one different, entirely different from the dissolution into existential humanity that has been worked out so far, during the prehistory of mankind. By Barth, or in theistic heteronomy, the great religious manifestations are called "impact craters" that show that a revelation has occurred. In Feuerbach, or in atheistic autonomy, these manifestations, the biblical ones above all, have the opposite and solely correct character of protuberances showing that a total wish extension of the *humanum* has occurred, with an equally total intention aimed at the sense of the world. What was intended in the great religions, instead of the many single *hopes,* was *hope itself;* it was to encompass and focus the many single ones, but not as an *ens realissimum* with the subjects' reflex of *proskynesis* and throne. The only truth of the divine ideal is the utopia of the kingdom, and the premise of that utopia is that no God remains on high, where none is or has ever been anyway.

THE SPACE INTO WHICH THE DEITY WAS IMAGINED OR UTOPIANIZED

But how strong were the forces positing a beyond! How self-evident did it seem for a long, long time that the world is full of upper and lower spirits! How tenaciously would people who had been conservatively raised and had remained so cling to a picture of something enthroned on the other side! Habit and unseriousness play a large part, but the very habit is here padding vague feelings until they loom larger than they are. Today no man, not even the most pious, believes in God in the same way in which the most lukewarm and skeptical believed in him two hundred years ago. But the hypostasis of strong wish forces or cravings for a solution has endured in habit and in its organized ecclesiastic tradition, and those will still permit a lukewarm theism, at least. Otherwise, in the huge bourgeois prosaic world, it would no longer be possible for the Church to occur at all—to occur as an exception to the atheistic rule, but an exception that knows very well how to get along with the rule whenever the maintenance of the bourgeois prose world's capitalist foundations is at issue. Until the triumph of the bourgeois Enlightenment, atheism was not the rule but a rare, startling exception, and one so hedged in with qualifications that we may ask whether Greek, Roman, Hindu atheism can be understood at all in our sense of the concept. The different figures denied in the divine world already make a difference in the resulting vacuum: the No to Jupiter looks unlike the No to Brahma, and even more unlike that to Yahweh. As for the latter—the only one somehow related to the atheism of today— there are only about three times when the Bible mentions it as a threat. The perils of apostasy, of following other gods, were innumerable, but atheism appears timidly, if not late. Nor is it denounced as a struggle, a profession, a liberation. It is a kind of obliviousness—"They have denied the Lord, and said, He does not exist" (Jer. 5, 12)*—or the manner of pride that gives no thought to God (Ps. 10, 4) or a fool's lack of the wit to ask about him (Ps. 14, 1). By now, however, the questioning of God does have the wit to make of atheism something positive: the appearance of the very things which the belief in God has transferred or devalued. In fact, on this positive aspect all atheisms come to agree again, regardless of the kind of deity they dispose of: they agree that to deny the reality of an enthroned deity puts an end to human fear of it, to human nullity before it.

That the age of despotism, of heteronomous fear, is past— this unites atheisms so abysmally different as that of Lucretius, that of the Sankhya philosophy (which Buddha is based upon), that of the son-of-man mystics (insofar as they made Yahweh disappear), and that of Feuerbach. Lucretius' sigh of relief recurs almost identically in the eighteenth-century Enlightenment,

---

* This is Bloch's own translation (*Es gibt ihn nicht*). Luther's German accords with the King James and Douay versions' "It is not he"—which does not, of course, so strongly support Bloch's thesis. The *Jerusalem Bible,* however, translates thus: 'he is nothing'. —Translator.

for all the differences in the form of the majesty dethroned. To Lucretius, Epicurus the materialist comes to be in science what Prometheus was in the myth; this is the source of the positivity which all atheisms share, and which Lucretius expresses in his didactic poem: "When human life on earth lay crushed under the weight of religion, whose grim face glowered from the heavens, as it menaced mortals—then a man, a man of Greece, dared to lift mortal eyes in defiance, first to stand erect and challenge it; a man whom neither the fables of gods, nor lightning and the sky's threatening menace cowed, whose valiant manhood they only spurred the first to smash the constraining locks of nature's doors" (*De rerum natura* I, 62–71).

Such liberation from fear might seem to contradict the altogether different deliverance linked with the wishful essence of *religion itself,* with the hypostasis of men's own wishful perfection into a *Deus Optimus Maximus.* But no atheism that freed men from fear has ever freed them from the wish contents and hope treasures of religion—with the sole exception of its scantiest and completely negative form: of the popular materialism of the nineteenth century, whose philistine practitioners required erudition to keep them from a total loss of those contents in nihilism. Atheism restored the transcendent treasures to immanence, rather; in Feuerbach's case it had them reflected entirely in man. What vanished in this most important and here probably least understood form of atheism, what it freed men from, was always the same thing: the positing of the *perfectissimum* as a reality. It was the oppressive throning above man that disappeared, that Above pure and simple which is peculiar to Caesarism—and which then, of course, could also involve a purely ideological sum of non-treasures pertaining to the *masters' Church* alone. But as far as Feuerbach's *religious* criticism proper is concerned, it is the *Jove Optimus Maximus* whose essence was atheistically cancelled, not the wish-content of an *optimum maximum* itself. And what counters the immanence of atheism is essentially the superstitious transfer into a beyond of a human mystery and *perfectissimum* posited as real; it is to this that atheism opposes its open space—initially as a void. But its void is not in immanence. On the contrary: the recovery of the treasures that had been wasted on heaven increased the importance of immanence; it now obtained the total Otherness of anthropological depth.

The significance of nature in the sense of Lucretius has not remained definitive, no more than the astral myths from which mundane piety had been brought down were worthy of definitive belief. But the significance of the *regnum humanum in nature* is definitive, and what atheism has inherited from this is nothing less than the whole self-injection of the founders into the religious mystery, and thus the strongest positive element in religion. Or we might say, fully conscious of the paradox which amounts here to the thing itself, that when Jesus proclaimed himself mediator between himself and the Father, he had become the Father, and that when he called himself the vine, with the community as his branches, he was speaking in the divinely vacated space of a mystical anthropology.

In this entrance into Yahweh—or, more, in this exodus from the Exodus God—he has been followed by every son-of-man mysticism. There is no room for any *hubris,* flat or daemonic, where the *sursum corda* proves itself against hypostases. And because of this probation, the son-of-man mysticism continues all the way into Feuerbach's anthropologization, continues even if, indeed precisely if there is no *Deus Optimus Maximus* dwelling above the stars. An atheist who has understood what was conceived as God, has understood it as a draft on the human content that has not yet appeared—such an atheist is not an Antichrist. Nor is he an Antichrist who sees the links between the unappeared human substance and the utopian one of nature which surrounds mankind with a far broader, fermenting openness of its incognito. "Sensest thou thy secret, world?" is a cry as Christian, that is, as apocalyptic, as the old "Sensest thy creator, world?" is mythical, even though contained in Schiller's "Song to Joy" which Beethoven put into his Ninth Symphony.

Such a utopian element is and remains irreligious in the sense of being strikingly meta-religious—that is, it belongs precisely to the advent of an *atheism whose depth dimensions have at last been understood.* But the concept of atheism, according to its final *positivum,* is the realm of freedom. This is the end to

which the forward path of the world is held open; this is why
Jupiter and the throne and the world-creating, world-encircling
specter of an extant *ens realissimum* have been removed. What
used to be designated as God designates no kind of fact, no enthroned existence whatever, but an utterly different problem, and
the name of the possible solution of the problem is not "God"
but "kingdom."

So, things here below have not proved as shaky in the long
run as those above. Man inherits the treasures of the beyond
insofar as they are treasures, not just caricatures of the things
one failed to understand. For what the beyond reflected, along
with pusillanimity and the frauds of the master class, was purely
pious ignorance. It was not only the mystery, which is and
remains a mystery; there was ignorance mixed with it. What
Engels has to say about fraudulent faith and its exposure is
striking: "In order to grasp existing social conditions, they had
to be stripped of their halo." What he has to say about pious
ignorance and the mythological side of faith is not quite so
exhaustive: "In the beginnings of history it was the forces of
nature which were at first so reflected: . . . But it is not long
before, side by side with the forces of nature, social forces begin
to be active; forces which present themselves to men as equally
extraneous and at first equally inexplicable, dominating them
with the same apparent necessity, as the forces of nature themselves. The fantastic personifications, which at first only reflected
the mysterious forces of Nature, at this point acquire social
attributes, become representatives of the forces of history"
(*Anti-Dühring*). Added thus to the "primeval forest," according to Engels, is the "higher nonsense"—a religious consciousness which, at the least, is very much pre-scientific.

All this is genetically correct and yet, as we have noticed, it
fails to cover the upward striving of the higher religions, the
striving that fills their by no means simply "higher nonsense"
with so much agony, so much imagery, so much hope. For the
huge shadow of ignorance is not the same as the twilight of the
depth of wishing where so many treasures are found, and to see
through the first is not yet to see through the second. They are
as different, to give an example, as the myths of river or town

gods are from the *tao* of Lao-tse, or as the tale of God making Eve of Adam's rib is from Isaiah's prophecy about the future Mount Sion.

Salvageable, inheritable after a *reformatio in capite et membris,* is nothing but the wish content and the depth of hope which in religious images have become visible through ignorance or sheer fantasizing. They are restored to the human subject, to the possible subject of nature, to the dusk of the *incognito* in both. Still, there is a *last question* which atheism poses once every doubt of its anthropological-utopian positivity has been removed: what about the *vacuum* that is left—or not left—by disposing of the God hypostasis? Is it another part of ignorance; is it, like the hypostasis itself, a mere chimera that has settled in it as a seeming reality? Is the problem of the place into which gods were imagined a sham problem that will dispose of itself as soon as the religious sham is disposed of? Is this place, this space, virtually just like the image a mirror reflects: the entire length of a hall lies in it, the entire view from a window including the spire of a church miles away, but the mirror surface itself is flat, and behind it there is nothing of the whole perspective? Or does the void which the divine illusions were projected into not exist, at least, as this void? Does not indeed mere reflection, to be able to occur, require a mirror, a thing which itself does not just seem to be when it seems to duplicate others?

Is the problem—or pseudoproblem—of the religious locale not therefore a repetition on another level of the whole crux of one sided sensualism or economism, in the form that a distinct field, no matter what its worth, must be posited for the introjections or illusions after all—a field which sensualism or economism will inveigh against, then, and which each will propose to clean out? The crux became visible when Leibniz commented on Locke's sensualistic citation of the old line, *Nihil est in intellectu, quod non fuerit in sensu.* *"Excipe: nisi ipse intellectus,"* Leibniz added with malicious acumen (*Nouveaux Essais* II, 1 § 2). The intellect may have received everything from the senses; it may be a total blank without them— but the senses have not supplied the intellect itself. To which we add in regard to economism: there may be nothing in the super-structure that has not been in the economic infrastructure—except for the superstructure itself.

And the same applies to the superstructure in the superstruc-ture, to the religious celestialization of wishful images and even of vague natural and historical forces. A field, a space, a specific *topos* must be methodically presupposed and objectively pre-disposed if the religious wish-pictures (including those due to ignorance and especially those of a genuine mystery relation about the incognito) shall be capable of projection in the manner in which they have really been projected in religious history. It thus turns out that, corresponding to Leibniz's qualifying clause, the problem of the *space of religious projection in and for itself is not a sham problem,* and while this space is anything but a reality in the sense of factual existence, *neither is it a chimera.* It is not a reality, and certainly not a supreme reality in the sense of Plato's two-worlds theory, with its ephemerality of all phenomena and its true being of the eternal ideas at some eternal Uranian location.

But something other than this—something implied precisely in the material unity of the world—is to keep this vacuum open for a possible, still undecided reality of the future. As such, the vacuum would only initially be defined as a void, and in no case as the same as outright nothingness; and nothing—if we are objectively, not just anthropologically, in earnest about atheism—nothing would be more wrong than the fake con-sistency of believing in a vacuum in which no kind of being might be found at all, not even the correlate of an utopian being instead of God's, of a not-yet-being like the kingdom's. Pure faith in a vacuum can lead either to nihilistic despair or to hectic joy at the simultaneous disappearance of God and all meaning—whereupon the surrounding night of nihilism would leave mankind merely phosphorescing or fluorescing, as in a Geissler tube, for lack of air.

This is not the case, however. The fact remains that emptiness is only the first definition of the space from which the certainty of being has been cleared out; its second, instantly following definition is *fermentation, an open effective sphere* for the human subject, as well as for a far from finished subject of the natural environment. The wishful world of religion forced even Feuerbach in later years into significant interruptions of his overly pure anthropology, which in this case means his subjective idealism. Not in the extinguished beyond, but in a nature equally cleansed of deities he could not help finding, continuing to find, things that made the projection seem not quite so freely suspended any more. With nature participating in the religious projection, he even had to add objects—those of external sense perceptibility—to the mere wish pictures. For the later Feuerbach, the man who wrote *Theogony,* the gods are not mere creatures of the wish, but creatures of nature at the same time: "The wish is the source of religion, the source of the gods, and the wish itself comes from man; but the object of the wish comes from external nature, from the senses . . . The gods as such are not deified and personified natural forces or natural bodies; they are personified, emancipated, objectified feelings, sensations, affects—but affects tied to the natural bodies by which they are awakened or brought about." Thus far, instructively, a Feuerbach who has become objective: his sense of objects refers to nature religions, and accordingly to sensual objects in them that have remained after deducting their deification. If the sense of objects refers to humanistic religions, on the other hand, whose deity was worshipped "beyond nature," then, of course, no object of its own—no transcendent object, that is —remains after the removal of the deity; but there does remain the *open topos of what lies ahead,* the novum in which the mediated train of human purposes continues.

Myths of perfection have been projected into this *topos,* but for so long as it is not blocked it may also be the goal, if not the site, of the realization of tendencies. The *topos* would be blocked only if nothingness, in the true sense of this concept or anti-concept, had really begun in it—nothingness as the definitive void, that is, without any possible fermentation and utopian reality, without a correlate of hope in the void. This genuine nothingness and its futility is doubtless just as latent in the vacuum of atheism as the "all" of fulfillment by the *regnum humanum* or kingdom—only: it is just as undecided. In the time that men have left, the *latency of nothingness* shows as frustration, as destruction, as the effective sphere of what we call evil. In the space men have left, the same latency of nothingness shows as disintegration, as irregular diversity, as threatening chaos. But equally evinced in the open world is the *latency of all*—so that destruction can here always turn into destruction of the inadequacy, and diversity into the diversity of self-qualifying and experimenting abundance. Above all, the utopian space once filled by gods makes itself known, positively known, in the *topos of order,* the order that cements the anthropologically grown hope contents and their freedom. As the social utopias have shown earlier, and as becomes clear now from the viewpoint of religious philosophy, this order is the kingdom proper in the realm of freedom; *but in the final analysis such kingdom-related matters would defy intentional reference if the field of religious hypostases were not more lasting than the religious hypostases in this field themselves.*

Nothing and all, chaos and kingdom, hang in the balance in the one-time field of religious projection, and it is human achievement in history that will weigh down the scale of nothingness or that of all. It was not only the order pertaining to hope for the kingdom that was anticipated in the formerly religious space, and remains standing in the field of projection, if not of anticipation; it was the chaos signaling the threat of nothingness as well. Since the vacuum may contain all or nothing, it used to be called either *heaven or hell;* and hell was conceived as the realm of definitive destructiveness or of Satan. The satanic is the horror of total annihilation, of complete unsubstantiality, of seclusion fleeing to the definitive void in which it is secluded. The reality that has so far been at work contains plenty of such destructiveness, plenty of such eruptions of original evil, but not yet its victory; once its victory were shown as definitive and hypostatized, the religious space would fill up negatively, with a Prince of Darkness and demonic substances, as it had filled up positively with God and angelic substances.

But even when the mythologies of a Prince of Darkness and a King of Heaven alike have departed, there is again the *topos* that remains—this time as the twofold space of projection and anticipation inscribed either Dante's "*Lasciate ogni speranza*" or else "Saved from the devil is the noble member of the spirit world," as the angels sing while bearing the immortal part of Goethe's Faust to heaven. All these are *utopian space problems from the religious heritage;* they belong to that future world trail that is now being blazed into the most consummate immanence, that of the anthropological incognito. They belong to what lies ahead, to the realm in which the core of mankind and of earth, the anthropological subject as well as that of the cypher of nature, will either bloom to its utopian end or not bloom to the end.

If there is no utopia of the kingdom without atheism, there is implicitly no such utopia without the utopian reality of the vacuum either, which atheism has both left and opened. Time and again, if we are to lift the *incognito,* the very extra-territoriality of the *incognito* presupposes that the vacuum created by the collapse of the God hypostasis has not also collapsed; if it had, the extra-territoriality of the incognito would rest neither on the new heaven nor on the new earth it points to.

The realm of lifting the *incognito* of human and mundane depth has been the one and only goal of all religious history; but that realm needs space. It needs so large a space that all past expressions and extensions are insufficient for it, and then again it needs so small, so intensely pervaded a space that the only suggestion of it lies in the closing-in of Christian mysticism. The Christian ideal would be no ideal if it did not directly strike this incognito landscape; but it strikes it as a veiled *landscape.* The ideal traveled with the Three Wise Men of the whole East; the star above the stable made them forget their own stars, but they did bring gifts from all the earlier religions, incense, myrrh, and gold; they brought the tradition along with the perdition of the myths of estrangement, and they delivered it at the birthplace of the moment that was finally touching itself. The star traveled as far as the stable, where God ceases—not in nothingness, but in the henceforth self-liberating *cur-Deus-homo* space of possible identification of whatever urges and seeks to be born in man and the world.

To this end the religious vacuum is no chimera and will not become one even though all the gods in it were chimerical.

UNITY OF THE *Nu* IN MYSTICISM

The best often lies near at hand, where one would not suspect its presence. So the Here and Now returns at this *highest point,* to say for itself what it is. All intensively utopian views together with their moral, musical and religious guidelines lead back to the darkness of the lived moment, for this is the place of universal ferment, the place where all is still utopian to itself, hidden and not yet come to be. Whenever we close in upon the hope content of a being-for-itself, we are approaching the moment and attempting more and more intensely to define this basic intensity.

The most intensive moment is religious, in the sense of man's self-injection into the mystery: the last beyond is our closest, most immanent proximity. This, however, is nothing but the driving force of each lived moment, what has not yet been halted as bliss, nor unearthed as gold. "Tarry awhile; thou art so fair"—this Faustian hope has its final religious fulfillment in mysticism or, more precisely, in the *nu* or *nunc aeternum* of mysticism. Of the mysticism that arose on the soil of richly subjectified, humanized religion, of religion that knows meditative *immersion,* that is not just orgiastic or indeed no longer orgiastic at all. A man in the grip of religious orgasm would also be pushed beyond his former stature and given forces and faculties that seemed to spring from a dark root; his rapture made him so much like the enrapturing god that the shamans and the initiates of Dionysus all felt "deified." But the self-injection in these cases is as external for the subject as are the gods it invades; they are nature gods not yet endowed with any human substance. This is why ecstasy flourishes chiefly in primitive and astral religions, among shamans and priests of Baal, but not in humanized religions or only on their fringes.

Christian mysticism, above all, is *immersion* without frothing at the mouth and being beside oneself, the kind of immersion that corresponds to the most deeply proximate effect of subjective effusion into God, and divine effusion into the subject. The noise of getting or being beside oneself yields to the stillness of becoming-for-oneself; the wilderness yields to the "powerful inhabitation of one's self," as Daniel Czepko, a Bohemian mystic, put it. The individual "I" is submerged as a mere part of transience and diversity; this submergence is the premise as well as the constantly attested basic trait of the mystical experience. Getting rid of one's individuality, of the way one is, as well as of the diversity of all things—this departure from everything is deemed the main road to finding everything, which means finding the unity of the essence with the true self. Mystical immersion is contact with the deity (with essence rather than appearance) by shedding the diversity—in other words, by simplification; this will grant everything, in the form of the unity of everything.

The neo-Platonists tried to distinguish the no longer individual self of this union in a special, actively concentrated function of consciousness—Plotinus, for example, in the supreme σύνεσις which, as insight, simultaneously contains the supreme σύνθεσις, a combination resulting in the supreme ἅπλωσις, or simplicity. It is in this self-combining ground of force, of self, of identity that all immersion has since been claimed to deify its practitioner in the three stages of purification, illumination, and union. Here is the point of a seemingly super-conscious, far from intoxicated self-deification, a point in order to describe which the medieval mystics later searched for the most poignant metaphors. Meister Eckhart, comparing the souls to little sparks, says, "If the whole man were like the spark, he would always be uncreated and uncreatural, above time, in eternity." St. Teresa's word for the same stage of apparent deification is "soul castle," and she lists the several quarters in it; all of these place names are related. The attitudes or approaches to this castle also come to relate, indeed to blend with one another, be they called ardor or light, love or contemplation, activity or passivity. In the *unio mystica* they have ceased to be alternatives. The question of the primacy of thought or will divided all Christian scholasticism, but in mysticism (for the same scholasticists) it became a moot point:

as mystics, *Doctor ecstaticus* Ruysbroek and *Doctor angelicus* Thomas are not at odds any more; love of the sublime and contemplation of the sublime are identical in the mystical *maximum*. Similarly superseded is the difference between suffering and action, passivity and activity: in the *summum mentis* their features are interchangeable.

The New Testament contains this united duality of rending and being rent, in such interwinings of humility and aggression as this: "From the days of John the Baptist until now the kingdom of heaven suffereth violence, and the violent take it by force" (Matth. 11, 12). But mysticism takes a dialectical view of humility and activity; it has these postures recoil and pass into each other as soon as they reach their peaks. Christian mysticism is consummate yielding to God, complete dissolution in God; but simultaneously at work in this passivity is an entirely different aggressive dissolution: a redemption from God. On the other hand, Christian mysticism is an invasion of God throughout; in fact, it is the overwhelming sense of an *apex mentis,* a pinnacle of the mind that pierces God. Yet at the same instant, this activity recurves into surrender as the deity transforms its master into its servant, into its carrier who seems himself to be carried by superior forces. What occurs in the mystical castle is a coalescing of dualisms which in the usual world are upheld by the concepts of "I" and "not I." It is this hold that fades in the mystical union in which the sharpest of the dualisms fades: the castle no longer has a partition between I and not-I, subject and object, subject and substance. The castle is built without otherness.

No more otherness—this has been the gigantically anticipating ultimate illusion of all mystics, a *phantasma utopicissime fundatum.* The wedge that splits the world into subject and object is psychically withdrawn by the mystic, whereupon every kind of detachment seems to void itself. The immediate moment is thus entered into as equally undivided and wholly esoteric: there is ingress into a moment which seems to the mystical experience to be no longer in time. Time and the moment have never been so close, so intertwined, as this moment is with eternity. It comes to be called *nunc stans,* or *nunc aeternum*—a name in which the seemingly most diametrical opposites, instantaneity and eternity, change places in complete dialectical union. The mystics' God was the *God of this nunc aeternum, hence the God of supreme instantaneity.* In mysticism Now is Always, Here is Everywhere. Even the antithesis of God and not-God is voided; it is another of the objectivities outside the castle. God dies as he is born in the *nunc aeternum.* To Eckhart, therefore, God is sheer nothingness—namely, the unpredicated all.

Tot capita, tot mentes is a widely applicable and widely divisive saying. But it is no longer divisive when the minds' eyes are closed, when believers go into a trance. Frothing at the mouth and immersion are incompatible, of course—except on the fringes, where orgiastic waves may rise—but otherwise immersion used to fuse all the dividing lines drawn by the children of the usual world. National borders would vanish, and so, above all, would the borders between forms of faith. In the unity of an illumination without Scripture, Thomas Münzer, the revolutionary among the mystics, could read an international unity across all the divisions: Jewish, Turkish, Papist, Lutheran —all of that belongs to the letter of the world, according to Münzer, not to the effusion of the spirit. "I preach a Christian faith that is uniform in the hearts of all the chosen on earth. If in all his life a man had neither heard nor seen the *biblia,* he might well have an unfailing Christian faith for himself by the right doctrine of the spirit, as all those have had it who wrote Holy Scripture without any books. If we Christians are now to accord together in harmony, Psalm 72, *with all the chosen among all the divisions and generations of all kinds of faith,* then we must know what is in the mind of one who has been raised among the infidels from childhood on and has learned the right works and the doctrine of God without any books." And as regards the harvest in Christendom, the separation of the wheat from the chaff: "To a chosen friend of God it is a wondrous ecstatic joy if his fellow brother also has come to the faith in such uniform advent as himself. The Church today is . . . against it, yet the time of the harvest is always at hand" (*Emphatic Exposure of the False Faith,* 1524).

229

This is the *unity* in which mysticism saw all of its children, a unity that voided the religions by laying the gulf between infidels and chosen athwart the several religions. It did, of course, require the great popular movement that had begun in the twelfth century with the Albigensian Wars and culminated in the German Peasant War: like the community of the disciples once upon a time, the mass of the chosen walked *in unity among the people,* not among masters' priests, much less among princes. Also eliminated by this unity was the loneliness which still enveloped the mysticism of Hugo and Richard of Saint Victor in the twelfth century, the loneliness of a soul with its God (*"Soliloquium de arrha animae"* was the significant title of one of Hugo of Saint Victor's principal works). The steps of the heavenly ladder came forth from psychology; Joachim di Fiore, the first prophet of Gothic mysticism, transformed the soul's travel-guide to God into a movement of history itself, into the dynamics of the last gospel. It is now *mankind as a whole* that moves into the Third Kingdom of mystical likeness unto Christ, where the pure will be saved and the impure will perish; the kingdoms of the law and of grace are transcended; *plenitudo intellectus* is attained. And this fullness of the mind corresponds exactly to the deification with which Christian mysticism surrounded its *illuminati;* it corresponds to the community of a universal Pentecost. Or, as the Brethren of the Free Spirit, a mystical sect that flourished about Eckhart's time, described this future or third age, quite in Joachim's sense, but also quite in the sense of the former lonely entrancement: "In the third age the Holy Spirit will show itself to be a flame, a fiery furnace of divine love, a cellar of spiritual drunkenness, a pharmacy of divine spices, spiritual oils and ointments, a constant prophesying of spiritual joys, whereby the truth of the incarnated Word of God will not only be seen in plain knowledge but tasted and touched in experience" (cf. Hahn, *Geschichte der Ketzer im Mittelalter,* 1847).

Eckhart, in fact, follows up mankind's union in "knowledge" with a cosmic, so to speak, or cosmogonic union: mysticism's movement towards God is not only "auto-motion," self-knowledge, self-revelation of God, his unfolding from his "unnatured nature" to "natural nature," but for this very reason it is the same as the world process. And as the mystical soul, divine in its inmost nature, returns from worldly alienation to the primal ground, to regain its divinity, so does the whole world process return to the primal ground by virtue of this "unbecoming": through cognition and conversion, being doubles back into its ground. Here the mystical function becomes a function of the turn in the world itself: *scintilla,* the mystical spark, burns on the dividing line of otherness and identity rather than in sheer solitude. In the end these are great modes of union; but all of them come from the revolutionary sense of the togetherness, the oneness, of the chosen—from the chiliasm, in other words— with which meditative immersion has been combined in full-fledged heretical Christianity. Advancing to this, in a socially and also cosmically broad-based mysticism, was glory—which in man's breakthrough to God burst forth as from a prison. It was sheer frustrated glory, after all, that burned and erupted in the *scintilla,* a freedom of God's children as after the Latter Day; they mean to have this freedom now, today, and in such anticipation feel free even from God as an object. *The glory of the core in the imprisonment of its inadequate world* is thus the ultimate base of the mystical union "among all the divisions and generations of all kinds of faith." Doubtless the unions of mysticism never will return in their old forms; the lightning in which "the indescribable is done" will unlock no more heavens for metaphorical glories to pour from, as at the end of Goethe's *Faust.* But in the depth of this enthusiasm there always lay an intended entrance of self-encountering, ground-encountering humanity into a realm that would contain no mysteries other than human ones, and no order other than that of a body of Christ with vine and branches. The kingdom of Christian mysticism was built to the measure of the son of man, with the suddenly opened moment for his manger. This *nunc stans,* emerging from the Here and Now itself, is very far from any beyond, and the nearest thing in life; *in a literal as well as in a central sense, the nunc stans of the mystics means the same as* "Tarry awhile; thou art so fair." And it is only in the problem of that *nunc stans* that the Faustian goal has the form and content of the *identity posited in it*. The perfect utopia or utopia of perfection, which religion placed in heaven, recoils here into the core of mankind as well as into the problematical subject of nature. *Nunc stans* is the precise formula for the most immanent immanence—that is to say, for the temporally so remote and still flatly undetermined world without any possible alienation.

MIRACLE AND WONDER

An awe-inspiring quality would often emanate from pious men. To the people they seemed to possess strange powers, which were thought of as magical, thaumaturgical, superhuman. The point of a feat of magic was partly to impress and influence those whom a sermon could not affect because they didn't understand it. But to some extent, beyond this spectacular aspect, miracle-working was produced by an explosive will. It was an attempt to lift the usual course of things (that to which men were not just subjectively but objectively accustomed) off its hinges. Both propagandist and objective magic are to be found in the Old Testament—the first as Aaron outdoes the Egyptian sorcerers with a rod that finally swallows up their rods, and the second when Elijah, with "his face between his knees," acts entirely like an African rainmaker (I Kings 18, 42ff.). However, in the Old Testament the miracle stories are told more or less incidentally, as if they did not really or not directly matter. Even such fantastic legends of Moses as the ten plagues and the parting of the Red Sea serve only as a framework for the greater, charismatic feat of leadership out of Egypt. There are two reasons for this relative subordination, and for the eventual receding of miracles in the Old Testament: neither prevails in the New Testament. First, the priestly editing of the Bible under Ezra, when the Jewish Levitical state was established, curbed the rank growth of the old magical popular faith, and the will to move in it regardless of the law. Many miracle accounts are likely to have vanished at that time, especially if they were concerned with phenomena tending to subvert Yahweh or even to improve upon him. And second, the

232

prophetic type had changed. Elijah's features are still largely thaumaturgical and orgiastic-magical like those of a shaman or Baal's priest; but only a hundred years later, with Amos, a pure, visionary utopianism begins and soon becomes literary. Thunderous language took the place of miraculous things, and the miracle itself, indispensable for purposes of religious propaganda, was reduced to visionary contact—in a particularly noble form by Ezekiel, the priest and scriptural scholar. Until "faith's favorite child" (as Goethe called the miracle) ran wild again in the New Testament, in a naïve resurgence most upsetting to the liberal theologians of today.

Jesus appears magical throughout, heals the lame, turns water into wine, feeds five thousand with five loaves of bread and two fishes, drives out sick devils, and revives the dead like Elijah. In other words: the popular base came to the fore again, and with it the miracle folklore undisturbed by Sadducees and Pharisees. Even Evangelists such as Luke the physician and the Hellenized author of the Gospel according to St. John do not suppress the miracle stories, but give them an additional spiritual significance by making them refer to still greater miracles. The bread distribution is tied to the Last Supper (John 6, 35), and the healing of the blind, to Christ as the light of the world (John 9, 30). Thus the evanescence and singularity of these miracles drops away: they are to benefit far greater multitudes than the five thousand who chanced to be there at the time, or the single blind man. What the possibility of these reinterpretations makes clear is that this was not just a sphere of primitive magic retailed by peasants and fishermen in the New Testament. The miraculous was stirred instead by wholly new definitions, and by those above all: by Jesus as the Messiah, by Jesus and the heavenly kingdom that was near at hand. These two were the fundamental miracles required to lay a foundation for the smaller ones expected of Jesus, which he himself felt were his "signs."

The older meaning of miracles, the one still connected with magic, was thus replaced by a *new, eschatological* meaning: miracles are *indications* of the coming end. Taken by themselves, without this background, the accumulated miracle tales about

Jesus are no different from all the others in history, whether
in the history of superstition and its mass psychoses (witch-
craft delusion), or among those paraphysical or parapsychical
phenomena for which we may still lack an explanation and a
systematic order. Rightly or wrongly, such parapsychical faculties as telepathy and such paraphysical ones as telekinesis are
reported from outside religion as well, and in this area many
New Testament miracles are found equally among fetish priests.
Legends like that of the transmuting of water into wine might
as well be told of the sorceress Medea as of the man who
taught the Lord's Prayer and gave the Sermon on the Mount;
and the Doctor Faustus of folklore even brought forth wine
from wood. Accordingly, on the basis of these isolated miracles,
a medieval Jewish squib on "Jesus the Hanged" has little more
to report than that Jesus learned magic in Egypt and used it
to lead Israel astray. But the *novum,* the source of the completely different values, consists of *messianic pretension* and
apocalyptic background: "Behold, I make all things new"—
this and this alone is what Christ's miracles live by, the most
primitive ones included. For those too pertained to the Messiah
and the end of time, as "signs," not merely as miracles (John
7, 31). And above all, the crucial point: in the New Testament,
which is eschatologically intended and enveloped throughout,
even the magical interventions stand in their singular place as
testimonies of a far greater transformation: from the miraculous
to the *wonderful.* Water turns into the *wine of wonder.*

Jesus himself, explaining these enormities as marks of the
Messiah and the approaching kingdom, had referred to Elias
as a forerunner of the Christ, not as a former miracle worker.
Hence the answer to the Baptist's question whether it was he
that should come or whether another was to be expected: "The
blind receive their sight, and the lame walk, the lepers are
cleansed, and the deaf hear, the dead are raised up, and the poor
have the gospel preached to them" (Matth. 11, 5). Hence the
reply to the Pharisees and Sadducees: "When it is evening, ye
say, It will be fair weather, for the sky is red. And in the morning, It will be foul weather today, for the sky is red and lower-
ing. O ye hypocrites, ye can discern the face of the sky; but

can ye not discern the signs of the times?" (Matth. 16, 2f.). The signs of the times combined such seemingly disconnected events as the healing of the lame and the preaching of the gospel to the poor—that too was meant to change the realities, to bring the state of laboring and being heavily laden to an end in a new aeon. Jesus is so definite about setting concrete change above a merely internal and invisible one that he can ask the following astounding question: "Is it easier to say to the sick of the palsy, Thy sins be forgiven thee; or to say, Arise, and take up thy bed, and walk?" (Mark 2, 9). The question contains the answer, to wit: "But that ye may know that the Son of man hath power on earth to forgive sins, he saith to the sick of the palsy: I say unto thee, Arise, and take up thy bed, and go thy way into thine house" (Mark 2, 10f.). The proof of their faith which the palsied man's getting up supplied to believers ranked above the power to forgive sin, according to Christ's own estimate.

A single material line, a line that does not remain inwardly, runs from the obligation to heal the palsied to the proverbial faith that moves mountains, not psychologies. And all this in the sign of the end, of the *basic miracle of the Apocalypse* that was believed and phenomenologically linked with the coming of the Messiah. Thus the miracle as exploding of the accustomed state of affairs attains in Jesus its most radical expression, for it is augmented by the *novum* itself: on a small scale, it is always meant to be a new heaven and a new earth already. There is, of course, no comparison between the habitual context of things as perceived in Jesus' day and environment, and the lawful causality with which the miracle concept has been contrasted since the sixteenth century. The context of knowledge differed even from that of scholastic Christianity, however full its world still seemed of demons, and however directly controlled by God and his angels. The world of Jesus was that of Mandaean-Persian dualism, with Satan as the ruler of this aeon, and the kingdom of light as that of the imminent new aeon. The Messiah is the bringer of the world conflagration—as in the Mandaean Book of John, where the spirit of light says to his begotten son: "Be thou a messenger unto me; go into the world of darkness, in which no ray of light falls." *Only against this world and its Satanic contexts* did the miraculous interruption occur. But it always occurred as an interruption, and a visible one at that; above all, it happened so as to advance the particular, substitutive visibility of a totally changed order—a wonderful order.

Thus, beyond the world image of his time, Christ's miracles agree in two main points with the concept we can still have today: *in the formal point of interruption, and in the material point of outright positivity*. It also remains essential that inner occurrences were not considered miracles. A miracle intends a tangible external change; the salvation whose appearance it is to serve comes via the world. Thomas Aquinas accordingly defines the Christian miracle—as distinct from mere Christian preaching and conversion—as follows: "*Miraculum est effectus sensibilis, qui divinitus fit praeter ordinem totius naturae*" (3. *Contra gentiles* c. 101). The forgiveness of sins was not counted as a miracle by Thomas, nor was transubstantiation, since neither is a sensually perceptible effect; and throughout scholasticism, when no one believed any more in the imminence of the heavenly kingdom, the miracle always dwelled at the natural world's point of fracture, at the point of a visible leap by a visible part of the visible world.

What all this makes clear is that no matter how far the miraculous has since been reduced to, or unveiled itself as, a banal occultism—no matter how its continued official existence has been confined to Catholic propaganda or business dealings, to hysterical virgins and to such pitiful gates of heaven as Lourdes—even so, apart from its transcendent superstitions, the miracle concept does, most significantly, contain a far from superstitious concept *derived from explosive faith: the concept of the leap*. That very concept has been acquired from the miracle; a purely mechanical causal world, antithetical to miracles in any form, had no room for the idea of a leap, but there was a place for it in a world no longer conceived as either static or finite. There, of course, the leap as a recoil resulting from strict dialectics shows a legality of its own, and its interruption of the purely mechanical progress of the same does not by any means locate it in an *intermissio legis* pure and simple, where the scholastically defined, mythical miracle resides. Nor will the self-evident elimination of all transcendent factors leave anything "exceptional" here, any space drained of legality, where a transcendent will might posit things impossible on earth. And yet: when Hegel writes about the qualitative leap and its portents that something is here "interrupted by the lightning-like inception which all at once puts up the structure of a new world," we may be sure that the concept of this lightning (though it may be the result of a law *sui generis*) is not unrelated to the past suddenness of the miracle as a basic archetype of religious, and especially of Christian, adventist imagination. *Natura facit saltus,* nature does make leaps—this much, at least, the old miracle faith has contributed to a no longer magical and even less transcendentally vaulted world. The idea of the leap first grew in the landscape of apocalyptic miracles, which it still has as its background.

And the leap is not all that the strange apparition left behind. Water turning to wine is an interruption only for him who believes it. But something else lives in the break, which can dispense with all magic—particularly with all magic that has turned into hocus-pocus. It has to do with the *hopes placed in* the miracle, and its name is *wonder*—a name which even a scion of the Enlightenment knows and takes quite seriously, unlike the hair-raising feats of magic. "I search for the wonderful," says Ibsen's Nora, a liberal woman far from all theological circles. She says it not in these exact words, but what she means is the same substance that lies in the radical leap and makes her husband add the superlative and questioning, "The most wonderful—?" on which note that most untheological anti-family play ends. So the wonderful retains its golden sound even if the wondrous (the interruptions of which provided the space it used to fill) has faded. Substantially, of course, not every miracle that was reported and imaginatively elaborated on seemed wonderful or even good. Legend also tells of punitive miracles; the most detailed are the ten plagues and the Egyptians' destruction in the Red Sea; the most diverse were illustrated by Ovid in his *Metamorphoses*. Even the total explosion of the *status quo* as conceived of in the Apocalypse involves as much horror (for the enemies of Christ) as it involves total joy.

And yet, in a substantial miracle, joy is essential. The Egyptians' destruction gave the non-Egyptians something to rejoice over: the fact of rescue, or the category of the triumph of the right. From this point of view there is no difference between the song of the prophetess Miriam about the wonderful rescue (Ex. 15, 21) and the announcement from stellar heights which the angel makes to the shepherds, and which even today's unbeliever hears in the chords of Bach's Christmas oratorio: *"Fürchetet euch nicht; siehe, ich verkündige euch grosse Freude"* (Luke 2, 10). Eventually, wonder remains the dominant, if not the only substance of the interruption that was intended in the miracle—so much so that the good in this world, not just its evil or inadequacy, is thought of as miraculously interrupted if the miracle contains *an extreme; and thus the true nature of wonder*. Viewed as such, a supreme interruption was mystical entrancement and the flatly superior content it may promise to a moment that seems to expand into eternity. This kind of downright superiority is of the essence of wonder, and is again most grandiosely suggested in the Pauline verse: "Eye hath not seen, nor ear heard, neither have entered into the heart of man, the things which God hath prepared for them that love him" (I Cor. 2, 9). And Paul speaks of "our glory"—the exact content of our most central and thus most radical wish dream. Considering what exists in the world, of course, and what has happened thus far, such extremes, such complete extravagances as are implied in the category of wonder seem hardly less magical than miracle-working itself. Empirically, the wonderful is nothing to brag about even in its simplest version, and to "our glory," to the utopia in which all nullities evaporate, we have a long way to go.

Unlike the superstition of miracle-working, however, the belief in wonder is hopeful, indeed paradoxical, from the outset; it is not a real, objective statement. Or, rather (to exclude the misconception of an "eternal ideal" here, as everywhere): it implies no statement referring, or capable of referring, to anything other than hints, presemblances, pre-experiences, or cyphers in the existing, objectively real world. But if even miracles are relatively true, if there is at least a converted truth to them in that the world moves in leaps (by means of history) and permits breakthroughs (without any transcendent alliances or interventions)—if that is the case for the miraculous, then these leaps and possible breakthroughs are partial pre-phenomena, or pre-appearances, and possibly full, real phenomena of the wonderful, for just as long as its opposite, (which is futility or nothingness) has not totally and really occurred yet. The hopeful faith in something *substantially still undetermined but unmistakably wonderful* is a superstition only in mechanical empiricism, or—which here amounts to the same thing—in abstract utopianism. But it is anything but superstitious in concrete utopianism, with its inconclusive world of the dialectical process. On the contrary, that faith is precisely what is not superstitious in religions; it is the part of religion which, along with man's self-injection into transcendence and on grounds of this self-injection, gives to religion the truth which it retains, the demythologized truth that comes not only from fear and want and ignorance but from the drive to the light. This truth lives essentially in the new and in the future that history brings; it does not consist of claiming reality for the hypostasis of a mythological beyond. Nor, of course, does it consist in the very partial preterite of things as they have become in merely causal-mechanical interpretation. "Our glory" resides and continues to reside here too in the *incognito of each lived moment.* This is the legacy of the most radical and as such most central wish dream: that of the intensive center of all things.

What I have tried to define and to identify in guiding images and charts, in the gist of Faust's wager (which is the real problem of Faust), and in the self-contents of music which are as direct as they are always still only half-manifest—this multivocal productive essence of ourselves has its last testimonial in the religiously pursued *unio,* in the union of the moment with eternity. Not time but the moment, the non-temporal in time, communicates with eternity, the sole measure of perfect joy. The communication of the moment, of wonder, and of eternity is in Paul's mind when he makes the enormous conjunction: "Behold, I shew you a mystery: We shall not all sleep, but we shall all be changed, in a moment, in the twinkling of an eye" (I Cor. 15, 51f.). And the non-mythological, though final, boundary sense here is that when the change into the opposite of sleeping, the opposite of nothingness comes, it will come in a moment, *as this moment*. . . .

Men are not alone with their moment; it exists in all the processes and forms of nature. Indeed it is only in cyphers of nature that it can be broadly read, and only in the scope of nature that it can be understood as the kingdom rather than as mere compressed intensity. But the kingdom's substance itself is small precisely because it is so large; it is as concentrated as that which in the mysticism of ethics we call the "highest good." Cyphers of nature and the highest good are the last testimonies in which the core of mankind demonstrates its identity with the core or kernel of the earth. This identical core is at the same time the one that has not appeared; so little about it is settled, and so little of it has become definitely phenomenal, that it remains most uncertain whether it will be completely manifested at all or whether it will wither. As a result of this continuing failure to appear, the essence of the core—which is what the religions mean—hangs in the balance of threatening nothingness or successful all, of futility or wonder. The Herods pointed to nothingness; the Orpheus, Zoroaster, Buddha, Moses, and Jesus figures point to wonder—it depends upon this century whether at least the attainable good will be realized, and whether the realm of freedom can come near enough to permit an entrance rather than an exodus. The goal of all higher religions was a land in which milk and honey will flow actually as well as symbolically; the goal of the substantial atheism that remains after the end of the religions is exactly the same: without God, but with the uncovered countenance of our *absconditum* and with the latency of salvation in the difficult earth.

240